P9-AGA-359

UNITS IN WOODWORKING

UNITS IN WOODWORKING

J. H. Douglass, R. H. Roberts, Forest L. Penny, and Douglas L. Polette

DELMAR PUBLISHERS
COPYRIGHT © 1981
BY LITTON EDUCATIONAL PUBLISHING, INC.

All rights reserved. Certain portions of this work copyright © 1946, 1955, 1962, 1967, 1973 by Litton Educational Publishing, Inc. No part of this work covered by the copyright hereon may be reproduced or used in any form or by any means — graphic, electronic, or mechanical, including photocopying, recording, taping, or information storage and retrieval systems — without written permission of the publisher.

10 9 8 7 6 5 4 3 2 1

LIBRARY OF CONGRESS CATALOG CARD NUMBER: 79-8737
ISBN: 0-8273-1333-0 Soft Cover
      0-8273-1332-2 Hard Cover

Printed in the United States of America
Published Simultaneously in Canada by
Delmar Publishers, A Division of
Van Nostrand Reinhold, Ltd.

Yavapai College Library
Verde Valley Campus

DELMAR PUBLISHERS • ALBANY, NEW YORK 12205
A DIVISION OF LITTON EDUCATIONAL PUBLISHING, INC.

preface

Wood is one of the oldest construction materials known. Since the beginning of time, wood has been used for a variety of purposes such as heat, tools, housing, and transportation. It is the raw material for such things as paper, special types of oils and solvents, plastics, and a variety of chemicals and compounds. No other material exists that can be used for so many things and is so easily available. Wood is one of our major renewable resources. Through proper conservation methods, we will continue to have an adequate supply of wood.

UNITS IN WOODWORKING is designed to teach the student the basics of working with wood. Because of the vast number of uses, it is important to gain a basic understanding of wood. Industrial education courses are an excellent way to learn about wood and how to work with it to produce useful products.

Whether woodworking is a hobby or an occupation, the basic fundamentals must be mastered before advanced woodworking projects can be completed. The first portion of the text deals with shaping wood using hand tools. A thorough understanding of these units is important. It is with the hand processes that habits and techniques are developed. This forms the foundation upon which power woodworking machines are better understood. The second section deals with the fundamentals of power woodworking machinery. Basic information is provided for the safe and efficient operation of power woodworking equipment. The third section deals with finishing materials and their application to wood. The final section provides the student with information on a variety of occupations that are closely related to the woodworking industry. After each unit there are Review Questions for the student to answer.

The drawings in the text are dimensioned in inches with the exception of the Working Drawings and Pictures in the back of the text. These are dimensioned in both inches and millimetres.

For further study in the woodworking field, the student may wish to refer to the following Delmar texts:

CABINETMAKING, PATTERNMAKING, AND MILLWORK
HAND WOODWORKING TOOLS
PORTABLE POWER TOOLS

REVISION AUTHOR

Douglas Polette has been a professor of Industrial Arts at Montana State University for 5 years. Previous to this, he was a professor at the University of Wyoming for 5 years and taught in the Wyoming Public School system for 9 years. He is a member of the American Industrial Arts Association, the American Vocational Association, and the American Council of Industrial Arts Teacher Educators.

contents

SECTION 2 MACHINE WOODWORKING

SECTION 3 WOOD FINISHING

SECTION 4 CAREERS IN WOODWORKING

section 1

general
woodworking

lumbering

OBJECTIVES

After completing this unit, the student will be able to:

- describe lumbering and sawmill operations.
- list the distinguishing characteristics of plain-sawed and quartersawed lumber.
- explain how lumber is seasoned.
- discuss the standard lumber dimensions for hardwoods and softwoods.

Two centuries ago the American continent was practically covered with virgin forests. The ravages of man, insects, fires, and storms have greatly reduced these forests. United States government estimates show approximately 488 million acres of commercial forest lands. There are 212 million acres of timber suitable for lumber production. Most of the remaining virgin forests are found in the northwestern part of the United States. Today, there are about 90 different species of trees that are commercially important.

CONSERVATION

Huge quantities of lumber are used for homes and other construction work, furniture, and paper products. Environmentalists and other government research agencies have done much to prevent tree damage caused by fire, insects, erosion, and pollution. Many stripped forest regions are being replanted. In recent years, the government has taken over extensive forest acreage for the purpose of conserving and establishing national parks.

LUMBERING OPERATION

Much waste in logging operations has been eliminated by carefully inspecting each tree before it is marked for cutting. Only mature trees are felled. After the fallen tree trunks have been cut to standard lengths, they are loaded on trucks or railroad cars, figure 1-1. They are then transported to the sawmill and cut to standard lumber dimensions.

The old method of floating logs to the mills on rivers and streams has been eliminated. Streams are not high enough to carry the logs during much of the year. Also, the development of hydroelectric power dams

Fig. 1-1 Loading logs for trip to sawmill

Fig. 1-2 Sorting logs in a millpond

Fig. 1-3 The bull chain elevates logs into the mill from the millpond

makes it impossible for open river channels to exist.

SAWMILL OPERATION

When logs arrive at the sawmill, they are dumped into the millpond and stored until they are ready to be sawed, figure 1-2. If they are allowed to season (dry) too rapidly, the logs lose too much moisture which can cause checking. *Checking* is the cracking of wood along the grain.

From the millpond, the logs are elevated to the mill by a large bull chain, figure 1-3. The log is then cut to desired lengths by a large cut-off saw, figure 1-4, mounted on carriages. These carriages travel past large band saws, figure 1-5, where boards are cut from the logs. After leaving the carriage, the lumber is hand sorted on the green chain, figure 1-6, and stacked into piles to be dried.

Cutting Methods

Two common methods of sawing hardwood lumber into boards are plain sawing and quartersawing, figure 1-7. *Plain-sawed lumber* is cut so that the annular rings form an angle less than 45 degrees with the surface of the

Fig. 1-4 Cut-off saw cutting logs to length

Fig. 1-5 Carriage operator controlling the carriage as the band saw makes its first cut through the log

Fig. 1-6 Lumber being sorted on the green chain

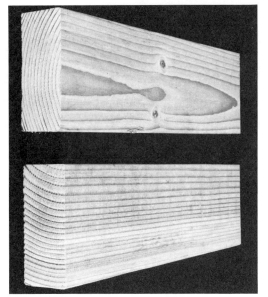

PLAIN SAWED

Fig. 1-7 Two common methods of sawing hardwood lumber into boards

QUARTERSAWED

Fig. 1-8 Dry kilns are used to speed the drying process of lumber.

board. *Quartersawed lumber* is cut so that the annular rings form an angle more than 45 degrees with the surface of the board. Quartersawing is more expensive and more wasteful than plain sawing, yet there is less warping and checking with quartersawing.

Seasoning Wood

The drying or seasoning operation of lumber is done by *air seasoning* or *kiln drying*. Soft, nonporous woods may be air dried satisfactorily. Hardwoods which are used in furniture should be put through the kiln-drying process before they can be used.

In the air-drying process, the lumber is stacked carefully in large piles and exposed to the open air. Thin strips are laid between each layer of boards. This allows for air circulation which prevents warping.

In the kiln-drying process, the lumber is placed in a large oven known as a *kiln,* figure 1-8. Here it is steamed for several days until the wood is thoroughly saturated with moisture. Warm, dry air is then forced into the kiln. The moisture content of the air is carefully controlled to keep the lumber from drying too quickly, which can cause checking. The kiln-drying process requires from two to five weeks.

Fan drying is sometimes used to accelerate seasoning before kiln drying. In this

Fig. 1-9 Electronic tester for testing moisture content of wood

process, air at a controlled temperature is forced through stacked lumber.

Radio-frequency dielectric heating is a recently developed method of drying woods. Other drying methods that are undergoing experimentation include solar energy, infrared radiation, and vacuum drying.

Thoroughly kiln-dried hardwood lumber has a moisture content of 4 to 8 percent. Construction lumber is considered dry if it has a moisture content of 19 percent or less. Figure 1-9 shows an electronic tester used to determine the moisture content of wood.

After the lumber has been dried, it is brought back to the mill to be surfaced to finished dimensions, graded, and shipped to the local lumber yards, figure 1-10.

Fig. 1-10 The planer is used to surface the lumber to finished dimensions.

Standard Dimensions into Which Lumber is Sawed

The sizes into which softwood lumber is sawed have been standardized. The standard lengths of lumber are from 8 feet to 20 feet in 2-foot intervals. Lumber usually ranges in widths from 2 inches to 12 inches in 2-inch intervals. The most common standard thicknesses are 1, 2, and 4 inches. Stock thicker than 4 inches, known as *timber*, is used for heavy construction.

Most lumber purchased at a lumber yard is surfaced (planed). Because surfacing removes some of the wood, its dimensions are less than those mentioned above. For example, 1-inch stock is actually 3/4 inch thick, while 2-inch stock is 1½ inches thick. The widths are also less. A board sawed 6 inches wide is actually 5½ inches wide after it has been planed.

Hardwoods are not sawed to standard lengths or widths. It is too wasteful, expensive, and most jobs using hardwoods do not require standardization. Some standardized hardwood stock is available in thicknesses only of ¼, ½, 1, 1¼, 1½, 2, 2½, 3, and 4 inches.

Grading Lumber

Softwoods are graded according to how much of the whole board can be used. Generally, they are classified in three ways. *Yard lumber* is available in retail lumber yards. *Timber* is used for heavy construction. *Factory and shop lumber* is used for the construction of doors, windows, and interior trim.

Hardwood lumber is graded according to the amount of usable lumber cut clear of defects from one piece. Many of these defects result from wood that is dried too fast or carelessly stored, and this directly affects the quality of lumber. When lumber dries, it has a tendency to *warp* (becomes distorted in shape). Problems in drying may cause *stains*. *Knots* occur where branches grow from the tree trunk. *Decay* may be caused by insects or fungi.

REVIEW QUESTIONS

A. Multiple Choice

1. The first operation to be performed when harvesting trees is to:
    a. load the trees onto trucks.
    b. mark the trees to be cut.
    c. transport the trees to the mill.
    d. push the trees over with dozers.

2. When the logs reach the sawmill, they are first stored in:
    a. large piles.
    b. large, open areas so they can dry.
    c. ponds.
    d. the form of lumber.

3. Large sawmills usually cut the log into lumber on a:
    a. buzz saw.   c. jigsaw.
    b. cut-off saw.   d. band saw.

4. The best method for drying hardwood is:
    a. air drying.
    b. kiln drying.
    c. fan drying.
    d. hardwood does not have to be dried.

5. Lumber to be used for cabinetmaking should not contain more than:
    a. 25 percent moisture.   c. 16 percent moisture.
    b. 20 percent moisture.   d. 8 percent moisture.

B. Short Answer

6. Explain why plain-sawed lumber is used more often than quartersawed lumber.

7. Explain why most hardwoods are not sawed to standard lengths or widths.

8. Explain how softwoods are graded and list the three ways in which they are classified.

9. Name and describe three common defects found in lumber.

classification, growth, and uses of common woods

OBJECTIVES

After completing this unit, the student will be able to:

- describe how hardwoods and softwoods are classified.
- identify common species of wood.
- list the major uses for a specific species of wood.

CLASSIFICATION

Woods are classified as hardwoods or softwoods. The evergreens are classified as softwoods, while those that shed their leaves annually are classified as hardwoods. However, some softwood trees produce harder wood than some hardwood trees.

The softwoods used in the building trades are dried either by air drying or kiln drying. However, hardwoods used for furniture construction are difficult to dry thoroughly by air drying.

GROWTH

Figure 2-1 shows the principal parts of the inner structure of a tree. The *pith* is the soft, center part of the tree which sometimes deteriorates and leaves the center hollow. The *heartwood* surrounds the pith and may be called mature wood because it does not aid in carrying food to the various parts of the tree. Surrounding the heartwood is the *sapwood*, which acts as the food carrier and is usually lighter in color than the heartwood. The *cambium* layer, between the sapwood and the bark, is a sticky fluid material. The tree grows when new cells are formed in the cambium layer. New wood cells develop on the inside of the layer, while cells that form bark develop on the outside of the layer.

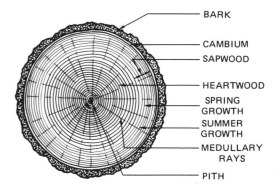

Fig. 2-1 Cross section of tree

Medullary rays are the hard, flaky growth that connects the center of the tree with the bark.

The pattern, or *grain*, of most woods is formed by the annular rings of the tree. Two growth rings, a hard one and a soft one, are formed each year. The soft ring is formed as the tree grows rapidly in the spring. The hard, narrow ring is formed during the slow summer growth. The approximate age of a tree may be found by counting the annular rings on the stump after the tree has been cut. In most cases, hardwoods grow slower than softwoods.

IDENTIFICATION

It is important for a woodworker to be able to recognize the various kinds of woods used. Each wood has its own identifying characteristics of growth. Some woods may

be identified by their highly figured grain, by their odor, or by their weight, color, or hardness, table 2-1.

A few of the woods having highly figured grains are walnut, chestnut, hickory, and oak. Cedar has a distinct figure due to the numerous knots. Basswood, cypress, redwood, poplar, and white pine have very little figure in the grain. Therefore, it is necessary to identify these woods by their color or odor.

Redwood has a reddish brown color and is much softer than mahogany. White pine and maple are both white, but maple is harder and heavier. Poplar has a yellowish green color but no distinctive grain and is not as heavy as yellow pine. Because of its aromatic odor, cedar is easily identified. Cypress, in addition to its peculiar odor, is light brown in color and has an oily appearance.

Kinds of Wood	Lasting Qualities (Outside Use)	Grain	Strength	Hardness	Weight
1. Basswood	Medium	Close	Weak	Soft	Light
2. Beech	Poor	Close	Strong	Hard	Heavy
3. Birch	Medium	Close	Strong	Hard	Heavy
4. Cedar (Red)	Good	Close	Medium	Medium	Light
5. Cedar (Western Red)	Good	Close	Medium	Soft	Light
6. Chestnut	Good	Open	Medium	Medium	Light
7. Cypress	Good	Close	Medium	Soft	Light
8. Douglas Fir	Good	Close	Strong	Medium	Medium
9. Gum (Red)	Poor	Close	Medium	Medium	Medium
10. Hickory	Medium	Open	Strong	Hard	Heavy
11. Mahogany	Medium	Open	Strong	Hard	Medium
12. Maple	Poor	Close	Strong	Hard	Heavy
13. Maple (Western Soft)	Poor	Close	Medium	Medium	Light
14. Oak (White)	Good	Open	Strong	Hard	Heavy
15. Pine (Western White)	Medium	Close	Medium	Soft	Light
16. Pine (Shortleaf)	Good	Close	Strong	Medium	Medium
17. Poplar (Yellow)	Good	Close	Medium	Soft	Light
18. Redwood	Very Good	Close	Weak	Soft	Light
19. Spruce (Sitka)	Good	Close	Weak	Soft	Light
20. Walnut (Black)	Good	Open	Strong	Hard	Medium

Table 2-1 Comparison of Common Woods

CHARACTERISTICS AND USES OF COMMON WOODS

Basswood *(Tilia americana).* The basswood tree grows best on lowlands along the rivers east of the Mississippi. It is a soft wood, works easily, and warps little. Some of its principal uses are for toys, paper pulp, drawing boards, picture frames, core stock in veneered panels, and food containers. It takes and holds nails well.

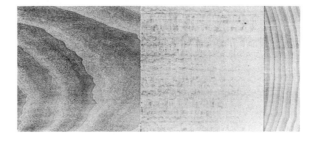

AMERICAN BASSWOOD

Beech *(Fagus grandifolia).* Beech grows best in the eastern part of the United States. Because beech is hard, strong, and elastic wood, it is used frequently for parts which must bear weight and stress, such as tool handles, chairs, frame parts, and sides of drawers.

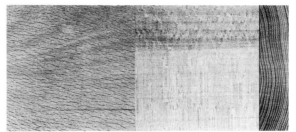

AMERICAN BEECH

Birch *(Betula lutea).* Birch grows best in the northern part of the United States and Canada. It is hard, tough, and elastic. The heartwood of birch is reddish brown, and the sapwood is white. Some uses of birch include cabinetwork, spools, shoe heels, dowels, and interior trim. The bark was formerly used for the making of canoes. Birch is a difficult wood to work because it is very hard and its grain is irregular. It is often used as a substitute for walnut and mahogany.

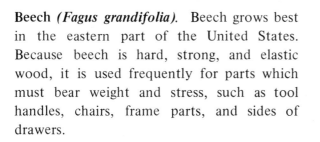

YELLOW BIRCH

Eastern Red Cedar *(Juniperus virginiana).* Red cedar is a popular wood used to line linen closets and chests because its odor is offensive to moths. The heartwood of cedar is dark red, and the sapwood is white. Due to the numerous knots found in this wood, it is difficult to plane. This wood is found in the eastern part of the United States.

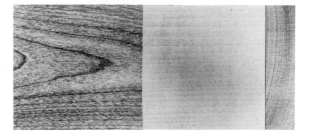

EASTERN RED CEDAR

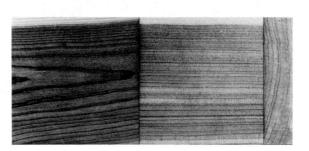

Cypress *(Taxodium distichum).* Cypress grows best in the swamps of the southern United States. Except for the sapwood which is nearly white, cypress is dark brown. The wood is light in weight and planes easily. Cypress is durable when in contact with soil or water. For this reason, it is used extensively for shingles, railroad ties, water tubs and tanks, porch boxes, and boats.

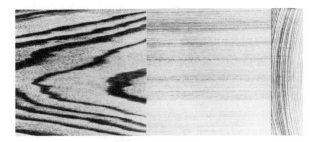

BALD CYPRESS

Douglas Fir *(Pseudotsuga taxifolia).* The several species of fir are so closely related to the spruce that it is difficult to distinguish between them. Douglas fir is strong, elastic, and widely used for plywood, packing cases, dimension lumber for interior use, heavy construction work, masts, piles, and railroad ties. It grows extensively in the western mountains and northwest coastal regions of the United States.

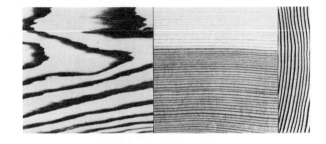

DOUGLAS-FIR

Mahogany *(Swietenia mahagoni).* There are several varieties of mahogany, and it is difficult to distinguish among them. It grows mostly in Cuba, Central America, the West Indies, and Africa. Mahogany has been used extensively for fine furniture, interior trim, and panel work. Mahogany works easily, warps little, and takes a fine finish.

MAHOGANY

Sugar Maple *(Acer saccharum).* Hard maple, which is used extensively in furniture and interior work, grows best in the northeastern part of the United States. It varies in color from light brown to white. Because of its toughness, it is difficult to work. Bird's-eye maple and curly maple are often used for fine furniture, but they are scarce. Bird's-eye maple shows a beautiful spotted design, resulting from an irregularity in growth.

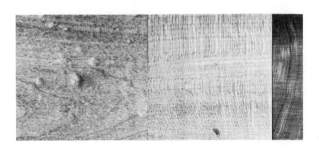

SUGAR MAPLE

Western White Pine *(Pinus ponderosa).* As its name indicates, the color of this wood is nearly white. It is used extensively in building construction for doors and window frames. White pine is light in weight, works easily, and warps little when properly seasoned. It grows in the western part of the United States.

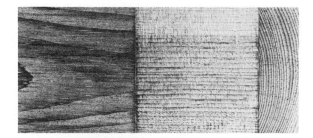

WESTERN WHITE PINE

White Oak *(Quercus alba).* White oak, which is most commonly used in cabinetwork, is found in the eastern part of the United States. It is light brown in color and has an open, noticeable grain. The medullary rays of oak are very prominent and produce a flaky surface when it is quartersawed. This wood is used for interior finish, cabinetwork, furniture, flooring, and implemental parts.

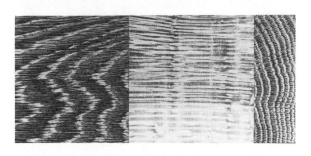

WHITE OAK

Yellow Poplar *(Liriodendron tulipifera).* Yellow poplar is used for vehicle bodies, core stock in plywood, furniture, interior trim, doors, siding, and paper pulp. It is dark yellow, easy to work, and grows best in the eastern third of the United States.

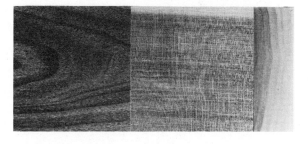

YELLOW POPLAR

Black Walnut *(Juglans nigera).* Black walnut, the ideal American cabinet wood, is noted for its richness in color, durability, and beauty. It grows mainly in the eastern half of the United States and requires a deep, rich soil. Stump and burl walnut are very valuable for veneer and panel work.

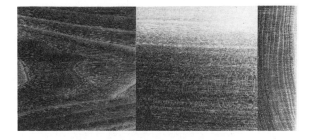

BLACK WALNUT

REVIEW QUESTIONS

A.   Identification

1.   Name the following parts in the cross section of a tree. Use the list provided.

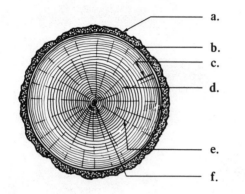

Pith
Medullary rays
Heartwood
Sapwood
Bark
Cambium

2.   Draw a cross section of a piece of lumber that has been plain-sawed and one that has been quartersawed.

3.   Name four ways in which woods can be identified.

B.   Multiple Choice

4.   How can softwood trees be identified?
   a. They lose their leaves annually.
   b. They remain green all year long.
   c. Those trees that have soft wood.
   d. They only grow in certain regions of the world.

5.   The growth of a tree occurs in the:
   a. heartwood.   c. cambium layer.
   b. sapwood.   d. pith.

6.   Which of the following woods is not native to the United States?
   a. Cypress   c. Mahogany
   b. Birch   d. Basswood

7.   Which part of the tree is responsible for carrying food to the other tree parts?
   a. Sapwood   c. Heartwood
   b. Pith   d. Bark

unit 3
wood products other than lumber

OBJECTIVES

After completing this unit, the student will be able to:

- explain how plywood is manufactured.
- describe how particleboard and hardboard are made.
- list the advantages of using sheet materials.

A large portion of harvested timber is used for making boards and lumber. However, a large amount of timber is also remanufactured into sheet-type materials such as plywood, particleboard, and hardboard.

PLYWOOD

Plywood is made of thin sheets of wood, called *veneers* (usually 1/28 inch thick), glued to *core stock*. Core stock can either be a piece of solid wood, thin sheets of veneer, or particleboard. The grain in each sheet of veneer runs crosswise in alternate layers. This gives the plywood added strength and prevents warping and shrinking.

Plywood which is made with waterproof glue is used for exterior purposes such as concrete wall and foundation forms, sheathing, and materials for boat building.

Interior plywood is made with nonwaterproof glue. The cheaper grades are often used for subflooring, while the better grades are used for paneling walls and cabinets. Hardwood plywood is used extensively in the manufacture of quality furniture, cabinets, and paneling.

Veneer for plywood is obtained from logs by slicing, sawing, or rotary cutting. Rotary-cut veneer is the most economical to manufacture. A section of a log is softened in hot water or steam for several hours. It is then placed in a veneer lathe and rotated against a long, sharp knife, figure 3-1. This knife peels off a continuous sheet of veneer, figure 3-2.

The thin veneers are then dried, inspected, and clamped in a plywood press with glue between each layer, figures 3-3 and 3-4. Upon leaving the press, the plywood is sawed square and inspected, figure 3-5. Douglas fir plywood is produced by the rotary cutting method. Millions of square feet of this plywood are manufactured each year for use in homes and commercial buildings.

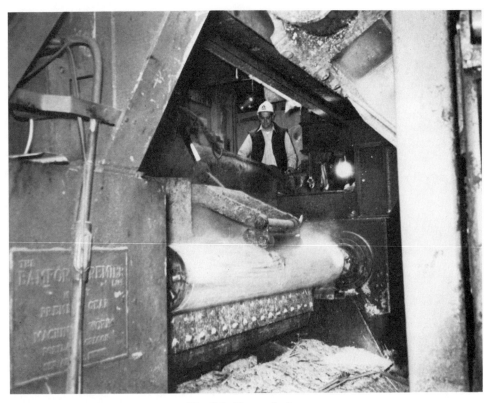

Fig. 3-1 Veneer lathe

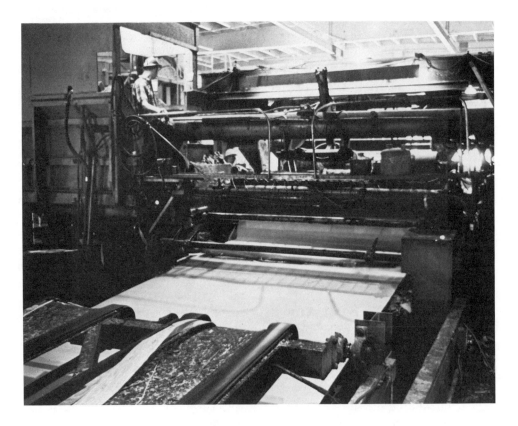

Fig. 3-2 Lathe peeling veneer from a log

Fig. 3-3 Grading and inspecting plywood veneers

Fig. 3-4 Plywood press

Fig. 3-5 Inspecting finished plywood

Veneer stock can be purchased separately by furniture manufacturers to use in making furniture and cabinets, figure 3-6. In this case, the cabinetmaker glues the thin veneer onto a less expensive piece of wood.

The crotch, burl, and stump sections of some hardwood trees provide valuable, highly figured veneer, figure 3-7. Careful selection of these veneers allows the craftsperson to produce attractive pieces of cabinetry, figure 3-8.

Fig. 3-6 A few of a large variety of fine veneers that are available to the cabinetmaker.

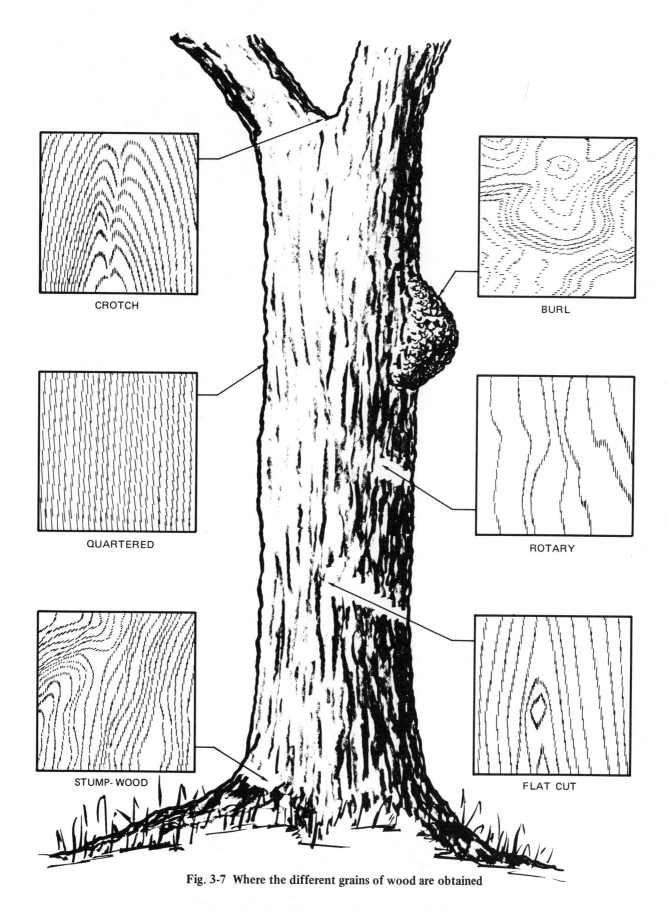

CROTCH

BURL

QUARTERED

ROTARY

STUMP-WOOD

FLAT CUT

Fig. 3-7 Where the different grains of wood are obtained

Fig. 3-8 A paneled office interior *(Courtesy of the Fine Hardwoods Association)*

PARTICLEBOARD

Particleboard is a flat slab, usually a standard size of 4' x 8', made from wood chips bonded together by glue, figure 3-9. Various thicknesses (¼ inch to 1½ inches) of particleboard are obtained when the board is formed in heated presses under very high pressure. Because of its grain regularity which minimizes warping, particleboard is often used as a plywood core. It is also used for sheathing, roofing, siding, and floor under-layment.

Fig. 3-9 Particleboard is made from small wood chips.

HARDBOARD

Hardboard is composed of wood fibers that are steamed, heated, and pressed by heavy rollers, figure 3-10. The sheets are fed into multiple presses where heat and pressure produce thin, hard, dry boards. From the presses, the boards are trimmed to standard dimensions and wrapped for shipping. Hard-board ranges in thickness from 1/8 inch to 3/4 inch, in width up to 5 feet, and in length up to 16 feet. Hardboard is useful for cover-ing large areas where wood-grain material is not required, such as the backs of bookcases, drawer bottoms, and the backs of cabinets. In construction, it is extensively used for siding of homes and interior paneling.

Fig. 3-10 Four common types of hardboard (Left to right — perforated pegboard, tempered hardboard, prism wood, and standard hardboard)

ADVANTAGES OF MANUFACTURED WOOD PRODUCTS

Because industry is able to remanufacture raw materials such as wood, they can combine the best advantages and remove most disadvantages of the original product. Some advantages of using sheet materials are:

- Checking, splitting, and warping are greatly reduced.

- The use of large sheet materials saves both time and materials in the construction industry.

- Plywood, hardboard, and particleboard come in several types and sizes so they can be suited to a particular job.

- Conservation is practiced by using the waste materials from the manufacturing of lumber to make particleboard and hardboard. The elimination of wasted sawdust is achieved by slicing the log with a knife rather than cutting it with a saw as in the manufacture of plywood.

REVIEW QUESTIONS

A. Multiple Choice

1. Plywood is made up of a number of thin sheets of wood called:
   a. hardboard.   c. veneers.
   b. core material.   d. strips.

2. Which of the following is particleboard made from?
   a. Wood chips   c. Plywood
   b. Lumber   d. Plastic

3. The standard size of a sheet of plywood, particleboard, or hardboard is:
   a. 2' x 6'   c. 4' x 8'
   b. 3' x 7'   d. 5' x 9'

4. Softwood plywood such as Douglas fir is used mostly:
   a. for fine cabinetwork.   c. for chair construction.
   b. for quality paneling.   d. in the construction industry.

5. Hardboard is useful in those areas that do not require:
   a. great strength.   c. a grain pattern.
   b. large pieces.   d. a thin material.

B. Short Answer

6. Name three advantages of using manufactured wood products such as plywood, particleboard, and hardboard.

unit 4
selecting a project

OBJECTIVES

After completing this unit, the student will be able to:

- recognize the considerations that must be made before selecting a project.
- explain the fundamentals of good design.
- list the steps in designing a project.

The woodworking project that is to be built should be one that the builder can be proud of. Therefore, the selection of a project should be carefully thought out. One way to do this is to answer the following questions about the proposed project.

1. Will the project be useful? An item may be either decorative or functional, however, it should be something that is needed.

2. Am I interested enough in this project to work on it until I complete it?

3. Do I have the materials, tools, and skills necessary to build the project? The necessary skills must be mastered and the necessary tools must be available to complete a project. If they are not, it would be advisable to think about some other project until the proper tools or experience is obtained.

4. The size of the project should be such that it can be planned and constructed in the allotted time. Until experience is gained with tools and materials, it is best to select projects that are less difficult. As skill develops, there will be many opportunities to work on the more difficult projects. Work is admired much more if it is a simple, well-done project than if it is a large project, but the workmanship is lacking.

5. What kind of wood should be used in the project? There are many varieties of wood available. Some woods are very easy to work, and others are difficult to cut and shape. Also, some are very expensive, while others are relatively inexpensive. With the first few projects, the work will be less difficult if a wood (such as pine or bass) is selected that is easier to work. As experience is gained,

work with the harder woods becomes easier.

6. Where will the project be used when completed? This will affect the style, type of wood, as well as the kind of finish that will be put on the project.

7. What will be the total cost of the completed project? Before construction begins, it is a good idea to figure out how much the completed project will cost.

8. Where can plans or ideas for projects be obtained? In the last section of this text there are carefully selected projects. Other places to look are in woodworking textbooks and magazines, catalogs, and furniture stores. Another choice is to design your own project. Although this is not an easy task, it is a rewarding one.

DESIGNING A PROJECT

Design is an essential element in the development of a project. The three fundamentals of good design are *function, appearance*, and *construction and workmanship*. The individual must consider each fundamental of design if the completed project is to have a pleasing appearance.

Function

In order for a project to be useful, it must fit the needs or requirements that it was originally intended for. It would be considered poor design if a chair were not comfortable to sit in, or if a gun rack did not properly hold the gun.

Appearance

The next consideration is how the finished project will look. The woodworker should strive for a design that has a pleasing appearance. Items are often selected over others based on looks alone. Generally, appearance deals with such items as balance, proportion, harmony, shape, and materials.

Construction and Workmanship

The construction features, such as the type of joints used, the direction the grain should run, the kind of wood to be used, the type of finish to be applied, and the woodworker's skill, should all be given careful consideration.

STEPS IN DESIGNING A PROJECT

1. Determine the requirements for the project. Write these requirements in list form with the most important first, etc., figure 4-1.

2. Develop five or six sketches of possible solutions. Try to be free with your ideas. Let your imagination for new ideas guide your thinking. These are only preliminary sketches, figure 4-2. Little time should be spent on detail.

3. Select one or two of the best ideas and further develop them. Keep in mind the three fundamentals of function, appearance, and construction, figure 4-3.

4. Refine the ideas and develop more detail. If desirable, construct a model of the design. Use simple materials such as paper, cardboard, or balsa.

5. If the project design is pleasing, then determine the particular joints, types of wood, and finish to use. If it is not pleasing, go back to one of the earlier designs and start the same process over again.

REQUIREMENTS FOR BOOK HOLDER

1. Holds books on desk.
2. Able to get the books out easily.
3. Able to replace the books easily.
4. Able to hold different sized books.
5. Looks good.

Fig. 4-1

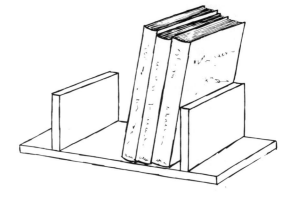

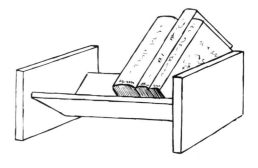

Fig. 4-2 Preliminary sketches for design purposes

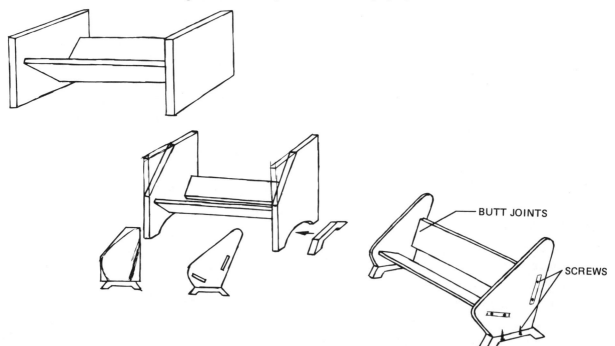

BUTT JOINTS

SCREWS

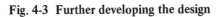

Fig. 4-3 Further developing the design

6. Begin to develop a working drawing and plan on how to actually construct the project. This step will include a bill of materials, a working drawing, a plan of procedure, and an estimate of time for project completion.

REVIEW QUESTIONS

A. Multiple Choice

1. It is best for the beginning woodworker to select a project that:
   a. contains several types of joints and construction techniques.
   b. is relatively simple.
   c. is only put together with nails and screws.
   d. is made from oak or maple.

2. A good place to look for good ideas for projects is:
   a. in the back of books pertaining to woodworking.
   b. in magazines that have articles on woodworking.
   c. in furniture stores.
   d. all of the above.

3. The first step in designing a project is to:
   a. make a complete bill of materials.
   b. develop the working drawing.
   c. list the requirements that the completed item should meet.
   d. make a model of the project.

B. Identification

4. Place the following steps in designing a project in the proper order.
   _____ Select the best idea.
   _____ Begin to develop the working drawing.
   _____ Determine the requirements for the project.
   _____ Determine the particular joint construction.
   _____ Further refine the ideas.
   _____ Develop five or six sketches.

5. Identify the three fundamentals of good design.

unit 5
developing and reading a working drawing

OBJECTIVES

After completing this unit, the student will be able to:

- identify the location of the views in a working drawing.
- list the names of various drafting instruments.
- identify various types of line symbols.

The beginning woodworker must be able to read and understand a working drawing before accurately constructing a project. Almost every manufactured article is constructed with the aid of a plan or drawing.

Projects constructed of wood are planned with the aid of a working drawing. A *working drawing* gives all the necessary information about the size, shape, and method of assembly of the project.

THREE-VIEW WORKING DRAWING

Because most objects have height, width, and depth, the working drawing usually shows three views. Figure 5-1 shows the *front view* located in the lower left-hand section of the plate. The *top view* is located directly above the front view. The *side* or *end view* is placed to the right of the front view.

Since the front view shows the most detail, it is usually drawn first. The arrowheads on the projection lines indicate that the width of the front view is then projected to the top view. To project the depth, it must first be measured in the top view. Both the height and depth are then projected to the space provided for the side or end view. The projections save much time and make the working drawing more accurate. A horizontal ground line and a vertical trace line are drawn between the views to aid in the projection. For this, a T square and 45-degree triangle or a drafting machine are used.

DRAWING INSTRUMENTS AND SYMBOLS

Other instruments used by the drafter include the 30-60-degree and 45-degree triangles, the T square, and drawing board, figure 5-2. Figure 5-3 illustrates a set of drawing instruments that are necessary for drafting work.

The drafter uses various types of lines to convey the meaning of the plans. Figure 5-4 shows some common line symbols. An

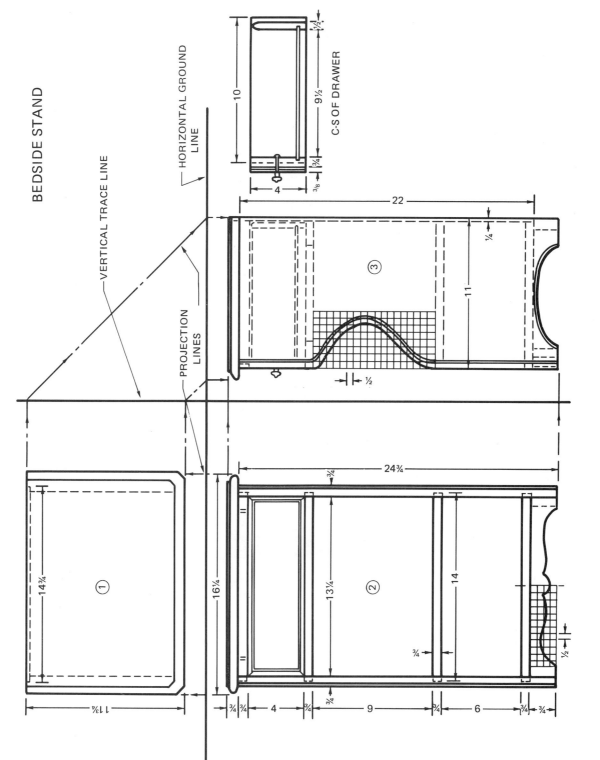

BEDSIDE STAND

Fig. 5-1 Three-view working drawing

Fig. 5-2 Drawing board, T square, and triangles

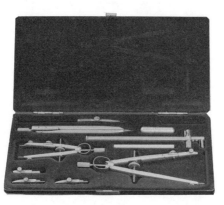

Fig. 5-3 Set of drawing instruments

BORDER LINE	————————————
VISIBLE OBJECT LINE	————————————
HIDDEN OBJECT LINE	– – – – – – – – –
EXTENSION LINE	————————————
PROJECTION LINE	—— — —— — ——
DIMENSION LINE	⊢——— 2 1/2 ———→
CUTTING-PLANE LINE	—— – – —— – – ——
CENTERLINE	—— – —— – —— ——

Fig. 5-4 Common line symbols

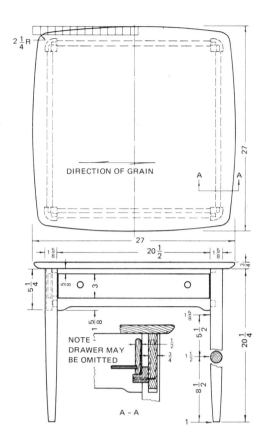

Fig. 5-5 Two-view working drawing

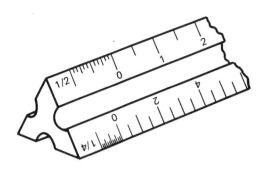

Fig. 5-6 Architect's scale

understanding of these symbols is essential to both the drafter and the beginning wood-worker.

Overall dimensions and detail dimensions are placed between the views when possible.

They are placed to read from the bottom or right side of the drawing. The radius is given when arcs are dimensioned. The diameter is given when circles or holes are dimensioned. If space permits, the dimensions are placed between dimension lines, figure 5-5.

SCALING

It is impossible to draw most objects to their actual size. Therefore, it is necessary to draw them to a reduced scale with the actual size dimensions given. The architect's scale is used for measuring in mechanical drawing, figure 5-6. The 3/32, 1/8, 3/16, 1/4, 3/8, 1/2, 3/4, 1, and 1 1/2-inch scales are usually found on the architect's scale. The architect general-ly uses a scale of 1/4 inch equals 1 foot, while most cabinet drawings are reduced to a scale of 1/8, 3/16, or 1/4 inch equals 1 inch.

REVIEW QUESTIONS

A. Identification

1. Name each of the following lines and instruments.

a. ----------------------------------

b. ————— – ——————— – – —————

c. ◄————————— 2 —————————►

d.

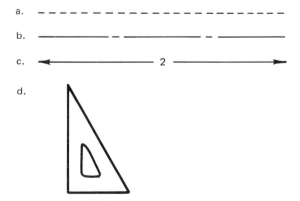

e.

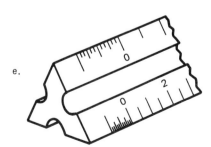

2. Identify the views in the working drawing given below.

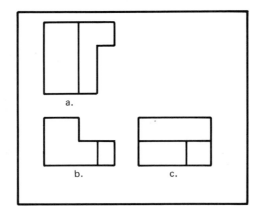

a.

b.   c.

B.   **Multiple Choice**

3. The name of the drawing that provides you with the necessary information tion to build the project is called a:
    a. two-view drawing.   c. perspective drawing.
    b. pictorial drawing.   d. working drawing.

4. A working drawing usually consists of _____ view(s).
    a. 4   c. 2
    b. 3   d. 1

5. Projection lines are used in drawing to:
    a. transfer measurements from one view to another.
    b. eliminate detail drawings.
    c. project the drawing onto a screen.
    d. draw a picture with a projector.

6. When a note at the bottom of a drawing reads 1/4″ = 1″, this means:
    a. it is a very small project.
    b. the project is drawn to scale.
    c. the material in the project is 1/4 inch thick.
    d. the drawing is 1/2 the size of the project.

7. Dimensions on a drawing read from:
    a. left to right.   c. the bottom and right side.
    b. right to left.   d. the bottom only.

unit 6
preparations for constructing a project

OBJECTIVES

After completing this unit, the student will be able to:

- describe how a bill of materials is developed.
- figure board measure.
- explain how a plan of procedure is developed.

Careful planning of a shop project saves time and materials, and improves the quality of work. Experienced cabinetmakers always make a simple sketch or drawing of an item before construction begins. If equipment and facilities are not available to make a drawing, a carefully done pencil sketch of the views and dimensions is satisfactory.

Fig. 6-1 Completed book rack

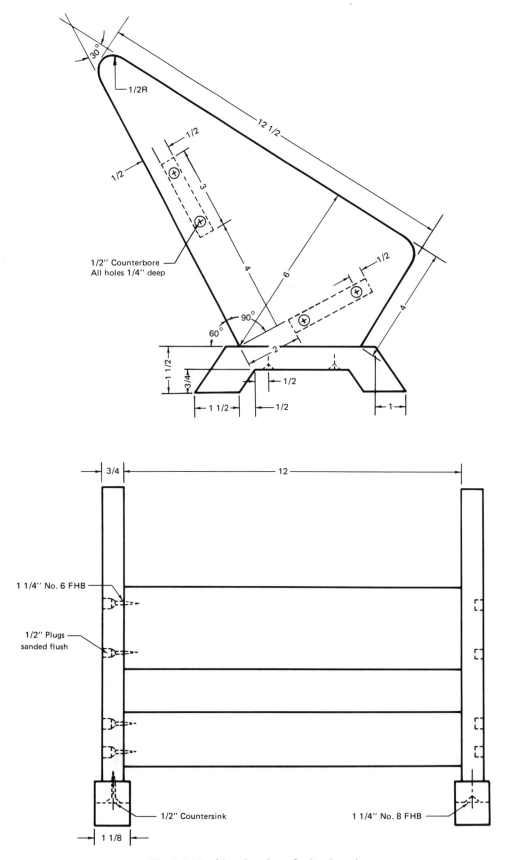

Fig. 6-2 Working drawing of a book rack

WORKING DRAWINGS

A working drawing of the book rack, figure 6-1, is shown in figure 6-2. This drawing shows the front and side views. It provides all necessary dimensions and details needed to build the project. To make a drawing complete, it is sometimes necessary to show the top view. Many times it is desirable to make a three-dimensional sketch, figure 6-3, to visualize how a project will look.

BILL OF MATERIALS

To begin the construction of a project, a bill of materials is developed, figure 6-4. The *bill of materials* is a detailed list of the number of pieces, name of the part, and the kind and finished sizes of stock needed. It also allows for a cost estimate before the project is started.

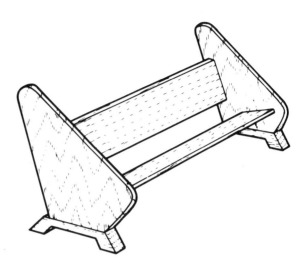

Fig. 6-3 Pictorial drawing of book rack

BILL OF MATERIALS

INDUSTRIAL ARTS DEPARTMENT					FLORENCE HIGH SCHOOL			

Name   Robert Jones   Class   7-B

Instructor   Mr. Carter

Project   Book Rack   Date   2/25/81

No. Pieces	Thick-ness (inches)	Width (inches)	Length (inches)	Part	Material	Bd. Ft.	Bd. Ft. Cost	Total Cost
2	1 1/8	1 1/2	8 1/2	Legs	Pine	.35	.60/ft.	$0.21
2	1/2	3	12	Rails	Pine	.50	.60/ft.	$0.30
2	3/4	6	13	Sides	Pine	1.08	.60/ft.	$0.65

Hardware and Finishing Materials:	
8 – 1 1/4″ No. 6 FHB wood screws	$0.20
8 – 1 1/2″ No. 8 FHB wood screws	$0.32
100-grit sandpaper (1 sheet)	$0.35

Fig. 6-4 Bill of materials for a book rack

FIGURING BOARD MEASURE

The standard method of listing lumber dimensions is thickness times width times length. The unit of measure for small quantities of the lumber is the board foot. Larger quantities are sold by the thousand board feet. A *board foot* is a piece of lumber with dimensions 1 inch thick by 12 inches wide and 12 inches long, or the equivalent. A piece of lumber that is 2″ x 6″ x 12″ is equal to one board foot, just as a piece 1″ x 6″ x 24″ is equal to one board foot, figure 6-5.

Stock listed as 2″ x 4″ is sawed to this size in the rough, but when surfaced, it is only 1 1/2″ x 3 1/2″. Surfaced 1-inch stock is actually only 3/4 inch in thickness. However, it is figured as a full inch when calculating board measure.

The board measure table in the appendix, pages 300 and 301, is a great aid in figuring board feet. Because this table is not always available, the formula for figuring board measure is:

$$\text{Bd. ft.} = \frac{\underset{\text{Pieces}}{\text{No. of}} \times \underset{\text{(in.)}}{\text{thickness}} \times \underset{\text{(in.)}}{\text{width}} \times \underset{\text{(in.)}}{\text{length}}}{1 \times 12 \times 12 \text{ (or 144)}}$$

Example: Compute the number of board feet contained in two pieces of stock that measure 1″ x 8″ x 32″.

$$\text{Bd. ft.} = \frac{\overset{2}{\underset{\text{pieces)}}{\text{(no. of}}} \times \overset{1}{\underset{\text{(thickness)}}{}} \times \overset{8}{\underset{\text{(width)}}{}} \times \overset{32}{\underset{\text{(length)}}{}}}{144}$$

$$= \frac{512}{144}$$

$$= 3\frac{5}{9} \text{ bd. ft.}$$

or

Approximately 3 1/2 bd. ft.

When the length of the stock is given in feet, the denominator is 12 instead of 144. This is because a board foot may also be defined as a piece of lumber that measures 1 inch thick by 12 inches wide by 1 foot long. Therefore, the formula is changed as follows:

$$\text{Bd. ft.} = \frac{\underset{\text{pieces}}{\text{No. of}} \times \underset{\text{(in.)}}{\text{thickness}} \times \underset{\text{(in.)}}{\text{width}} \times \underset{\text{(ft.)}}{\text{length}}}{1 \times 12 \times 1 \text{ (or 12)}}$$

Example: Compute the number of board feet contained in four pieces of stock that measure 1″ x 6″ x 5′.

$$\text{Bd. ft.} = \frac{\overset{4}{\underset{\text{pieces)}}{\text{(no. of}}} \times \overset{1}{\underset{\text{(thickness)}}{}} \times \overset{6}{\underset{\text{(width)}}{}} \times \overset{5}{\underset{\text{(length)}}{}}}{12}$$

$$= \frac{120}{12}$$

$$= 10 \text{ bd. ft.}$$

Fig. 6-5 Each piece of lumber contains one board foot.

PLAN OF PROCEDURE

A procedure for constructing a project must be carefully planned. Otherwise, time and materials will be wasted during construction. A plan of procedure may be in list form and contain enough information to indicate the processes involved. The following is a plan of procedure for the book rack:

PLAN OF PROCEDURE

Process	Tools Required
1. Select stock for two legs and cut two pieces 1 1/2" x 1 3/4" x 8 1/2".	Handsaw
2. Select the best face and adjacent edge and plane smooth and square.	Jack plane
3. Plane to proper thickness and width (1 1/8" x 1 1/2").	Jack plane
4. Lay out and cut outside angles on legs.	Rule and backsaw
5. Lay out and cut inside angles.	T bevel and backsaw
6. Remove waste stock with wood chisel being careful not to split material beyond layout lines.	Wood chisel and mallet
7. Select stock for two rails and rough cut to length.	Handsaw
8. True one face.	Jack plane
9. Plane to thickness.	Jack plane
10. Joint one edge.	Jack plane
11. Rip to width plus 1/16 inch.	Handsaw
12. Plane to finish width.	Jack plane
13. Square one end.	Block plane
14. Cut to length.	Handsaw and block plane
15. Lay out the two sides of the book rack on the same board. Material may be saved by making layout with pointed ends facing each other, figure 6-6. It is not necessary to round corners at this time.	
16. Make the necessary cuts on the two ends making sure to leave at least 1/16 inch for planing.	Handsaw

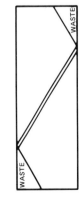

Fig. 6-6 Layout for book rack ends

17.	Clamp ends to-gether and plane to finished dimensions. Check for squareness while planing.	Plane and try square	
18.	Lay out rounded corners. Note that the base corners are not rounded.	Compass	
19.	Cut rounded corners.	Coping saw	
20.	Locate holes and counterbore with 1/2 inch bit to 1/4 inch depth.	Drill press	
21.	Drill shank hole for 1 1/4-inch No. 6 flathead wood screw.	Drill press	
22.	Sand all pieces.	100-grit sand-paper	

23.	Lay out location of screws in legs and attach to ends with 1 1/4-inch No. 8 flathead wood screws.	Hand drill, awl, and screwdriver	
24.	Attach sides to rails with one screw in each end of each rail.	Hand drill, awl, and screwdriver	
25.	Set book rack on a flat surface and mark and install remaining screws.	Hand drill, awl, and screwdriver	
26.	Make plugs from scrap material.	Plug cutter and drill press	
27.	Install plugs and trim flush with surface.	Glue and wood chisel	
28.	Sand.	100-grit abrasive paper	
29.	Apply finish.	Finishing materials	

REVIEW QUESTIONS

A.   Multiple Choice

1. The plan of procedure is:
   a. not necessary for small projects.
   b. a list of steps in the proper order for the construction of a project.
   c. the same as a working drawing.
   d. a set of blueprints for constructing a project.

2. A working drawing is:
   a. not necessary for small projects.
   b. the same as the plan of procedure.
   c. a drawing or sketch that shows the details and dimensions of the project.
   d. a three-dimensional drawing of the project.

3. The proper order for listing lumber dimensions on the bill of materials is:
   a. thickness, length, width.
   b. thickness, width, length, number of pieces.
   c. length, width, number of pieces, thickness.
   d. number of pieces, thickness, width, length.

4. To help visualize how a project will look when completed, it is sometimes desirable to draw a:
   a. three-dimensional sketch.
   b. front-view sketch.
   c. top-view sketch.
   d. side-view sketch.

B. Short Answer

5. Write the formula for figuring board feet.

6. Calculate the number of board feet of material in three pieces of stock that measure 1″ x 8″ x 40″.

7. Calculate the number of board feet of material in ten pieces of stock that measure 2″ x 4″ x 8′.

8. The bill of materials should list the kind and finished sizes of stock needed, the number of pieces, and the _____.

unit 7
layout tools

OBJECTIVES

After completing this unit, the student will be able to:

- name and properly use different layout tools.
- explain the English and metric systems of measurement.
- lay out distances and angles.
- make common geometric layouts.

The group of tools used first in the construction of an item is known as *layout tools*. Layout tools are those used for measuring, laying out, and checking angles.

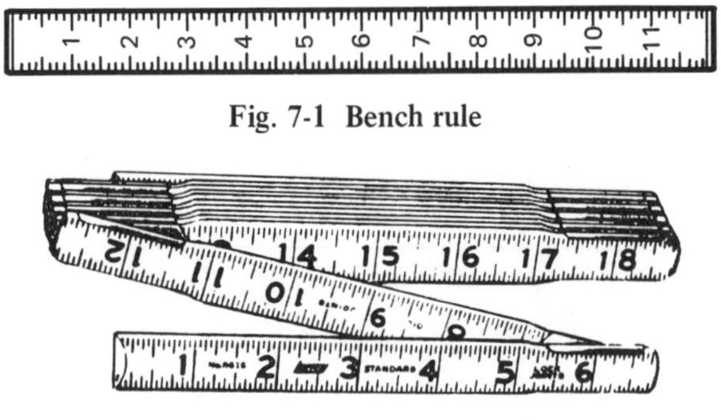

BENCH RULES

Bench rules are commonly used for short, simple measurements on bench projects. They are made of wood or metal. Bench rules are available in 1-, 2-, or 3-foot lengths and also come with metric divisions, figure 7-1.

FOLDING RULES

The folding rule is often used by the woodworker for measuring long stock, figure 7-2. It is made of wood and can be folded into a small compact size that is easy to carry.

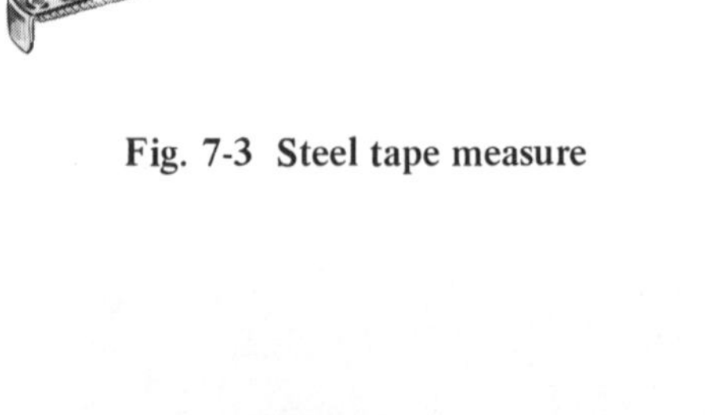

STEEL TAPE MEASURE

The steel tape measure comes in sizes from 3 feet to 24 feet, figure 7-3. To make

Fig. 7-1 Bench rule

Fig. 7-2 Folding rule

Fig. 7-3 Steel tape measure

the scale easier to read, the blades are white or yellow with black numerals. Graduations are marked on one or both edges. A clear, tough finish is applied to the blade to decrease wear on it. Because this special coating is used, measurements may be marked on the blade with a pencil and then erased.

TRY SQUARE

The try square is used to test the squareness and levelness of small surfaces and to lay out 90-degree angles, figure 7-4. The blade and the handle form a 90-degree angle. Both sides of the blade are divided into eighths of an inch. The blade is made of toughened steel and the handle is either metal or wood. To keep the tool accurate, avoid dropping it or using it as a hammer.

FRAMING AND FOOT SQUARES

The framing square, figure 7-5, is a large, right-angled piece of steel. It is used to square lines across rough stock before cutting, test large surfaces for levelness and squareness, and test for squareness when assembling. Each inch is divided into halves, quarters, eighths, tenths, twelfths, sixteenths, and thirty-seconds.

The foot square is similar to the framing square but smaller, and the inch is only divided into eighths and sixteenths.

T BEVEL

The T bevel is similar to the try square, but has an adjustable blade used for laying out and testing angles, chamfers, and bevels, figure 7-6.

COMBINATION SQUARE

The combination square, figure 7-7, has a sliding, adjustable head used for laying out and testing 90-degree and 45-degree angles. It usually has a spirit level in the handle which can be used for testing vertical and horizontal surfaces.

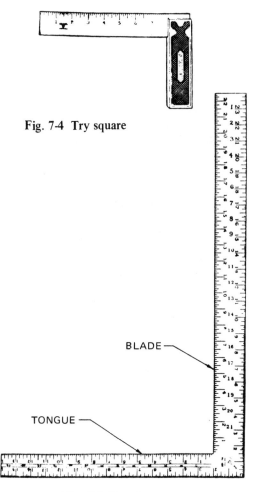

Fig. 7-4 Try square

BLADE

TONGUE

Fig. 7-5 Framing square

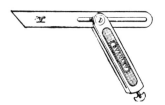

Fig. 7-6 T bevel

Fig. 7-7 Combination square

MARKING GAUGE

The marking gauge, figure 7-8, is made of wood or metal. It is used for marking a line parallel with an edge. The three parts of a marking gauge are the head, beam, and spur. The beam has a scale which is divided into sixteenths of an inch. A sharp spur in one end of the beam does the marking. The head is square or oval and contains the thumbscrew which holds the gauge in adjustment. A hole may be bored in one end of the beam and a pencil inserted when it is necessary to lay out chamfers and bevels.

MORTISE GAUGE

The mortise gauge is a marking gauge with three spurs instead of one, figure 7-9. Two of the spurs are on one side of the beam. They are adjustable to various widths for marking parallel lines, widths, and thicknesses. Both sides of a mortise or tenon can be marked at one time with the mortise gauge.

SCRATCH AWL

The scratch awl has a sharp, hardened steel point, figure 7-10. It is used to mark lines on both wood and metal surfaces. The scratch awl is also used for making small anchor holes for wood screws. The wood handle has flat sides on it to keep it from rolling off the workbench.

DIVIDERS

Dividers resemble a compass except that both points are metal, figure 7-11. They are used to transfer measurements and lay out circles and arcs. The points should be straight to do accurate work. Some dividers have a removable leg so that a pencil may be used in place of the metal marking point.

TRAMMEL POINTS

The trammel points, figure 7-12, are used for scribing large circles and arcs that

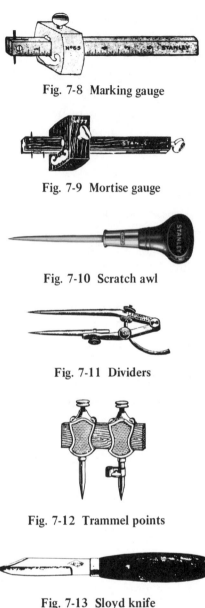

Fig. 7-8 Marking gauge

Fig. 7-9 Mortise gauge

Fig. 7-10 Scratch awl

Fig. 7-11 Dividers

Fig. 7-12 Trammel points

Fig. 7-13 Sloyd knife

cannot be made with dividers. These points are clamped to a wooden bar by adjustable thumbscrews. The length of the bar determines the maximum size a circle or an arc can be scribed.

KNIVES

When extreme accuracy is needed in marking a board or preparing to cut the gain for a hinge, a knife is often used. Figure 7-13 shows one type of knife that can be used for this purpose. A pocket knife is also a good marking tool.

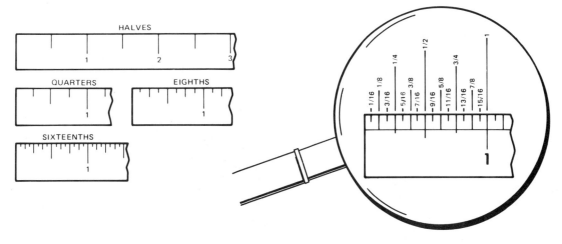

Fig. 7-14 English graduations applied to a rule

HOW THE RULE IS GRADUATED

The *rule* is a device to transfer a measurement from one point or set of drawings to another. Dividers may also be used to transfer measurements. The divisions on rules and other measuring devices are either in English units of feet, inches, and parts of an inch (1/2, 1/4, 1/8, 1/16, etc.), or they use the metric system of metres, centimetres, and millimetres. The beginning woodworker should gain an understanding of both systems.

In the English system, typical division lines on a rule are shown in figure 7-14. Start with the inch as the major division and divide it into two equal parts. The result is two 1/2-inch parts. If the inch is divided into four equal parts, the result is four 1/4-inch parts. In beginning woodworking it is common to

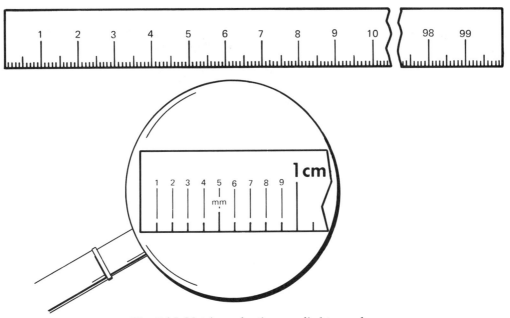

Fig. 7-15 Metric graduations applied to a rule

divide the inch into sixteen equal parts. The result is sixteen 1/16-inch parts.

The standard division line for the metric system is the centimetre which is 1/100 of a metre, figure 7-15. The centimetre may be further broken down into millimetres. There are ten millimetres (mm) in one centimetre (cm). The projects in the back of the text are dimensioned in the English and metric systems so you become familiar with using both.

PROCEDURE FOR MEASURING LENGTH OF STOCK

1. If the end of the stock is irregular or checked, square a line across the board a short distance from the end before measuring the stock to the desired length. Figure 7-16 shows the proper procedure for using the framing square to square a line.

2. Lay the rule on the stock parallel to the edge of the stock. Place one end of the rule even with the squared line. If extreme accuracy is desired, the rule should be placed on edge and the length marked with a knife.

3. Mark the length desired with a sharp pencil and square a line through this point.

4. Lay the rule in place again and check the measurement. Long stock is best measured with a folding rule or a steel tape measure. This reduces the chances for error in measurement since measuring with a short rule adds to the possibilities of inaccuracy.

PROCEDURE FOR MEASURING WIDTH OF STOCK

1. Place the rule on edge across the face of the stock and at right angles with the edges of the stock, figure 7-17. Figure 7-18 shows how stock should be marked to width with the framing square. By

Fig. 7-16 Squaring line with framing square

Fig. 7-17 Measuring width with rule

using the forefinger of either hand, the outside edge of the square is kept even with the edge of the stock.

2. When the stock is too wide to be marked with the marking gauge, the width can be marked near each end, and the points connected with a straightedge and pencil.

3. To mark the width of the stock into several equal divisions, place one end of the rule even with the edge of the surface to be divided. Swing the rule

Fig. 7-18 Measuring width with framing square

Fig. 7-19 Dividing equal spaces with tape rule

diagonally across the surface until the reading of the rule allows an even division, figure 7-19.

PROCEDURE FOR USING THE SQUARE

1. To square a line across the end of the stock, place the tongue of the framing square firmly against the straightest edge of the stock. Have the blade of the framing square extending across the surface to be marked. Square a line along the outside edge of the blade, figure 7-16.

2. To square lines across narrow stock, use the try square, figure 7-20.

3. The try square is also used to extend face lines across the edge of the stock, figure 7-21. In this case, the handle of the try square is against the face side of the stock. Note the position of the hand holding the try square.

4. When marking on the edges of the stock to locate joints or when laying out duplicate parts, place the edge of the stock on the workbench. Use the try square to line up the ends and then mark all pieces as one unit, figure 7-22.

Fig. 7-20 Squaring lines with try square

Fig. 7-21 Continuing face line

Fig. 7-22 Marking duplicate parts

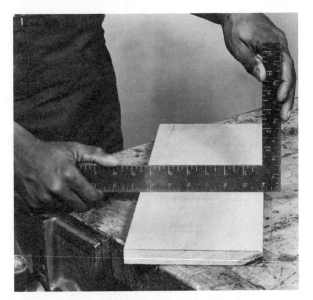

Fig. 7-23 Testing flatness of stock with framing square

5. When testing flatness of stock with the foot square or the framing square, place the blade of the square on the stock. Keep the tongue in an upright position, figure 7-23.

PROCEDURE FOR USING THE MARKING GAUGE

1. Adjust the desired distance between the head and the scribing pin. Tighten the thumbscrew.

2. Place the head of the marking gauge against the board you wish to mark.

3. Tip the gauge in the direction you wish to move the gauge, as shown in figure 7-24, and slowly advance the gauge.

4. Use only light pressure to scribe the line. If heavy pressure is used, the pin may catch in the wood grain and cause a mistake.

PROCEDURE FOR MAKING PATTERNS AND GEOMETRIC LAYOUTS

The principles of geometric construction are used constantly by the woodworker. When designing furniture, it is often desirable to add outline or surface designs to produce a

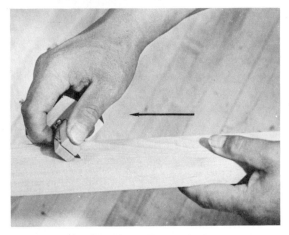

Fig. 7-24 Scribing a line with the gauge

pleasing appearance. The following are the procedures for making patterns and geometric layouts.

Procedure for Marking Rounded Corners

1. Determine the amount of curve (radius A) to be used, figure 7-25.

2. Measure the desired distance A in both directions from the corner and mark this distance on the edges.

3. With a try square, draw lines through these points to meet at point C.

4. Set the compass with a radius equal to A and draw an arc using C as the center.

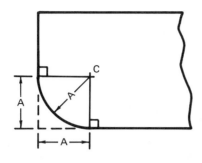

Fig. 7-25 Marking rounded corners

Procedure for Laying Out a Hexagon

1. Draw the diagonals of the square to locate the center C.

2. With this center, draw a circle having a radius equal to one-half the length of one side of the square, figure 7-26.

3. Beginning at point A and using the same radius, step off six equal parts on the circle.

4. Connect these points as in figure 7-26.

Procedure for Laying Out an Octagon-Method 1

1. Draw the diagonals of the square to locate the center C.

2. From each corner of the square and in both directions, lay off a distance equal to one-half of diagonal A, figure 7-27.

3. Join the points just located to form the octagon.

Procedure for Laying Out an Octagon-Method 2

1. Lay out a square equal to the width or height of the desired octagon, figure 7-28.

2. Lightly draw diagonal lines from corner to corner crossing at center O.

3. Using point A as the center, set the compass with a radius equal to AO and lightly scribe lines on the sides of the square at E and F.

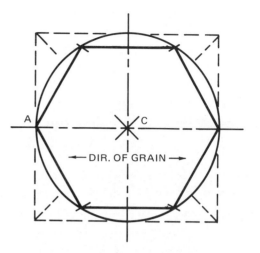

Fig. 7-26 Laying out a hexagon

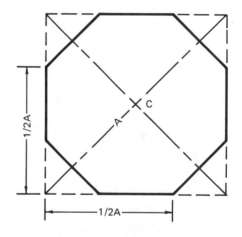

Fig. 7-27 Method 1 for laying out an octagon

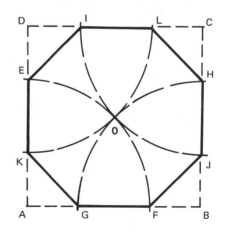

Fig. 7-28 Method 2 for laying out an octagon

4. Repeat Step 3. Using corners B, C, and D as centers, mark points G, H, I, J, K, and L.

5. Connect these points to form an octagon.

Compass Method for Laying Out an Ellipse

1. Draw the major axis AB and the minor axis CD, figure 7-29.

2. Make OE and OF equal to AB minus CD.

3. Make OG and OH equal to three-fourths of OE. It is possible that E and F may be inside of C and D, depending on the length of the minor axis.

4. Draw lines through G and H from E and F.

5. Using F as the center and a radius equal to FC, scribe the arc as indicated in figure 7-29. Repeat this operation from E.

6. Using H as the center and a radius equal to HB, draw the arc as indicated. Repeat this operation from point G.

Pin-and-String Method for Laying Out an Ellipse

1. Draw major axis CD and minor axis EF, figure 7-30.

2. Using E as the center and a radius equal to one-half of the major axis (distance XD), strike an arc to intersect the major axis.

3. The arc drawn in Step 2 cuts CD at points 1 and 2.

4. Insert pins at points 1, 2, and E.

5. Tie a string around pins 1, 2, and E.

6. Remove the pin at point E and replace it with a pencil point.

7. Keeping the string tight with uniform outward pressure, move the pencil point clockwise inside the string to complete the ellipse.

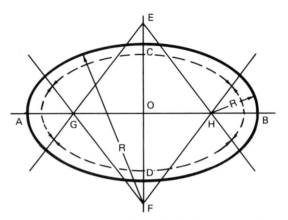

Fig. 7-29 Compass method for laying out an ellipse

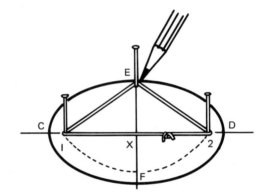

Fig. 7-30 String method for laying out an ellipse

Procedure for Laying Out a Five-Point Star

1. Draw a circle that circumscribes the required star.

2. With a compass, mark off points on the circumference by trial and error until it is divided into five equal parts, figure 7-31, or measure 72-degree divisions with a protractor.

3. Connect points A-C and A-D, B-E and B-D, C-A and C-E, D-B and D-A, and E-B and E-C.

4. Erase the dotted construction lines shown in figure 7-31.

5. If a symbol design is desired, a smaller circle may be drawn inside the star, figure 7-31.

6. If a pentagon is desired, connect the points of the star.

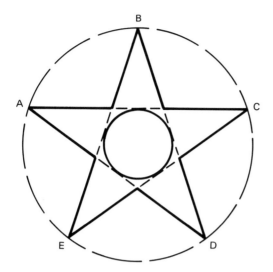

Fig. 7-31 Laying out a five-point star

Procedure for Developing a Design Pattern

Intricate curves are often transferred from the working drawing to a pattern graph that is used to trace the design on the project stock. The pattern is a full-size outline of the required design.

1. If the design is symmetrical, obtain a piece of heavy cardboard or light plywood large enough to make either half of the design, figure 7-32.

2. The outline of the design on the working drawing is usually not full size. Therefore, it needs to be enlarged. After laying out a grid of small squares on the working drawing (if not already included), lay out larger squares on the pattern. The size of the larger squares depends on the scale of the working drawing. For example, if the scale is 1/4″ = 1″ and the smaller squares are drawn 1/4 inch wide, the larger squares should be 1 inch wide.

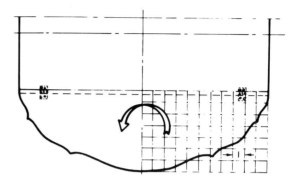

Fig. 7-32 Pattern graph for one-half of a drop-leaf table

One edge of the pattern acts as the centerline. The larger squares are numbered to correspond with the smaller squares on the working drawing.

3. Mark off on each square of the pattern the point that corresponds to the intersection of the curve and square of the working drawing.

4. Lightly sketch the curve by connecting the points on the grid of the pattern.

5. Retrace the curve on the pattern with a large French curve.

6. Cut out the pattern along the heavy, curved line.

7. Draw a centerline on the project stock. With the straight edge of the pattern on this line, mark half of the design.

8. Reverse the pattern and mark the other half of the design, being careful to match the second half to the first half just marked.

9. Saw out the design and smooth the edges.

REVIEW QUESTIONS

A. Identification

1. Name each of the following layout tools.

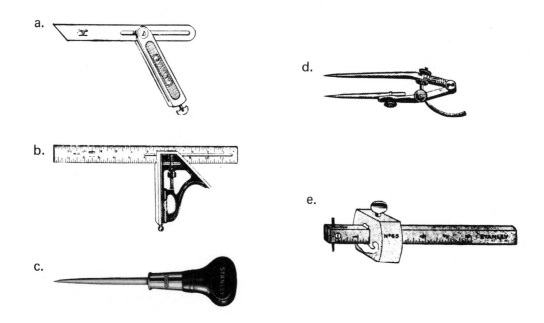

a.

d.

b.

e.

c.

B. Multiple Choice

2. Which of the following layout tools has a scale where the inch is divided into twelfths?

    a. Try square   c. Framing square
    b. Combination square   d. T bevel

3. When extreme accuracy is needed in layout work, which of the following tools would be the best to use?

    a. Pencil   c. Trammel point
    b. Pen   d. Knife

4. Which of the following tools allows you to lay out both 90-degree and 45-degree angles?

    a. Marking gauge   c. Try square
    b. Combination square   d. Framing square

5. The 1/16-inch division on the English rule divides the inch into _____ divisions.

    a. 8   c. 32
    b. 16   d. 12

6. In the metric system of measurement, the metre is divided into 100 smaller divisions called _____.

    a. millimetres   c. decimetres
    b. centimetres   d. kilometres

7. The radius of a circle is the same as the distance:

   a. from one side to the other.
   b. from the center to the edge × 2.
   c. around the circle.
   d. from the center to the edge.

8. The spur of the marking gauge should not be used for:

   a. marking stock to width.
   b. marking stock to thickness.
   c. marking bevels and chamfers.
   d. none of the above.

9. When using graph paper to develop a symmetrical design, how much of the pattern must be developed?

   a. 1/3   c. 3/4
   b. 1/2   d. The full pattern

10. Which of the following geometric figures has a major and minor axis?

   a. Hexagon   c. Five-point star
   b. Octagon   d. Ellipse

unit 8
handsaws

OBJECTIVES

After completing this unit, the student will be able to:

- select the proper handsaw for a job.
- use a handsaw safely and properly.
- properly care for a handsaw.

Each of the handsaws discussed in this unit are designed to perform a particular job. There are, however, several power saws that can perform the same jobs as handsaws. The operation of power woodworking tools will be covered in later units. The techniques learned with handsaws will help you to do a better job when using power tools.

CROSSCUT SAW

The crosscut saw is usually from 20 to 26 inches in length, figure 8-1. It has teeth that are sharpened to a knife-like point and designed to cut wood across the grain, figure 8-2A. Figure 8-2B shows how the crosscut saw cuts across the wood grain. Each tooth is bent alternately to one side and then the other. This provides clearance for

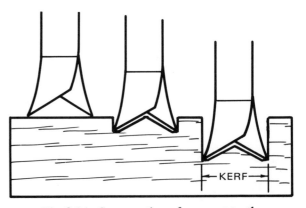

Fig. 8-2A Cross section of crosscut teeth

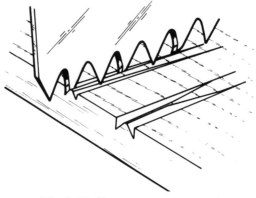

Fig. 8-2B How a crosscut saw cuts

Fig. 8-1 Crosscut saw

the saw to operate freely. This bending of the teeth is called *set,* and the groove made by the saw is called the *kerf.*

The teeth of the saw may be coarse or fine. This depends on the number of points per inch. *Points to the inch* is the term used to designate the size of teeth on a saw. There is always one more point than teeth per inch, figure 8-3. A saw with a smaller number of tooth points to the inch, six points for example, makes a rough cut, but it cuts faster. A saw with eight to ten points cuts slower but makes a finer and smoother cut. For general purpose work, you should select a saw with about eight to ten points to the inch. If fine finish work is necessary, select a saw with more points per inch.

RIPSAW

The ripsaw is designed to rip or cut parallel with the grain of the wood. The ripsaw is identical to the crosscut saw except for the shape of the teeth. The teeth are shaped like a chisel with a flat cutting edge, figure 8-4A. Its cutting action is much the same with each tooth chipping out a small portion of the wood from the kerf, figure 8-4B. Ripping may be done with the crosscut saw. However, a ripsaw leaves a very ragged edge when cutting across the grain.

BACKSAW

The backsaw, figure 8-5, is a fine-toothed saw with a thin blade. The blade is reinforced with a heavy rib of steel on the top edge. Because of its thin blade and fine teeth, the backsaw is ideal for doing fine, accurate work. It may be used for cutoff sawing as well as for making various joints.

DOVETAIL SAW

The dovetail saw, figure 8-6, is similar to the backsaw except that it is smaller, has a thinner blade with finer teeth, and a straight

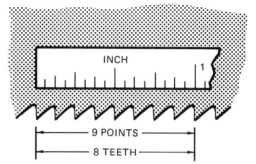

Fig. 8-3 Points and teeth per inch

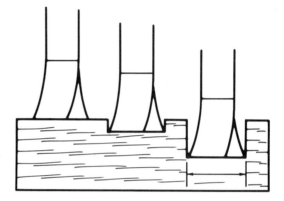

Fig. 8-4A Cross section of ripsaw teeth

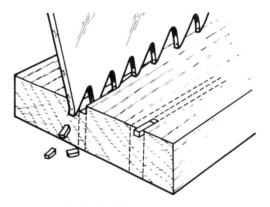

Fig. 8-4B How a ripsaw cuts

Fig. 8-5 Backsaw

Fig. 8-6 Dovetail saw

handle that is fitted on the end of the reinforced metal backing. It is used for cutting dovetail joints in drawer construction, model building, pattern sawing, and for fine sawing.

COPING SAW

A coping saw has a very narrow blade and is used for cutting inside or outside curves in thin stock, figure 8-7. It has a steel frame which holds the replaceable blade under tension.

COMPASS SAW

The compass saw consists of a narrow, tapered blade attached to a wooden handle, figure 8-8. It is used to cut curves and circles in wood that is 1/2 inch to 3/4 inch thick. The cut is usually started from a hole bored near the line to be cut. A keyhole saw is similar to the compass saw except the blade is smaller and thinner.

MITER SAW

The miter saw, figure 8-9, is a large version of the backsaw designed for use in the miter box. The frame of the miter box holds the saw rigidly in a vertical position. To provide various cutting angles, the guides that hold the saw are fastened to a pivoting base. For positioning the saw at the desired angle, a protractor scale is located on the front edge of the miter box frame. Graduations on the dial range from 90 degrees in the center to 45 degrees right-and-left of center. The most common settings are the 90-degree setting, which gives a right-angle cut, and the 45-degree setting. These settings are often used for cutting picture-frame joints.

PROCEDURE FOR USING
THE CROSSCUT SAW

The crosscut saw is used for sawing stock to length. However, the backsaw is the

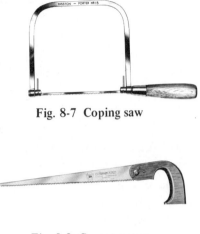

Fig. 8-7 Coping saw

Fig. 8-8 Compass saw

Fig. 8-9 Miter box saw

appropriate tool for sawing stock one inch or less in thickness and six inches or less in width.

1. Lay the board on a sawhorse with the stock to be removed extending over the edge. Measure the length desired and square a line across the stock with a square and sharp pencil.

2. If the stock is long, a second sawhorse may be used for support.

3. Grip the handle of the saw in the right (or left) hand with the first finger extending along the handle.

4. Assume a comfortable position with the left (or right) knee holding down the stock. Adjust yourself so your right (or left) wrist, elbow, and shoulder are in line with your cut, figure 8-10.

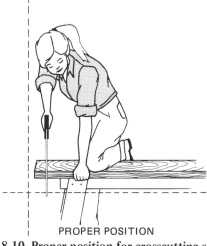

PROPER POSITION

Fig. 8-10 Proper position for crosscutting stock

5. Start the saw on the waste side of the line but as close to the line as possible. Place the thumb of your free hand against the saw blade to act as a guide. Draw the blade toward you.

6. Use short strokes until the saw is cutting straight with the line. Take long, even strokes with the saw under control at all times. This method of cutting gives the best results.

7. Sight along the side of the saw blade and the line to be followed so that a straight kerf may be cut.

8. Do not ride the saw to make it cut faster. The weight of the saw is enough to make it cut as fast as it should. Any additional weight tends to clog the gullets of the teeth. If the saw is not cutting as fast as it should, this is an indication the saw should be set and sharpened.

9. With the try square, as shown in figure 8-11, test to see that the side of the saw blade and the surface of the stock are at right angles. The direction of the cut may be changed by twisting the handle slightly in the direction to be followed.

10. Keep the cutting edge of the saw at approximately 45 degrees with the surface of the stock.

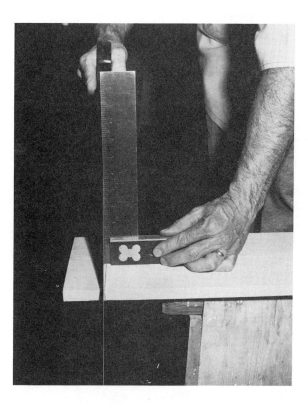

Fig. 8-11 Testing saw cut with try square

Fig. 8-12 Crosscutting stock held in vise

11. When nearing the end of the cut, support the waste side of the stock. This prevents it from splitting. This may be accomplished by using your free hand or with the help of an assistant.

12. With short strokes, finish cutting off the stock.

The vise or bench hook, instead of the sawhorse, may be used to hold small stock when cutting it to length, figure 8-12. Refer to figure 18-9 for an illustration of a bench hook.

PROCEDURE FOR USING THE RIPSAW

The ripsaw is used for ripping stock to width. If the material is long, it may be supported on the sawhorse. If it is short, it should be held in the vise.

Procedure For Ripping Long Stock

1. Place the board lengthwise on the sawhorse with one end extending beyond the end of the horse, figure 8-13.

2. Mark the cutting line on your board with the marking gauge or straightedge.

3. Grasp the saw as you would for crosscutting and position yourself above the board so you can easily see the line. Start the cut by pulling the saw towards you, while guiding it with the thumb of either hand.

4. As you continue to cut, move the board out further until you can turn it around to complete the cut. While sawing, maintain an angle of 60 degrees between the tooth edge and the board surface.

Procedure For Ripping Short Stock

1. Clamp the stock in the vise, figure 8-14, with the grain pattern vertical. Do not clamp the stock in the vise with the grain pattern horizontal. This causes the saw to bind in the kerf.

2. Keep the cutting edge of the saw approximately even with the top of the vise. This can be done by raising the stock in the vise from time to time as the ripping proceeds. If the sawing is done too far above the vise, the stock tends to vibrate.

3. Keep the heel of the saw lower than the toe when ripping stock in the vise. The *heel* is the toothed end nearest the handle, while the *toe* is the toothed end farthest from the handle.

Fig. 8-13   Long stock in position for ripping

Fig. 8-14   Ripping stock in vise

4. When the cut is nearly finished, hold the waste side of the stock with the free hand to steady the stock and prevent it from splitting.

PROCEDURE FOR USING THE BACKSAW

The backsaw is frequently used by the cabinetmaker. It is a fine-toothed saw which produces smooth, accurate work. After skill has been developed with the backsaw, several types of joints may be cut accurately. The blade of this saw is thin and its teeth are small. Therefore, use the backsaw carefully to prevent it from being damaged.

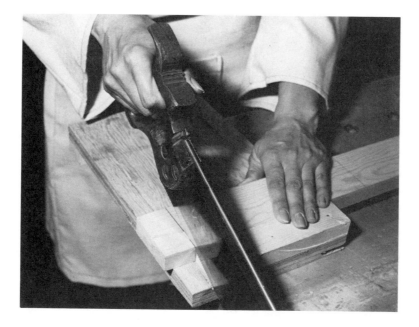

Fig. 8-15 Starting saw on back stroke with stock supported on a bench hook

Procedure For Crosscutting Stock

1. Fasten the stock securely in the vise or hold it on the bench top with the aid of a bench hook.

2. Grasp the handle of the backsaw, extending the forefinger along the side of the handle. This aids in guiding the saw.

3. Hold the stock against the bench hook with the free hand while allowing the thumb to act as a guide in starting the cut.

4. To start the cut, raise the handle of the saw slightly and begin sawing on the edge of the stock farthest away, figure 8-15.

Fig. 8-16 Taking a full cut

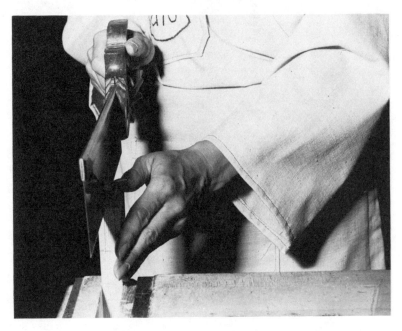

Fig. 8-17 Cutting cheeks of tenon

5. Gradually lower the handle as the sawing proceeds until the cutting edge is parallel with the surface of the stock, figure 8-16. This results in a smoother and more accurate cut than when sawing at an angle.

6. Follow the line marked on the edge of the stock until the stock is cut through or to the depth desired.

Using The Backsaw To Cut Joints

1. The backsaw is used for ripping the cheeks of a tenon, figure 8-17.
2. Refer to figure 17-40, which illustrates cutting the shoulders of a tenon with the backsaw.
3. When extreme accuracy is desired in cutting the sides of a dado joint or

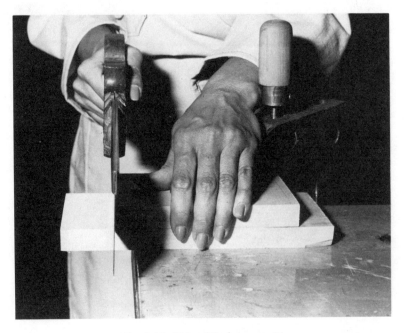

Fig. 8-18 Using block as a guide

cross-lap joints, clamp a piece of waste stock on the surface of the stock being sawed to act as a guide, figure 8-18. Although this method does not develop as much skill as sawing without the guide, it is sometimes faster.

PROCEDURE FOR CUTTING CURVES WITH THE COPING SAW AND COMPASS SAW

Both the compass and coping saw are designed to cut either inside or outside curves in wood.

Using The Compass Saw

1. Mark the desired shape on the piece of stock and support the wood.

2. Hold the saw almost perpendicular to the workpiece. Begin the cut by pulling the saw in an upward motion, figure 8-19.

3. As the sawing action proceeds, gently guide the saw by turning the handle in the direction of the cut. *Caution*:

Fig. 8-19 Cutting curves with a compass saw

Fig. 8-20 Sawing on a V block with a coping saw (teeth pointing toward handle)

Forcing the blade too much may cause it to bend or break.

4. If you are making an internal cut, use a bit to bore a hole within the area to be cut out. This hole must be large enough to admit the point of the saw. From this starting point, proceed to cut as in Steps 1, 2, and 3.

Using The Coping Saw

1. Mark the desired shape on the piece of stock and support the wood.

2. If the workpiece is supported flat, make sure that the teeth of the coping saw blade are pointing toward the saw handle, figure 8-20.

3. Hold the saw perpendicular to the workpiece with the handle below the piece of wood to be cut.

4. Start the cut on the down stroke and proceed to cut along the line. Make sure the blade is perpendicular to the wood. Use full, easy strokes. Make sure the workpiece is supported to prevent excess blade breakage. Continue to shift the work or rotate the blade to accommodate the saw frame.

5. If the workpiece is held in a vise, it is necessary to point the teeth away from the saw handle. The cutting is done on the push stroke.

6. If an internal cut is desired, it is necessary to bore a hole at least as large as the coping saw blade and assemble the saw after the blade is inserted in the hole.

CARE OF HANDSAWS

Taking good care of a tool assures a long tool life at the least amount of expense. The following suggestions will keep your saws in the best possible condition:

- Hang up or put the saw away when not in use.
- Never pile tools or materials on top of the saw.
- Carefully inspect each piece of lumber to assure that nails or other hard objects will not be cut into.
- Never twist off strips of waste stock with the saw.
- Properly support work so that it will not bind the saw or splinter the wood when nearing the end of a cut.
- Support the work in such a manner that the saw point will not strike obstacles while cutting.
- Never force the saw into the cut. If it is not cutting properly, the saw needs to be sharpened.
- If a saw is not going to be used for an extended period of time, the blade should be lightly oiled to prevent rusting.

REVIEW QUESTIONS

A. **Multiple Choice**

1. The term that describes the alternate bending of the teeth on a saw is:
   a. turned.
   b. filed.
   c. bent.
   d. set.

2. Which of the following saws is similar in construction to the backsaw?
   a. Crosscut saw
   b. Miter saw
   c. Ripsaw
   d. Coping saw

3. The clearance on each side of the blade of the saw while cutting a board is provided by:
   a. filing.
   b. twisting the saw.
   c. setting the teeth.
   d. the points of the saw.

4. A saw with ____ points to the inch will give the smoothest cut.
   a. 6
   b. 8
   c. 10
   d. 12

5. The word that best describes the shape of the teeth on a crosscut saw is:
   a. flat.
   b. knife-shaped.
   c. square.
   d. chisel-shaped.

6. While cutting, a crosscut saw should be held at an angle of _____ with the surface of the wood.
   a. flat
   b. 45 degrees
   c. 60 degrees
   d. 90 degrees

7. A ripsaw should be held at an angle of _____ with the surface of the wood while cutting.
   a. flat
   b. 45 degrees
   c. 60 degrees
   d. 90 degrees

8. A backsaw should be held _____ with the surface of the wood while cutting.
   a. perpendicular
   b. parallel
   c. at an angle of 60 degrees
   d. at an angle of 45 degrees

9. The teeth of the coping saw blade should point _____ when using the saw to cut material that is held flat on the bench top.
   a. toward the handle
   b. toward the material to be cut
   c. away from the handle
   d. either direction

10. The groove that is made in a board while the cut is taking place is called the:
    a. sawdust.
    b. kerf.
    c. set.
    d. groove.

11. To make the smoothest and most accurate cut with a saw, you should:
    a. make short, rapid strokes.
    b. force the saw into the cut.
    c. take long, smooth strokes.
    d. take short strokes near the tip of the saw.

12. The cut should take place:
    a. directly on the layout line.
    b. 1/8 inch from the layout line.
    c. next to the line on the stock that you will be using.
    d. next to the line on the waste side.

B. Short Answer

13. Explain the term *points to the inch*.

14. How would you care for a saw blade if it is not going to be used for a long period of time? Why?

C. Identification

15. Name each of the following saws.

a.

c.

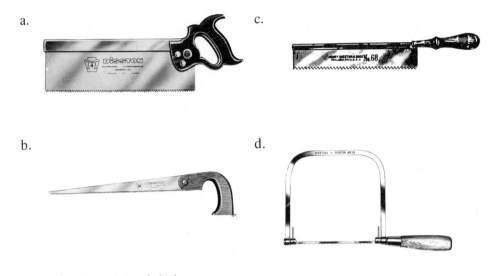

b.

d.

16. Identify the saw teeth below.

a.

b.

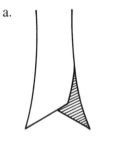

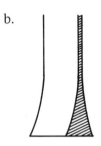

unit 9
hand planes

OBJECTIVES

After completing this unit, the student will be able to:

- select the proper plane for a job.
- use the hand plane safely and properly.
- sharpen a plane iron.
- assemble and adjust a plane.

Hand planes are used for smoothing rough wood surfaces and edges of boards. All hand planes operate on the cutting-wedge principle. The cutting portion of the plane is shaped like a wood chisel. The only difference is the plane has a frame to securely hold the plane iron in position.

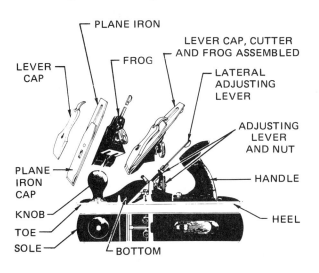

Fig. 9-1 **Parts of a plane**

The main parts of the plane are shown in figure 9-1. The cutting is done by the plane iron. The plane iron cap, attached to the surface of the plane iron, breaks the shavings as they enter the throat of the plane. On the back part of the frog there is an adjusting nut which regulates the plane-iron cutting depth. On the same part there is a lever which adjusts the plane levelness.

The following descriptions will help the beginning woodworker select the proper hand plane for a job.

JACK PLANE

The jack plane is an all-purpose plane used for smoothing and jointing boards, figure 9-2. The bed, or bottom, of the plane is 14 inches long.

SMOOTHING PLANE

The smoothing plane is similar to the jack plane except for size. It is only 6 inches

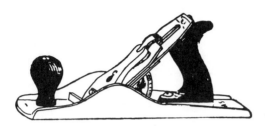

Fig. 9-2 Jack plane

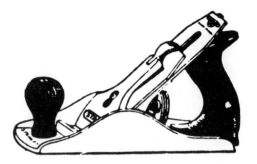

Fig. 9-3 Smoothing plane

Fig. 9-4 Jointer plane

to 10 inches long, figure 9-3. It is used for smoothing level surfaces and for small, fine work.

JOINTER PLANE

The jointer plane, figure 9-4, is also like the jack plane but is 22 inches to 30 inches long. It is used almost exclusively for jointing the edges of long boards.

BLOCK PLANE

The block plane is designed for planing end grain and has no plane iron cap, figure 9-5. The plane iron is set at a lower angle than those planes already mentioned. The *bevel*, slope of the cutting surface, is turned up. It is designed to be used with one hand. The block plane ranges from about 4 inches to 8 inches in length.

BULLNOSE RABBET PLANE

The bullnose rabbet plane is somewhat similar to the block plane but narrower, figure 9-6. The plane iron is located near the front end of the bed and, unlike any previous planes, makes a cut the full width of the bed.

Fig. 9-5 Block plane

Fig. 9-6 Bullnose rabbet plane

The bullnose rabbet plane is about 4 inches long and is used for planing rabbets, corners, and other surfaces with limited space to work with. It is also useful for dressing the cheeks of a tenon to fit the mortise. For a description of the mortise-and-tenon joint, refer to Unit 16.

RABBET PLANE

The rabbet plane is used for cutting rabbets and grooves with the grain. Like

Fig. 9-7 Rabbet plane

Fig. 9-8 Router plane

Fig. 9-9 Circular plane

Fig. 9-10 Spokeshave

the bullnose, the blade is the full width of the bed, but the rabbet plane is larger, figure 9-7.

ROUTER PLANE

The router plane has a wide, oval-shaped bed, figure 9-8. It is useful in smoothing bottoms of trays and removing surplus wood from dadoes after their sides have been cut with a saw.

CIRCULAR PLANE

When rounded edges are desired, either concave or convex, the circular plane is used, figure 9-9. The sole of this plane is flexible and may be adjusted to fit several curved edges.

SPOKESHAVE

The spokeshave is another tool designed for smoothing curved edges of stock. The cutting principle of the spokeshave is similar to that of a plane. It has two handles and resembles a cabinet scraper, but it is smaller, figure 9-10.

PROCEDURE FOR USING THE SMOOTHING, JACK, AND JOINTER PLANES

A properly adjusted plane should take off a long, thin, tissuelike shaving. For a deeper cut turn the adjusting nut clockwise, and for a lighter cut turn it counterclockwise. When edges or ends of stock are planed, make sure the full length of the plane is on the stock and level at all times.

1. Hold the plane bottom side up with the knob of the plane toward you and the heel toward the light. While sighting over the sole, adjust the plane iron with the lateral adjusting lever. The cutting

Fig. 9-11 Checking plane iron for levelness

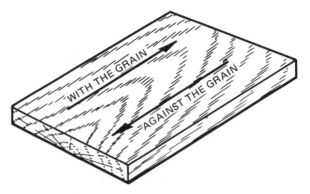

Fig. 9-12 Determining direction of grain

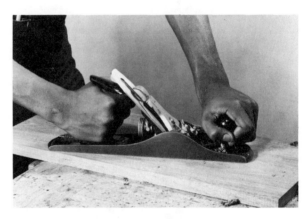

Fig. 9-13 Smoothing surface with jack plane

edge should be parallel with the sole of the plane, figure 9-11.

2. Stand in a straight position with your right (or left) side toward the bench.

3. Determine the grain direction before starting, figure 9-12. If it is difficult to determine the grain direction by sight, take a stroke or two with the plane to find it. Planing with the grain produces a smooth surface. Planing against the grain produces a rough surface.

4. Hold the plane with hand on the knob and the free hand on the handle, figure 9-13.

5. With the toe of the plane flat on the stock, push the plane the full length of the piece. Apply pressure on the knob when starting the stroke and on the handle when finishing the stroke, figure 9-14. If this procedure is not followed, a convex surface results rather than a straight, level surface.

6. Continue planing until the surface is smooth.

7. Test for levelness by turning the plane on its side and sighting under it, figure 9-15.

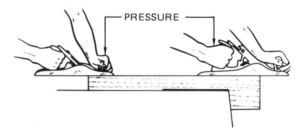

Fig. 9-14   Change pressure from plane knob to handle as the cut is made

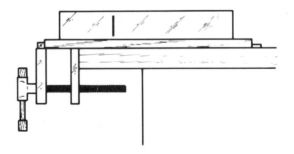

Fig. 9-15 Testing for levelness

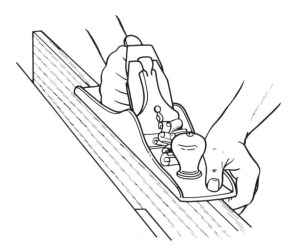

Fig. 9-16 Keeping side of plane parallel to face of stock.

Fig. 9-17 Proper position for plane when not in use

Fig. 9-18 Using block plane

8. If necessary, use short strokes to remove high places on the stock.

9. Keep the side of the plane parallel to the face of the stock when planing edge grain, figure 9-16. To help determine where the plane is cutting, draw lines across the edge of the board before beginning.

10. The plane will stay sharp much longer if you lay it on its side when not in use, figure 9-17.

PROCEDURE FOR USING THE BLOCK PLANE

Since the block plane is used for planing the end grain of small stock, it does not have a plane iron cap, figure 9-18. To cut end grain smoothly and to prevent vibration, the plane iron must be set at a low angle. Therefore, the bevel is turned up. In many cases, the smoothing plane or jack plane may be used instead of the block plane for planing end grain. There are three methods shown in figure 9-19 that may be used to prevent the splitting of end grain while planing.

1. Sight down the sole of the plane to see that it is properly adjusted.

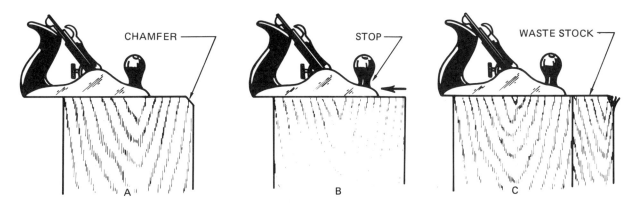

Fig. 9-19 Three methods of planing end grain

2. Grasp the plane in one hand, figure 9-18.

3. Take a light stroke on the stock to determine if the plane is set at the proper cutting depth. A very shallow cut will produce the best results.

4. Plane alternately from opposite edges. Stop before planing to the edge and repeat planing in the reverse direction, figure 9-19B. Avoid planing across the end of stock because it splinters the edges, as shown on the waste stock in figure 9-19C.

5. With the try square, test the end for squareness.

PROCEDURE FOR GRINDING THE PLANE IRON

When the plane iron becomes dull, it must be removed and whetted (sharpened) on an oilstone. The plane iron may be whetted on an oilstone several times before it has to be reground on the grinder. The following procedure should be followed when grinding or shaping the edge of the plane iron.

1. Lift up the lever on the lever cap and remove the double plane-iron assembly.

2. Loosen the cap screw with a screwdriver. Remove the plane iron cap from the plane iron.

3. Grip the plane iron in one hand with the thumb on the top and the index finger underneath, resting against the edge of the tool guide. Place your other hand on top of the plane iron to help guide it. Apply the plane iron to the grinding wheel with its bevel turned down, figure 9-20.

4. Apply the plane iron lightly at first and inspect it for proper width of bevel. Figure 9-21 shows the bevel width should be from 2 to 2 1/2 times the blade thickness. For hard wood, a shorter bevel keeps a sharper edge than a

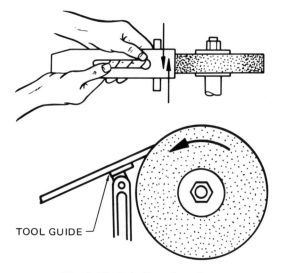

TOOL GUIDE

Fig. 9-20 Grinding plane iron

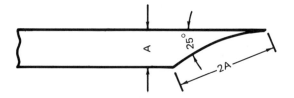

Fig. 9-21 Correct bevel width

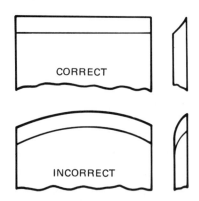

CORRECT

INCORRECT

Fig. 9-22 Correct and incorrect edge

longer one does. When the proper bevel width is obtained, keep the same grip so that the bevel remains uniform.

Caution: Always wear eye protection when grinding the plane iron.

5. Work the plane iron from one side of the stone to the other, figure 9-20. When the cutting edge of the plane iron is moved from side to side across the wheel, move the entire plane iron in a straight line with the cutting edge of the

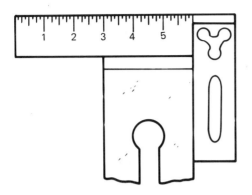

Fig. 9-23 Testing plane iron for squareness

wheel. If this is not done, a rounded, incorrect cutting edge will be produced, figure 9-22.

6. Continue grinding until the bevel reaches the correct cutting edge.

7. Test the edge for squareness and straightness by placing the try square head against the side of the plane iron, figure 9-23.

8. During grinding, dip the plane iron in water frequently to prevent the edge from turning blue. A blue edge indicates overheating, which destroys temper. If the plane iron has been ground straight and true, it will be slightly hollow ground.

9. Inspect the plane iron closely to see if a wire edge has been turned on the side opposite the bevel.

10. If a wire edge has been formed, remove it by drawing the edge lightly over a piece of wood, figure 9-24.

PROCEDURE FOR WHETTING THE PLANE IRON

A light dressing of kerosene or very light oil should be applied to the oilstone before whetting the plane iron. This carries off the steel particles and prevents them from being embedded in the stone.

1. Place the plane iron near the end of the oilstone with the bevel flat on the stone.

Fig. 9-24 Removing wire edge

Fig. 9-25 Whetting plane iron on an oilstone

Move it forward to collect oil on top of the plane iron.

2. Return to the starting point and begin to raise the back of the plane iron slowly until the oil on top runs onto the stone. At this position, the bevel is flat on the oilstone. Continue to raise the plane iron slightly so only the cutting edge rests on the stone, figure 9-25.

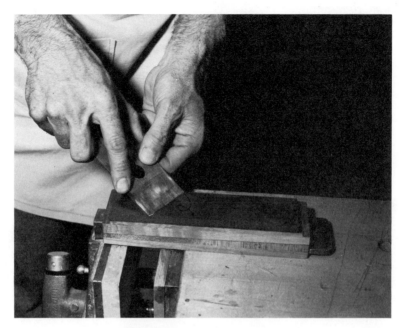

Fig. 9-26 Using circular motion

Fig. 9-27 Whetting flat side of plane iron

3. While maintaining this angle, whet lengthwise on the stone being careful not be let the plane iron slip off the ends. A circular motion may be used, figure 9-26.

4. Remove the sharp corners of the plane iron by giving them a light stroke on the stone.

5. Turn the plane iron with its bevel side up and hold it flat on the stone, figure 9-27.

6. Whet on this side until all traces of the wire edge have been removed.

7. Test the finished edge of the plane iron for sharpness by applying it to a piece of paper as shown in figure 9-28. The plane iron is sharp when it cuts the paper

Fig. 9-28 Testing for sharpness

smoothly. The plane iron is sometimes given a final whetting on a leather strap to give it a finer cutting edge.

8. When the plane iron has been thoroughly sharpened and whetted, the plane iron cap should be installed in position. Turn the plane iron cap at right angles to the plane iron. Insert the head of the screw through the hole and slide it up the plane iron until the end of the plane iron cap clears the cutting edge. Rotate the plane iron cap into final position, as shown in figure 9-29.

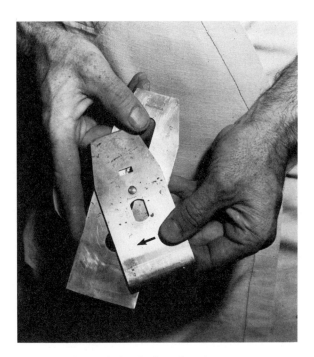

Fig. 9-29 Replacing plane iron cap

9. The distance the tip of the plane iron cap is placed from the cutting edge of the plane iron varies according to the hardness of the wood to be planed. When planing hard wood, the distance should be approximately 1/16 of an inch and for soft wood, 1/8 inch. The plane

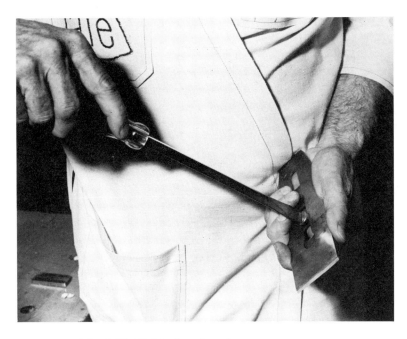

Fig. 9-30 Tightening plane iron cap screw

iron cap must fit firmly against the surface of the plane iron.

HOW TO ASSEMBLE AND ADJUST THE PLANE IRON

1. Tighten the plane iron cap with a screwdriver, figure 9-30.

2. Place the assembled plane iron in the plane with the beveled edge down, figure 9-31.

3. Lay the lever cap over the plane iron. Tighten the cap.

4. Adjust the plane iron with the lateral adjusting lever. The cutting edge should be parallel with the sole of the plane.

5. To regulate the depth of cut, turn the adjusting nut clockwise for a deeper cut and counterclockwise for a lighter cut.

PROCEDURE FOR PLANING CHAMFERS AND BEVELS

Figure 9-32 shows the difference between chamfer and bevel angle cuts. The *bevel* extends the entire thickness of the stock, while the *chamfer* extends only partway. Generally, the chamfer is made at a 45-degree angle with the edge and surface of the stock. This means that an equal amount of the edge and face of the stock are removed.

Two kinds of chamfers, the through chamfer and the stop chamfer, are also shown in figure 9-32. Through chamfers are cut with a plane; stop chamfers are cut with a chisel.

Procedure For Planing Through Chamfers

1. Mark the width of the chamfer on the face and edge of the stock. Do this by measuring from the edge the desired amount that will be replaced by the chamfer.

2. Place the head of the pencil gauge against the edge of the stock and set

Fig. 9-31 Installing plane iron

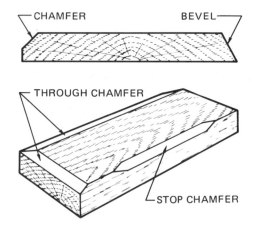

Fig. 9-32 Chamfers and Bevels

it to the mark, figure 9-33. Another method of marking is to hold the pencil in the hand and use the fingers to guide the pencil at the proper distance, figure 9-34.

3. Mark a line entirely around the surface to be chamfered.

4. With the head of the gauge against the face of the board, mark lines on the edges and ends.

5. Clamp the stock in the vise with the edge up. Another method is to clamp the stock in a hand screw. Then clamp the stock in a vise at an angle that keeps the

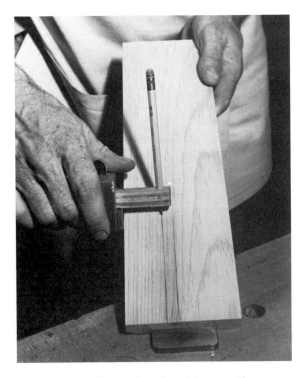

Fig. 9-33 Marking a chamfer with a pencil gauge

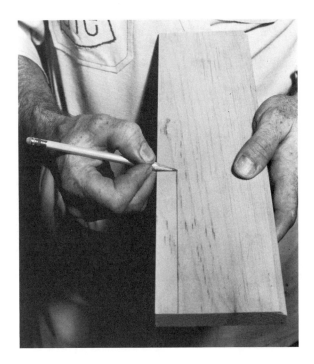

Fig. 9-34 Method of holding pencil to mark a line parallel to edge

bottom of the plane in a horizontal position, figure 9-35.

6. Plane straight with the stock until the finish cut barely removes both pencil marks. If this is done carefully a flat, straight surface is obtained.

7. Set a T bevel to the proper angle as shown in figure 9-36.

8. To set the T bevel to an angle of 45 degrees, line up the inside edge of its blade with equal numbers on the tongue and blade of the framing square. For

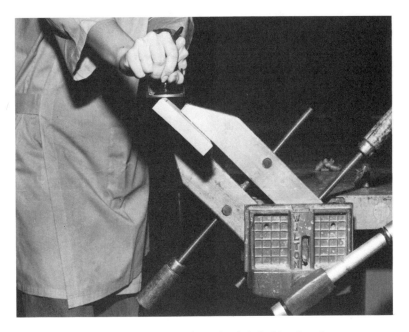

Fig. 9-35 Chamfering side of stock while held in hand screw

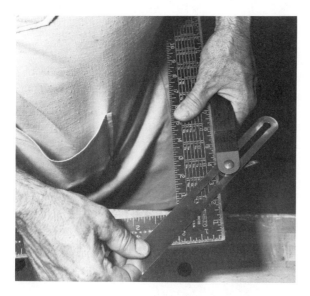

Fig. 9-36 Setting T bevel for 45° angle

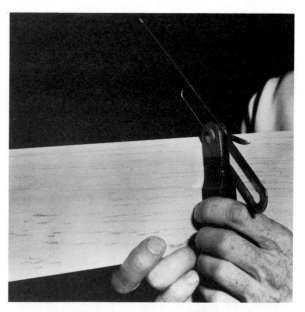

Fig. 9-37 Testing chamfer with T bevel

example, figure 9-36 shows the 3-inch marks being used.

9. Test the angle of the chamfer by placing the T bevel across the grain of the chamfer, figure 9-37. Also, test the surface to see that it is flat and straight by using the framing square, figure 9-38. The combination square is sometimes used for testing chamfers. The sliding, adjustable head of this tool makes extremely accurate work possible.

10. Plane and test the chamfer on the opposite edge if the chamfer is to extend around the face of the stock.

11. Clamp the stock in the vise with the ends up and plane chamfers on the ends, figure 9-39. Hold the plane so that its cutting edge is about a 45-degree angle to the end of the stock. This shearing cut prevents splitting off the ends of the finished chamfer on the edge.

Procedure For Cutting Stop Chamfers

1. Lay out the stop chamfer as shown in figure 9-32.

2. With a chisel, pare from both ends of the stop chamfer toward the center.

Fig. 9-38 Testing chamfer for straightness with framing square

3. Continue paring until a flat, even surface has been obtained and the gauge lines have been reached.

4. With the T bevel, test for the proper angle, figure 9-37. With the framing or foot square, test for straightness, figure 9-38. If the stop chamfer is long enough, the center may be cut with a smoothing plane. Then it is necessary to

cut only the ends of the chamfer with the chisel.

In carpentry, the draw knife is often used for cutting chamfers. The spokeshave may also be used for smoothing the stop chamfer.

Procedure For Planing Bevels

1. With a pencil gauge, mark on the face of the stock the distance the bevel is to extend in from the edge.

2. Plane the edges to be beveled in the same manner as planing through chamfers, figure 9-35.

3. When planing bevels on ends of stock, plane from the edges toward the center (refer to figure 9-19).

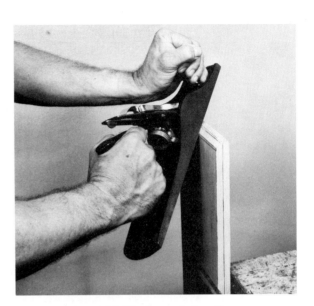

Fig. 9-39 Planing end chamfers

REVIEW QUESTIONS

A. Identification

1. Name each of the following hand planes.

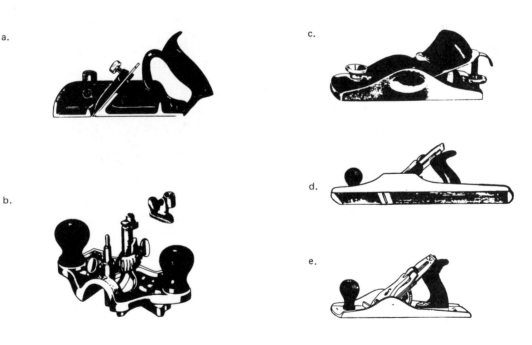

B. Multiple Choice

2. Before grinding a plane iron, you should always:
    a. wear eye protection.
    b. check the plane with a T bevel.
    c. grind on the side of the wheel.
    d. whet the plane iron first.

3. The proper bevel on a plane iron should be from _____ times the thickness of the blade.
   a. 1 to 2
   c. 2 1/2 to 3
   b. 2 to 2 1/2
   d. 3 to 3 1/2

4. Kerosene or very light oil is added to the oilstone to:
   a. reduce friction.
   c. make the plane iron slide easier.
   b. carry off steel particles.
   d. keep the stone cool.

5. After the bevel side of the plane iron is whetted, you should then:
   a. put the plane iron back in the plane.
   b. test the plane iron for sharpness.
   c. turn the bevel side up and whet the flat side to remove all traces of a wire edge.
   d. place the lever cap on the plane iron.

6. The bevel is turned down on all plane irons except the _____ plane.
   a. jack
   c. smoothing
   b. jointer
   d. block

7. The plane should be tested for cutting levelness by:
   a. sighting over the sole of the plane.
   b. taking a trial cut.
   c. placing the lateral adjustment straight up and down.
   d. it is not necessary to adjust it because it is set at the factory.

8. Which of the following planes would be best to use for smoothing the bottom of a dado joint?
   a. Bullnose plane
   c. Rabbet plane
   b. Block plane
   d. Router plane

9. Which of the following planes has the longest bed?
   a. Block plane
   c. Jointer plane
   b. Smoothing plane
   d. Jack plane

10. To keep the plane iron sharp when you lay it down, you should:
    a. lay it on its side.
    b. lay it with the bed down.
    c. set it on the floor so it will not drop.
    d. take the plane iron out.

11. A *bevel* is an angle cut on the edge of a piece that:
    a. extends from the face to the edge.
    b. extends from one face to the other.
    c. extends from the face to the end.
    d. extends from the edge to the end.

C.   Short Answer

12. What indicates that a blade has been overheated in grinding? What should be done during the grinding procedure to prevent this from happening?

unit 10
wood chisels

OBJECTIVES

After completing this unit, the student will be able to:

- select the proper chisel for a job.
- safely and properly use the wood chisel, gouge, and other carving tools.
- sharpen a wood chisel.

The wood chisel is used to remove large amounts of wood and to finish cut. One way chisels are classified is by the method that the handle is fastened to the chisel. There are three classifications: tang, socket, and molded. These chisels are controlled by hand, or a mallet is used to exert additional pressure.

SOCKET CHISEL

The socket chisel is designed for heavier work which requires the use of a mallet to force the chisel into the wood. The handle fits into the conically-shaped end, or *socket*, of the chisel, figure 10-1A. The handle head (top) is reinforced with a leather cap which acts as a cushion and prevents the handle from splitting. Another type of socket chisel has a metal core that extends through the handle and forms a metal cap at the head. This provides a more durable handle for heavy work.

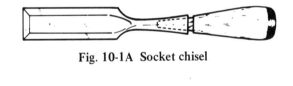

Fig. 10-1A Socket chisel

Fig. 10-1B Tang chisel

Fig. 10-1C Molded chisel

TANG CHISEL

The tang chisel differs from the socket chisel in that it has a ferruled handle into which the tapered end, or *tang*, of the chisel fits, figure 10-1B. This chisel is used chiefly for *paring*, or cutting away thin strips or layers, where it is not necessary to force it with a mallet.

MOLDED CHISEL

The molded chisel is designed to do heavy work. The plastic handle is molded around the ferruled end of the chisel blade. There is also a metal cap on the driving end of the chisel, figure 10-1C. For heavy cuts, it is permissible to use a hammer or mallet to drive this chisel into the wood.

TYPES OF CHISEL BLADES

Another way chisels are classified is by the shape and width of the blade, figure 10-2. A *mortise chisel* is designed to be used for cutting mortises. Therefore, it has a long, thick blade to withstand the force of prying out wood chips from the bottom of mortise cuts. The *butt chisel* has a shorter blade and is designed to do a variety of chisel jobs. The *paring chisel* has the handle attached to it with a tang and is only used for light cuts. The *firmer chisel* has a socket for attaching the handle and is used for both light and heavy cuts.

Most chisels mentioned can be purchased in varying widths. The blade widths indicate the size of the chisel. These widths commonly range from 1/8 inch to 1 inch with 1/8-inch increments and from 1 inch to 2 inches with 1/4-inch increments.

GOUGES

The *gouge* is a chisel used for grooving, fluting, shaping edges, and modeling. Gouges are classified into groups, depending upon whether the bevel is on the inside or outside of the blade, figure 10-3. All gouges have concave blades, but some have a much sharper curve than others. The blades range in width from 1/4 inch to 1 inch with 1/8-inch increments, and from 1 inch to 2 inches with 1/4-inch increments.

CARVING TOOLS

Carving tools are specifically designed chisels which are made in a large variety of

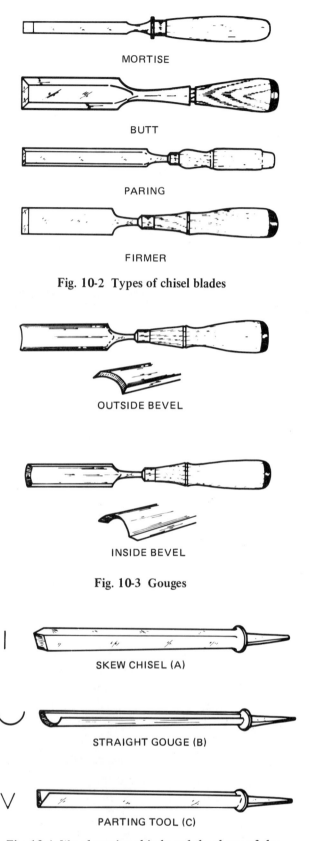

MORTISE

BUTT

PARING

FIRMER

Fig. 10-2 Types of chisel blades

OUTSIDE BEVEL

INSIDE BEVEL

Fig. 10-3 Gouges

SKEW CHISEL (A)

STRAIGHT GOUGE (B)

PARTING TOOL (C)

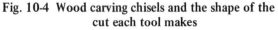

Fig. 10-4 Wood carving chisels and the shape of the cut each tool makes

shapes and sizes. These chisels are forced into the wood by hand or with very light tapping from a wood-carving mallet, figure 10-5. Although a complete set of carving tools may contain 45 to 50 individual carving chisels, there are basically three shapes. The *skew* chisel, figure 10-4A, is used for light cuts and smoothing. The *gouge*, figure 10-4B, is used the most and comes in a large variety of sweeps (blade curvatures). It is used to remove large amounts of material and work out intricate shapes. The *parting tool*, or veiners, is V-shaped and is used for outlining, rounding edges with straight sides, and adding detail work to the carving, figure 10-4C.

PROCEDURE FOR PARING HORIZONTAL, CROSS-GRAIN SURFACES WITH THE CHISEL

1. Clamp the stock in a vise or hold it firmly against a bench hook.

2. When cutting dadoes or other flat, horizontal surfaces, hold the chisel in the position shown in figure 10-6. Grasp the handle of the chisel in either hand. With either hand resting against the piece of stock, hold the blade of the chisel between the thumb and fingers of your free hand. The bevel is turned up for this type of work.

3. Push the chisel with the right (or left) hand. At the same time, move the handle from right to left. Take thin cuts and stop each time before the opposite edge is reached.

4. Alternately, pare from each edge toward the center until the depth line is reached and the bottom of the cut is level, as shown in figure 10-7.

5. Test for levelness with the try square.

PROCEDURE FOR PARING END GRAIN WITH THE CHISEL

1. Fasten the stock firmly on the bench, or between the vise dog and bench stop,

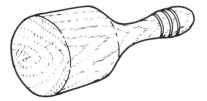

Fig. 10-5 Wood carver's mallet

Fig. 10-6 Paring across grain

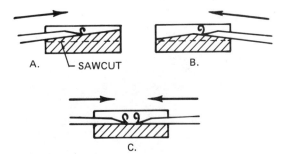

Fig. 10-7 Sequence of cuts for cutting out a gain

with a piece of thin scrap stock under the stock to be pared, figure 10-8. The scrap piece prevents the chisel from marring the bench top.

2. Turn the bevel away from the end grain. Start cutting a short distance from the finish line and work across the end and back to the line. Keep the chisel in a vertical position, figure 10-8.

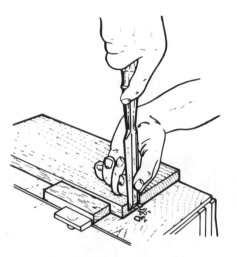

Fig. 10-8 Paring end grain

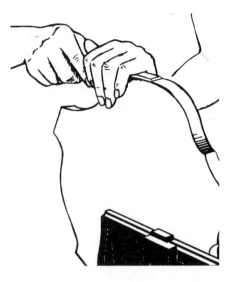

Fig. 10-9 Smoothing convex edge with chisel

3. Stand so that you can sight the proper cutting direction.

4. Apply pressure to the chisel with the palm of the right (or left) hand and rock the chisel slightly from left to right to give a shearing cut. For rough, deep cuts, use the mallet to drive the chisel. Cut with only one-half to one-fourth the width of the cutting edge of the chisel. Use the remainder as a guide for keeping the cutting line straight.

5. A wood chisel is sometimes used to smooth the curved edges of stock, figure 10-9.   The bevel is turned up when smoothing the edges of convex curves. The bevel is turned down when smoothing concave curves.

PROCEDURE FOR CUTTING
STOP CHAMFERS WITH THE CHISEL

1. With the beveled side of the chisel turned down, start paring from one

Fig. 10-10 Cutting stop chamfer with chisel

end of the stop chamfer. Cut about half the length of the chamfer from this end.

2. Continue paring this half of the chamfer with light cuts until the pencil line has been reached.

3. Reverse the stock and cut the other half of the chamfer from the opposite end, figure 10-10.

SHARPENING WOOD CHISELS

To do quality work in a safe manner, the wood chisel must be sharp. Improperly sharpened or dull chisels are common causes of accidents when working with hand tools. Accidents happen when too much force is used on the chisel because it is dull. The wood chisel is sharpened in the same manner as the plane iron (refer to Unit 9).

PROCEDURE FOR USING THE GOUGE

1. Choose the correct width and properly shaped gouge for the job. For example, if a deep, narrow groove is to be cut, a narrow, sharp-curved gouge is used. When shaping the edge of curved stock, figure 10-11, use the inside-bevel gouge. When fluting or doing light grooving, use the outside-bevel gouge, figure 10-12.

2. Grip the gouge firmly, figure 10-11, using either hand to guide and control it.

3. Take light cuts in the direction of the wood grain.

4. When cutting across the grain, rock the gouge slightly from left to right to produce a shearing cut.

5. For deep or large concave surfaces in stock, such as trays and hulls of model boats, use the mallet to drive the gouge.

PROCEDURE FOR USING THE BASIC CARVING TOOLS

1. Clamp a piece of practice stock, soft pine or bass, in the vise or on the bench

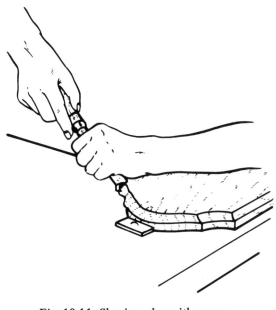

Fig. 10-11 Shaping edge with gouge

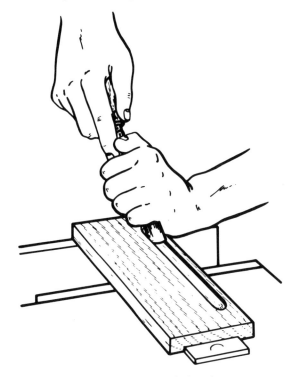

Fig. 10-12 Using outside bevel gouge

top. Draw lines about an inch apart using a soft pencil. These lines should be in the shape of a circle.

2. Start the carving with the veining tool and outline the pattern with it. Make sure to go with the grain while carving. It will be necessary to change direction

several times as the outline of the circle is being carved, figure 10-13.

3. Next, take the gouge and remove the material between the two carved lines. Make sure that you are going with the grain at all times. Take small cuts and never allow the tool to bury itself.

4. If the cutting is difficult, use the mallet to drive the tool.

5. Continue to carve away the wood in layers while working around the carving. Do not try to remove all of the wood down to finished dimensions in only one place at a time.

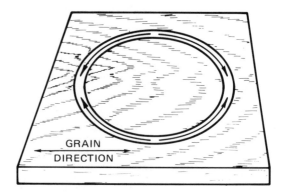

Fig. 10-13   Arrows showing proper direction of cuts

REVIEW QUESTIONS

A.   Identification

1. Name each of the following chisels.

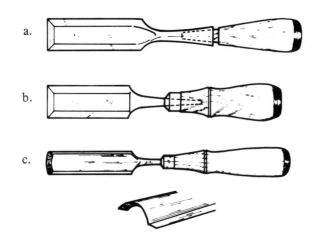

B.   Multiple Choice

2. Wood chisels are sharpened with a bevel on:
   a. one side only.   c. all sides.
   b. both sides.   d. none of the sides.

3. Which of the following chisels should not be forced into the wood with a mallet?
   a. Socket chisel   c. Molded chisel
   b. Tang chisel   d. Butt chisel

4. More accidents are caused by _____ tools.
   a. sharp   c. new
   b. old   d. dull

5. The most often used carving tool is the:
   a. veining tool.
   b. gouge.
   c. skew chisel.
   d. wood chisel.

6. When paring the end of a board with a chisel, it is a good practice to lay the board:
   a. on the bench.
   b. on the edge of a bench.
   c. on the floor.
   d. on a piece of scrap wood.

7. When using the wood chisel, you should always cut:
   a. in the direction the grain is running.
   b. against the grain direction.
   c. towards the center of your workpiece.
   d. towards the edge of your workpiece.

8. Which of the following chisels has the thickest blade?
   a. Tang chisel
   b. Socket chisel
   c. Paring chisel
   d. Mortise chisel

9. Which of the following tools should be used to drive the chisel when you are making a heavy cut?
   a. Claw hammer
   b. Rubber mallet
   c. Wood mallet
   d. A scrap piece of wood

C. Short Answer

10. How is the size of a chisel determined?

unit 11
scraping and filing tools

OBJECTIVES

After completing this unit, the student will be able to:

- name and properly use the various scraping and filing tools.
- sharpen scrapers.
- properly care for files.

SCRAPING TOOLS

Scrapers are used to smooth cross-grained or knotty stock which is difficult to do with a plane. Scrapers differ from cutting tools in that the surface of the stock is removed by a *scraping burr* instead of a cutting edge. The two common types of scrapers are the hand scrapers, figures 11-1 and 11-2, and the cabinet scraper, figure 11-3. Two other scrapers are shown in figures 11-4 and 11-5. Rasps and files are also classified as scraping tools.

Hand Scraper

The hand scraper is a thin, flexible, rectangular-shaped piece of steel. However, the edges are sometimes rounded, as in the swanneck scraper, figure 11-2, to fit various molding types. The scraper, when properly sharpened and used, removes a very thin shaving similar to the shaving from a plane. When the scraper removes only fine dust, it is

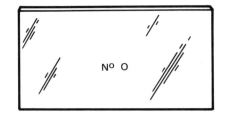

Fig. 11-1 Hand scraper

Fig. 11-2 Swanneck scraper

an indication of improper sharpening. The scraper is either pulled or pushed. This depends upon the position of the surface being scraped. The hand scraper is very

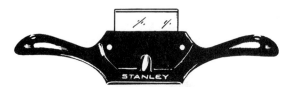

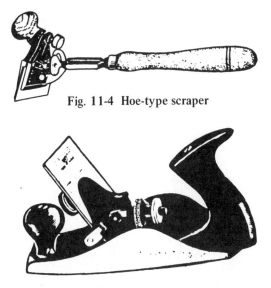

Fig. 11-4 Hoe-type scraper

Fig. 11-3 Cabinet scraper

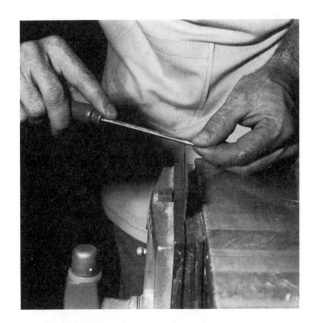

Fig. 11-5 Scraper plane

convenient to use in recesses and corners where it is difficult to use the cabinet scraper.

Cabinet Scraper

The cabinet scraper blade is similar to the hand scraper, but it is fitted into a handled frame, figure 11-3. The bottom of the cabinet scraper is similar in design to the plane, and the scraper blade is held rigidly in the frame. This makes it possible to produce a truer surface with the cabinet scraper than with the hand scraper. The cabinet scraper also cuts faster than the hand scraper because the handles make it possible to apply more pressure. Cabinet scrapers are useful for smoothing red cedar and other knotty, cross-grained woods. It is also used to remove glue from the surface of boards.

Hoe-Type Scraper

The hoe-type, or box, scraper has a socket adjustment on the end of the handle, figure 11-4. This allows the scraper blade to be adjusted to various angles. The working principle of this scraper is similar to the hand scraper. The only difference is the scraper blade is held in a frame instead of the hands. This scraper is convenient for scraping floor surfaces that are close to the wall and cannot be reached with a floor sander.

Scraper Plane

The scraper plane, figure 11-5, has a frame similar to other planes, but the blade produces a scraping cut like the cabinet scraper. It should be gripped like any other plane. An adjustment screw is located in

Fig. 11-6 Burnishing a hand scraper

front of the handle. This allows the blade to be adjusted to various angles. The scraper plane can be used for heavy scraping work. Since the scraper plane bed is large, it produces a reasonably level surface.

Burnisher

The *burnisher*, shown in figure 11-6, is a hardened steel tool used to produce a scraping burr on the scraper blade edge. The burnisher

Fig. 11-7 Filing scraper blades

Fig. 11-8 Whetting scraper blade

has an oval-shaped blade and is about 4 inches long.

PROCEDURE FOR SHARPENING SCRAPERS

1. Clamp the scraper blade in a vise with the cutting edge projecting about 1 inch above the vise jaws, figure 11-7.

2. Test the edge of the scraper for straightness. If the edge is not straight, file it lengthwise with a flat mill file.

3. Remove the remainder of the scraping edge by filing the scraper blade lightly on the flat side.

4. File a beveled edge on the scraper at an angle of about 35 degrees, figure 11-7. Use a flat mill file, putting firm, even pressure on the forward stroke and raising the file on the return stroke. Stop filing when a wire edge has been turned on the edge opposite the bevel.

5. Remove the scraper from the vise. Whet it with the beveled edge flat on an oilstone, figure 11-8.

6. Whet the flat side of the scraper on the oilstone to remove the wire edge, figure 11-9.

7. Remove the sharp corners by rubbing them lightly over the oilstone.

8. Place the scraper back in the vise in the same position as before, figure 11-6.

Fig. 11-9 Removing wire edge

9. Lay the burnisher on the edge of the scraper. Raise the handle until the angle of the burnisher is 5 degrees less than the angle of the bevel. Apply even pressure on the burnisher and push it across the sharpened edge, from one end to the other, figure 11-6.

10. Raise the handle of the burnisher to nearly a horizontal position and repeat the operation as before. This should leave a sharp scraping burr on the side opposite the bevel. To get a good, even scraping edge, it is essential that firm, even pressure be applied to all parts of the edge. The burnisher is better controlled by gripping the handle in one hand and the point in the other, figure 11-6.

11. If the scraper is used in the cabinet scraper frame, set the frame in a working position on a flat surface and drop the scraper blade into place. Tighten the

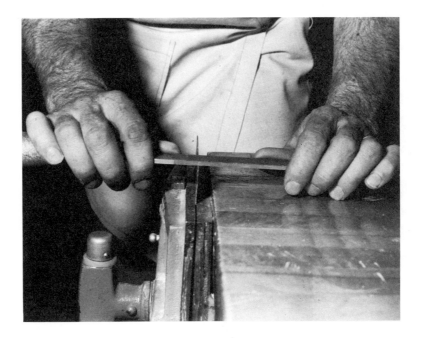

Fig. 11-10 Drawfiling

thumbscrews at the edges of the scraper. To control depth, adjust the thumbscrew found on the back of the blade.

The flat hand scraper is sometimes *draw-filed*, and a scraping burr is turned on both sides. In drawfiling, the file is held at right angles to the scraper and pushed from one end of the cutting edge to the other, figure 11-10.

For best results, the scraping burr must be kept sharp at all times. It is sometimes possible to burnish the scraping edge two or three times without filing it.

The swanneck scraper, figure 11-2, is useful when it is necessary to scrape curved moldings and other irregular surfaces. The entire edge of this scraper is sharpened so that any part of it may be used.

PROCEDURE FOR USING THE HAND SCRAPER

1. Grasp the scraper in the hands, figure 11-11.

2. Push the scraper over the surface with long, even strokes while keeping uniform pressure during the entire stroke.

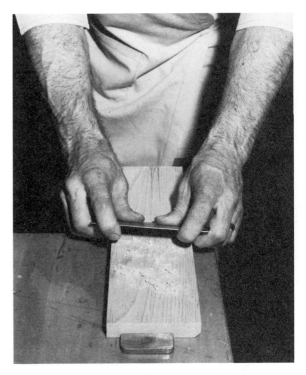

Fig. 11-11 Pushing a hand scraper

When scraping surfaces that are next to corners, moldings, and other vertical surfaces, the scraper is pulled instead of pushed, figure 11-12.

When removing blemishes from a wood surface, it is best to scrape a large surface

Fig. 11-12 Pulling a hand scraper

around the blemish to avoid leaving a low spot.

PROCEDURE FOR USING THE CABINET SCRAPER

1. Grasp the scraper handles firmly in both hands with the thumbs resting on the frame, figure 11-13.

2. Press the sole of the scraper firmly against the wood surface and push the scraper in the direction of the grain. The scraper should not be pulled. If the cabinet scraper is held at an angle, the skewed cut, figure 11-13, results in a smoother cut on cross-grained stock. The scraper blade also holds its edge longer.

3. If the scraper cuts too deep, turn the depth adjustment screw counterclockwise. If the scraper is set too shallow, turn the adjustment screw clockwise.

4. With long, even strokes, continue scraping with the grain until the entire surface is smooth.

Fig. 11-13 Using a cabinet scraper

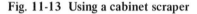
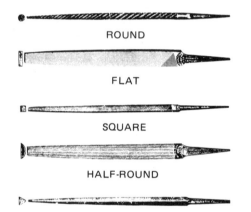

ROUND

FLAT

SQUARE

HALF-ROUND

TRIANGULAR

Fig. 11-14 Shapes of files

5. Scrape away from the ends of the stock rather than toward them. To produce a level surface, more pressure should be applied to the scraper when starting at the end of the stock.

If it is difficult to obtain a smooth surface with a scraper, sponge the surface lightly with water before the surface is scraped.

FILING TOOLS

Files are used where it is difficult or impossible to use other edge-cutting tools such as the chisel or plane. Files are made in several shapes and sizes. The most common cross-sectional shapes are round, half-round, flat, square, and triangular, figure 11-14. The

Fig. 11-15 How the length of a file
is measured

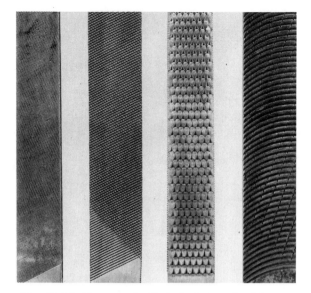

Fig. 11-16 The cut of a file: single cut, double cut,
rasp cut, and curved tooth

Fig. 11-17 Surform®tool

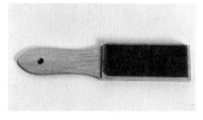

Fig. 11-18 File card

file length varies from 4 inches to 14 inches and is measured as shown in figure 11-15.

The *cut* of the file refers to the spacing of the teeth and the angle at which they cross the file surface. Files may be obtained with single-cut, double-cut, rasp-cut, or curved-cut teeth, figure 11-16. Furthermore, each file cut may be classified as to coarseness of teeth for that particular tooth shape. The most common classification of tooth coarseness is rough, bastard, second cut, and smooth.

Single and double-cut files are used to file metal, to sharpen woodworking tools, and for smoothing work. The rasp and the curved-tooth files are used where considerable surplus stock is to be removed on wood, plastics, or soft metals. The *Surform*^{R} *tool*, figure 11-17, is a forming tool shaped somewhat like a file and used for several types of cutting and trimming. Because it has open teeth, the tool does not plug up as easily as the standard file. Files should never be used without a handle. The tang can puncture the palm of your hand and cause serious injury.

As the file is used, it will often plug up with chips or finish. When this happens, the file will have to be cleaned with a file card, figure 11-18.

PROCEDURE FOR USING WOOD FILES

1. Select a medium-coarse wood file, bastard or second smooth, for the first smoothing. Do not select a coarse file for plywood.

2. Push the file across the edge of the stock with a forward and side motion, figure

Fig. 11-19 Filing concave edge

Fig. 11-20 Filing convex edge

11-19. This produces a shearing cut and prevents the opposite edge from splintering. Be very careful to avoid splintering when filing plywood.

3. Continue filing until the line is reached and the curve is uniform.

4. With the try square, test to see that the edge is at right angles with the face of the stock.

5. Finish smoothing the curved edge with a smooth or dead-smooth wood file. Examine figures 11-20 and 11-21 carefully. The flat side of the file is used for smoothing convex curves. The rounded side of the file is used for smoothing concave curves. The round, or rattail, wood file is used for smoothing small, sharp curves or circular holes. It is used in the same way as the other wood files.

CARE OF FILES

The following are suggestions for caring for files:

- Properly store files so they are not in contact with one another.

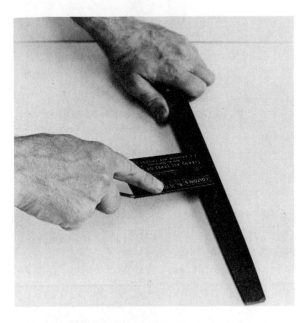

Fig. 11-21 Cleaning file with a file card

- Keep files stored in a dry place to avoid rusting.

- Do not strike files against one another or on hard surfaces.

- Do not pry with files. They are brittle and can easily break.

- Keep teeth clean by using a file card and file pick.

- Never use a file without a handle.

REVIEW QUESTIONS

A.   Identification

1. Name each of the following scraping and filing tools.

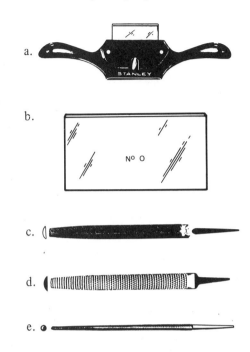

a.

b.

c.

d.

e.

B.   Multiple Choice

2. Which of the following file cuts has the coarsest teeth?
    a. Single cut   c. Rasp
    b. Double cut   d. Mill

3. When the hand scraper is properly sharpened and used correctly, it
    should remove:
    a. the wood in the form of fine sawdust.
    b. the wood in thin shavings.
    c. the wood in one pass.
    d. the wood in large, thick shavings.

4. Which of the following woods requires a scraper to give it a smooth
    surface?
    a. Sugar pine   c. Mahogany
    b. Basswood   d. Red cedar

5. Which of the following tools works well for removing glue from the
    surface of a board?
    a. Cabinet scraper   c. Hand scraper
    b. Scraper plane   d. Wood file

6. When drawfiling the edge of a hand scraper, the file should be held at
    an angle of _____ to the face of the scraper.
    a. 45 degrees   c. 90 degrees
    b. 100 degrees   d. 180 degrees

7. Files should only be used:
   a. when the material is soft.
   b. when the material can be held in a vise.
   c. on wood.
   d. when the handle is properly attached.

8. Which of the following tools can be either pushed or pulled for the proper operation?
   a. Cabinet scraper   c. Hoe-type scraper
   b. Hand scraper   d. File

C.   Short Answer

9. Explain the term *cut of the file*.

10. The tool used to produce a scraping burr on the edge of the scraper blade is called a _____.

unit 12
wood bits

OBJECTIVES

After completing this unit, the student will be able to:

- describe the uses of different wood bits.
- select the proper wood bit for a job.
- name the hand-operated tools used to hold bits.
- sharpen auger bits.

All drilling and boring operations require a bit and a device to turn the bit. Wood bits are used to bore holes for dowels, screws, bolts, and other wood fasteners. They are available in a large variety of types and sizes.

Bits are made to fit into holding devices, or *chucks*, which are used to turn the bits. Some chucks require a bit with a square tang, while others require a round shank. Square-tang bits are used in a bit brace. Round-shank bits are used in automatic drills, hand drills, electric drills, and drill presses.

AUGER BIT

An auger bit is used for drilling holes in wood and other soft materials. It is spiral-shaped and comes in three lengths. The main parts of the auger bit are the twist, tang, and body or shank, figure 12-1. The point of the bit is composed of the screw, lips, and spurs. The screw is the screw-shaped point which pulls the bit into the wood.

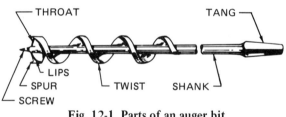

Fig. 12-1 Parts of an auger bit

The number stamped on the tang of the bit indicates the size in sixteenths of an inch, from 1/4 inch to 1 inch. For example, a number 9 on the tang indicates that it is a 9/16-inch bit.

POWER BIT

The power bit, figure 12-2, is a fast-cutting wood bit that may be used in a portable electric drill or a drill press. The sizes range from 3/8 inch to 1 inch with 1/8-inch increments. These bits may also be called spade or speed bits.

Fig. 12-2 Power bit

Fig. 12-3A Plug set over flathead screw

PLUG CUTTER BITS

The plug cutter bits, figure 12-3B, are used to cut plugs of various sizes for covering screwheads, figure 12-3A. Another use is to fill holes where knots and other defects are bored out of wood surfaces. For best results, the plug cutter should be used in the drill press. Sizes range from 3/8 inch to 1 inch with 1/8-inch increments.

Fig. 12-3B Plug cutter bit

AUGER BIT FILE

The auger bit file is used to sharpen auger bits, figure 12-4.

Fig. 12-4 Auger bit file

STRAIGHT SHANK DRILL BIT

The straight shank drill bit, figure 12-5, is used in drill presses, portable electric drills, and hand drills. A special chuck is required to hold the bits, which range in size 1/16 inch to 1/2 inch, or larger, with 1/64-inch increments.

Fig. 12-5 Straight shank drill bit

DOWEL BIT

The dowel bit, figure 12-6, is a short auger bit. This shorter length makes it more accurate when drilling holes for dowels.

Fig. 12-6 Dowel bit

AUTOMATIC DRILL BIT

The automatic drill bit is used for boring small holes in wood, figure 12-7. A spiral automatic hand drill is used to hold the bit.

Fig. 12-7 Automatic drill bit

COUNTERSINK BIT

The countersink bit is used to shape the top of a hole so it can receive a flathead screw. The bit head is tapered to a point or cone-shaped. A rosehead countersink, figure 12-8, is the one most commonly used. It may be used for countersinking holes in soft metal and wood.

Fig. 12-8 Rosehead countersink

Fig. 12-9 Expansive bit

Fig. 12-10 Forstner bit

EXPANSIVE BIT

The expansive bit is used to bore holes larger than 1 inch in diameter, figure 12-9. The bit is equipped with extra cutters of various lengths and with a gauge for setting it to diameters of up to 4 inches.

FORSTNER BIT

The forstner bit, figure 12-10, is used for boring holes in cross-grained wood. It is also used when it is necessary to bore a larger hole where a small hole has already been bored. A hole can be bored close to the edge without danger of splitting the wood. A hole can also be bored nearly through the stock because the bit does not have a screw to penetrate the wood and mar the other surface, figure 12-11. It is numbered the same as the auger bit in sixteenths of an inch.

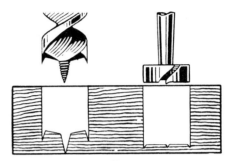

Fig. 12-11 Advantage of using forstner bit when boring nearly through stock

COMBINATION DRILL AND COUNTERSINK

Figure 12-12 shows a combination tool that drills holes for inserting screws as well as countersinking the screwhead. These are available in sets for installing various diameters and lengths of screws.

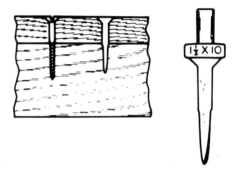

Fig. 12-12 Combination drill and countersink

BRACES

The ratchet brace is a crank-shaped tool used for holding and providing leverage to turn a bit when boring holes. The main parts are the knob, sweep, and chuck, figure 12-13. The chuck has a ratchet which permits the boring of holes where a complete revolution of the crank, or sweep, is impossible.

HAND DRILL

The hand drill, figure 12-14, is used for drilling small holes, 1/4 inch or less, in wood

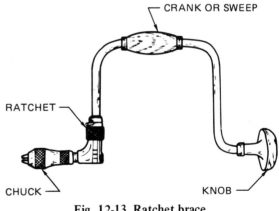

Fig. 12-13 Ratchet brace

and metal. The chuck is made to grip round-shank drills up to 1/4 inch.

AUTOMATIC HAND DRILL

The automatic hand drill, figure 12-15, is designed to rapidly drill small holes. This drill is made so that when pressure is applied to

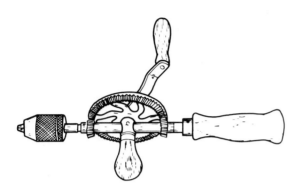

Fig. 12-14 Hand drill

Fig. 12-15 Automatic hand drill

the handle, the bit is revolved by action of a spiral following a groove inside the barrel of the drill. When pressure is released from the handle, a spring returns the drill to its original position. The handle of this drill holds various sizes of bits.

PROCEDURE FOR VERTICAL BORING WITH THE BIT AND BRACE

1. Locate the center of the hole to be bored.

2. Select the kind and size of bit needed.

3. Hold the chuck in either hand. Revolve the crank with the free hand until the jaws are open far enough to allow the tang to be inserted.

4. Insert the tang into the chuck so that the corners of the tang fit into the jaws of the chuck.

5. Revolve the crank in a clockwise direction until the chuck is tight and the jaws grip the round shank below the tang.

6. Clamp the stock in the vise and assume the position shown in figure 12-16.

7. Place the point of the bit on the center mark. Sight from two sides of the bit to get it as perpendicular to the surface of the stock as possible.

8. While sighting for straightness as the bit enters the wood, revolve the crank in a clockwise direction.

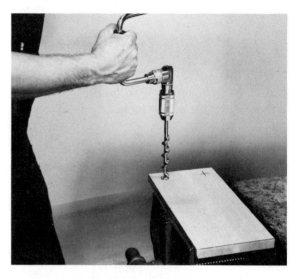

Fig. 12-16 Vertical boring with bit and brace

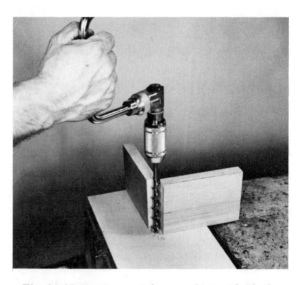

Fig. 12-17 Testing straightness of bit with blocks

9. Make a second test for straightness by placing try squares on two sides of the bit. Two blocks of wood with squared ends may also be used for this test, figure 12-17.

10. Continue boring until only the screw of the bit extends through the opposite surface of the stock.

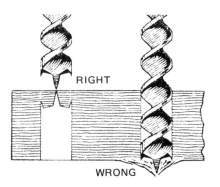

Fig. 12-18 Correct method of boring through stock

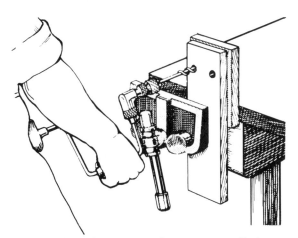

Fig. 12-19 Using scrap stock to prevent splitting

11. Remove the bit from the hole. Do this by rotating the brace counterclockwise and reverse the face of the stock in the vise.

12. Place the screw of the bit in the hole made by it when boring from the other side, figure 12-18.

13. While being careful to keep the bit perpendicular to the wood, finish boring from this side. This procedure is called *reverse boring* and prevents the stock from splitting. Splitting may occur when the stock is bored entirely from one side, figure 12-18. Another method to prevent splitting is to clamp a piece of scrap stock behind the stock to be bored, figure 12-19.

Wood is often counterbored to set screwheads and bolts below the surface. A hole for the head is first bored to the required depth. Then, a smaller hole is made to fit the shank. The larger hole is often fitted with a wooden plug to cover the screwhead or bolt, figure 12-3A.

PROCEDURE FOR HORIZONTAL BORING WITH THE BIT BRACE

1. Clamp the stock in the vise and assume the position shown in figure 12-20.

2. Sight carefully as the bit enters the wood. Make sure the bit is kept at right angles to the wood surface.

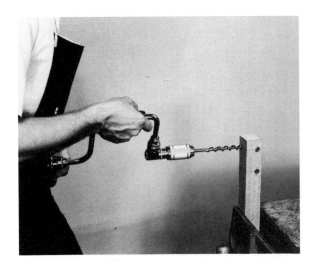

Fig. 12-20 Horizontal boring

3. Use a try square to test the accuracy of the horizontal boring. It is sometimes more convenient to have an assistant test the boring with a try square or by sighting.

4. When the spur of the bit projects through the opposite face of the stock, remove the bit. Then, reverse the stock in the vise and finish boring the hole.

STOP BORING

It is often necessary to bore a hole to a predetermined depth in stock. This is called *stop boring*, figure 12-21. It is done with the use of a bit stop clamped around the bit. A bit stop may also be made in the shop. This is

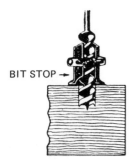

Fig. 12-21 Bit stop in use

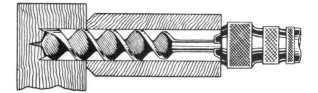

Fig. 12-22 Bit stop made of wood

done by boring a hole through a block of wood which is then fitted over the bit. The wood is cut to length so the bit extends past the block enough to bore to the necessary depth, figure 12-22.

Figure 12-23 shows the correct method of setting a bit stop to the proper depth. When two or more holes are to be bored to the same depth, the bit stop makes a quick, accurate job possible.

1. Determine the depth of the hole to be bored.

2. Clamp the bit stop around the bit and adjust it to the required depth. The depth measurement is taken from the edge of the cutting lips to the bottom of the bit stop.

3. If a block of wood is used as a bit stop, select soft wood about 1 1/2 inches square or larger, depending upon the bit size.

4. Place the bit in the brace. Determine the length of the block necessary to allow the bit to bore the required depth hole.

5. Cut the block to the proper length.

6. Using the same bit, clamp the stock in the vise. Bore a hole lengthwise through the block.

7. With the bit stop in place, bore a test hole in a scrap piece of stock to the depth allowed by the stop. If this gives the required depth hole, proceed to bore the desired holes.

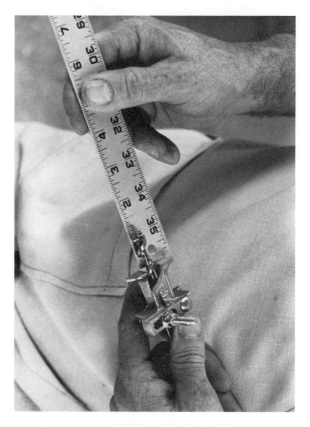

Fig. 12-23 Setting bit stop to proper depth

PROCEDURE FOR DRILLING SMALL HOLES WITH THE HAND DRILL

1. Locate the center of the hole to be drilled.

2. Select the proper drill.

3. Install the drill into the chuck. Tighten the drill by holding the chuck and turning the handle forward as shown in figure 12-24.

4. Place the drill point on the center of the hole to be drilled. Begin to rotate the drill while applying light pressure. Keep the drill perpendicular to the surface, figure 12-25.

Fig. 12-24 Installing a bit in the hand drill

5. When the hole is near completion, ease up on the pressure while continuing to rotate the drill. This allows the drill to clean the sawdust from the hole.

PROCEDURE FOR DRILLING WITH THE AUTOMATIC DRILL

1. Select the proper size drill from the tool handle.

2. Insert it into the chuck by pushing forward on the chuck and sliding the bit into position. Then release the chuck as shown in figure 12-26.

3. Place the drill point in the desired position and push the handle straight down. This pressure causes the drill to rotate and drill into the wood, figure 12-27.

4. Release the pressure on the handle while the spring returns it to the starting position. Repeat as desired to complete the hole.

5. Remove the drill from the chuck and return it to the handle.

Fig. 12-25 Using a hand drill

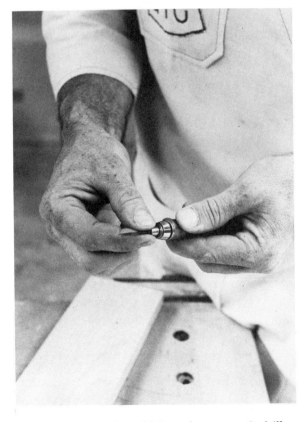

Fig. 12-26 Inserting a bit into the automatic drill

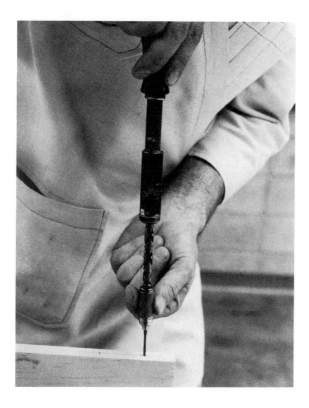

Fig. 12-27 Using an automatic drill

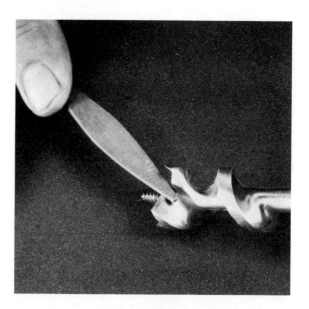

Fig. 12-28 Sharpening lips of auger bit

Fig. 12-29 Sharpening spurs of auger bit

PROCEDURE FOR SHARPENING AUGER BITS

Most drill bits are sharpened by a grinding jig. Auger bits are sharpened by filing with a special auger bit file. The following steps explain how to sharpen auger bits.

1. When sharpening the lips of the auger bit, place the bit on the bench as shown in figure 12-28.

2. File the upper side of the lips with the flat side of an auger bit file until a keen cutting edge is obtained.

3. To file the spurs of the auger bit, the bit should be placed against the edge of the workbench, figure 12-29. The inside surface of the spurs should be filed until a sharp knife edge is obtained.

4. Special auger bit whetstones may also be used to give a keener edge after filing the auger bit.

REVIEW QUESTIONS

A. Identification

1. Name each of the following boring tools.

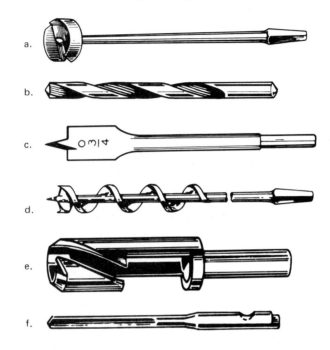

B. Multiple Choice

2. The hand drill has a chuck that holds drill bits with:
    a. a square shank.
    b. a triangular tang.
    c. a round shank.
    d. both a and c.

3. The spurs on the auger bit should be sharpened on:
    a. the inside.
    b. the outside.
    c. both the inside and outside.
    d. none of the above.

4. Which of the following bits cannot be used in the drill press?
    a. Speed bit
    b. Auger bit
    c. Straight shank drill bit
    d. Plug cutter

5. If a larger hole needs to be bored in a piece of wood directly over a small hole, the best bit to use is the:
    a. speed bit.
    b. auger bit.
    c. drill bit.
    d. forstner bit.

6. The number 7 stamped on the tang of an auger bit indicates that its size is:
    a. 7/8 inch.
    b. 7/16 inch.
    c. 7/32 inch.
    d. 7/64 inch.

7. Which of the following bits is used to cut the taper for the head of a wood screw?
    a. Plug cutter
    b. Straight shank drill bit
    c. Countersink
    d. Screwhead bit

8. When boring holes with the bit and brace, the brace should be turned in a:
   a. clockwise direction.
   b. counterclockwise direction.
   c. either a or b, depending on the bit.
   d. forward direction.

9. The part of the brace into which the tang of the bit fits is called the:
   a. ratchet.
   b. chuck.
   c. socket.
   d. bit holder.

10. When a hole is completed by boring from both sides of the stock, the process is called:
    a. counterboring.
    b. stop boring.
    c. reverse boring.
    d. speed bit.

11. Which of the following bits pulls itself into the wood?
    a. Auger bit
    b. Twist drill
    c. Forstner bit
    d. Speed bit

12. Which tool or machine should be used when using the plug cutter?
    a. Hand drill
    b. Brace
    c. Automatic drill
    d. Drill press

13. What device should you use when boring several holes to a particular depth using an auger bit?
    a. Bit block
    b. Bit stop
    c. Stop bit
    d. Hole stop

14. Which of the following bits produces a flat-bottomed hole?
    a. Speed bit
    b. Auger bit
    c. Forstner bit
    d. Combination bit

unit 13
squaring stock to dimensions

OBJECTIVE

After completing this unit, the student will be able to:

- describe the proper procedure for squaring stock to dimensions.

Squaring stock is the process of planing or cutting the edges, surfaces, and ends of stock at a 90-degree angle to each other. Stock that is squared has smooth and true surfaces. The quality of the finished project is largely determined by the ability to square stock quickly and accurately. Each part must be accurately squared to dimensions. This insures a proper fit when parts are joined together.

A correctly sharpened plane iron is necessary if the stock is to be squared easily. If a careful job is done when squaring stock with a hand plane, little sanding is required to prepare the surfaces for finishing.

PROCEDURE FOR WORKING THE FACE

1. Select the best surface of the stock as the working face. Consider the grain and

Fig. 13-1 Stock clamped between vise dog and
bench stop

Fig. 13-2 Planing the working face

Fig. 13-3 Testing across grain for levelness

amount of planing necessary to get a perfect surface.

2. Examine the working face to determine the grain direction. If it is not possible to determine the grain direction by examining the surface, place the stock in the vise, figure 13-1. Take two or three light test strokes with the plane. If the wood fibers seem to lift, leaving a pitted surface, this indicates that the planing is being done against the grain. Therefore, reverse the position of the stock in the vise.

3. After removing the stock from the vise, test the surface for flatness with a straightedge. Make light cross marks on the high places with a pencil.

4. Clamp the stock between the vise dog and the bench stop so the stock is held lengthwise with the grain running away from you, figure 13-1. If the stock is too long to be clamped this way, turn the stock so it is clamped across the grain. Do not clamp the stock too tightly. This may buckle the stock and

Fig. 13-4 Testing with the grain for levelness

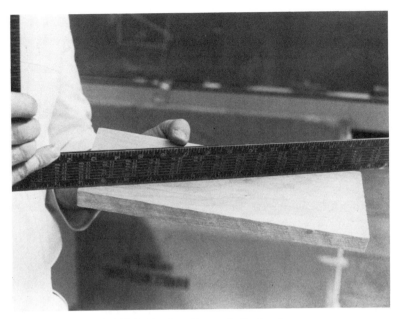

Fig. 13-5 Testing diagonals for levelness

make it difficult to plane to a level surface.

5. Plane the high places until they appear to be level with the remaining surface, figure 13-2. Remove as little of the surface as possible to get it smooth and level.

6. Remove the stock from the vise and test for levelness across the grain, figure 13-3.

7. With a foot square or framing square, test for levelness lengthwise, figure 13-4.

8. Test for wind. This is the diagonal test for levelness from corner to corner, figure 13-5.

9. If the surface is not true, mark the high places and continue planing.

10. When the surface is true, lightly mark it *WF* (working face) with a pencil.

PROCEDURE FOR WORKING THE EDGE

1. Select the better of the two edges as the *working edge.*

2. Clamp the stock in the vise with the better edge up and the grain running in the same direction as the planing, figure 13-6.

Fig. 13-6 Planing first edge

3. Plane the edge until it is level and square with the working face. Remove the stock from the vise to test for squareness with the working face, figure 13-7. Test for levelness with the framing square, figure 13-8.

4. When the edge is straight, smooth, and square with the working face, lightly mark it *WE* (working edge) with a pencil.

Fig. 13-7 Testing edge for squareness

PROCEDURE FOR WORKING THE END

1. Select the better of the two ends as the *working end.* Test it for squareness with the working edge and working face.

2. If the end is not square with the working edge, square a line from the working edge with a square, figure 13-9.

3. Measure and mark the stock to the desired width with a marking gauge. When the marking gauge is adjusted, check the setting carefully with a rule. This is done by measuring the distance between the head of the gauge and the point. The steel point of the marking gauge must be kept filed to a sharp, chisel point. Hold the gauge as shown in figure 13-10. The marking gauge should be pushed and not pulled. The depth is controlled by rotating the head of the gauge until the point makes a fine, shallow line.

4. Use a rule or straightedge, figure 13-11, for marking to width if the stock is too wide for the marking gauge. Or, use the panel gauge, figure 13-12.

5. Determine if there is enough waste for chamfering the corner. Refer to Unit 9 for planing chamfers. Chamfering the corner prevents splitting when planing the end of the stock. If there is enough

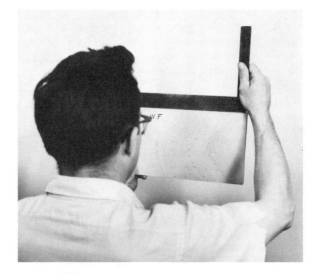

Fig. 13-8 Testing edge for levelness

Fig. 13-9 Marking working end for squareness

Fig. 13-10 Marking stock to width with marking gauge

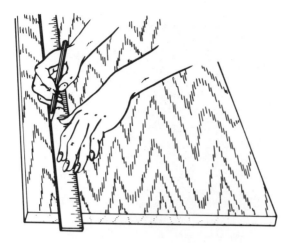

Fig. 13-11 Marking wide stock with straightedge

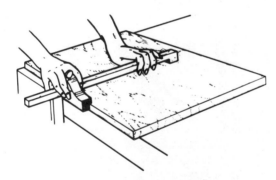

Fig. 13-12 Marking stock to width with panel gauge

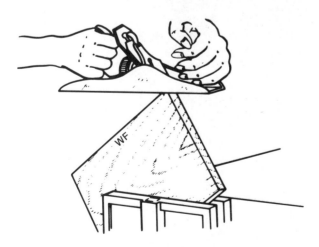

Fig. 13-13 Planing corner off to prevent splitting

waste, plane off the corner (outside of gauge line) as shown in figure 13-13. If preferred, cut this corner with a backsaw. If there is not enough waste to allow for chamfering, follow the methods shown in figures 9-19B and 9-19C for planing end grain of stock.

6. Place the stock in the vise and plane the end square to the working face and working edge, planing toward the chamfered edge, figure 13-14.

7. Remove the stock from the vise. Test the working end for squareness with WF and WE, figures 13-15 and 13-16.

8. When the stock is square and smooth, lightly mark the end *WE* (working end) with a pencil.

Fig. 13-14 Squaring first end with plane (Notice the chamfer to prevent splitting.)

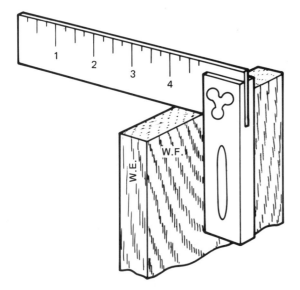

Fig. 13-15 Testing end for squareness with working face

PROCEDURE FOR WORKING THE SECOND END

1. Measure the stock from the working end to the desired length, figure 13-17.

2. Square a knife or sharp pencil line around the stock by resting the handle of the try square against the working face and working edge.

3. With a backsaw or a crosscut saw, cut off the end about 1/16 inch outside the line, figure 13-18.

4. Place the stock in the vise and remove the corner on the waste side, figure 13-19, as was done in planing the working end.

5. Plane to the line while testing for squareness, figures 13-15 and 13-16. The second end must be square with the WF and WE when the line is reached.

PROCEDURE FOR WORKING THE SECOND EDGE

1. Measure and mark the stock to the desired width, figures 13-10, 13-11, and 13-12.

Fig. 13-16 Testing end for squareness with working edge

Fig. 13-17 Measuring for length

Fig. 13-18 Sawing off waste stock with backsaw

Fig. 13-19 Planing to length

Fig. 13-20 Marking stock to thickness with a marking gauge

2. If the waste stock to be removed is more than 1/4 inch to 3/8 inch wide, rip off the surplus stock to about 1/8 inch outside the width line.

3. Place the stock in the vise. Plane the edge of the stock to the width line. Test for squareness with the WF, figure 13-7, and for levelness, figure 13-8. Stop planing exactly on the width line.

PROCEDURE FOR WORKING THE SECOND FACE

1. With the head of the marking gauge held firmly against the working face, mark the stock to thickness, figure 13-20. Mark the thickness on both edges and ends of the stock. Some woodworkers prefer to use a pencil gauge instead of the steel-pointed marking gauge for this procedure. A hole is bored through the beam, an inch or more back of the pin,

and a medium-hard pencil is inserted. The hole should be just large enough to provide a tight fit for the pencil. Make sure the pencil is kept sharp.

2. Clamp the stock in the vise. Plane the surface down to the thickness line, while testing for levelness and wind, figures 13-3, 13-4, and 13-5. When planing the last face, it is advisable to protect the ends of edges. To do this, use pieces of scrap stock between the vise dog and bench stop and the finished ends or edges.

3. Check the stock for proper thickness by measuring carefully at several points on both edges and ends.

4. Set the plane for a very light cut and plane carefully to remove any high spots that remain.

REVIEW QUESTIONS

Identification

Below are twelve operations for squaring stock to size. Place each in the correct order from number 1 to number 12.

_____ Square first end.

_____ Square second edge.

_____ Plane stock to thickness.

_____ Cut stock to length.

_____ Square second end.

_____ Mark stock to length.

_____ Square working face.

_____ Square working edge.

_____ Mark stock to width.

_____ Mark stock to thickness.

_____ Select working face.

_____ Rip stock to rough width.

unit 14
wood screws

OBJECTIVES

After completing this unit, the student will be able to:

- name the different kinds of wood screws and screwdrivers and their uses.
- explain how the sizes of wood screws are determined.
- properly fasten stock with wood screws.

KINDS OF WOOD SCREWS

Wood screws are made in many sizes and kinds. They are made of steel or brass, but may also be nickel or chromium-plated. They are classified according to the material, finish, shape of head, length, and diameter (or gauge) of wire from which they are made. Figure 14-1 shows the various shaped screwheads.

Roundhead screws are used on surfaces where the screwhead shows, figure 14-2. They are not countersunk. The screw should be left with the slot in the screwhead parallel with the wood grain. Ovalhead screws are used to fasten hinges and other hardware to wood.

Flathead bright screws (FHB) are used where they do not show on a finished surface. They should be countersunk until the screwhead is level or slightly below the adjoining surface. If used on a visible surface, they should be recessed below the surface and a plug set over them, figure 14-3. This process

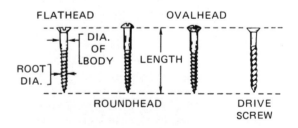

Fig. 14-1 How length of wood screws is designated

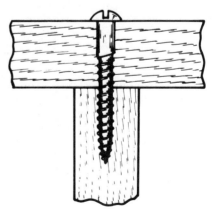

Fig. 14-2 Roundhead screw installed

107

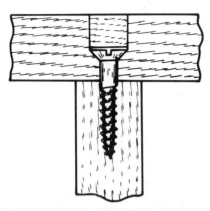

Fig. 14-3 Plug set over flathead screw

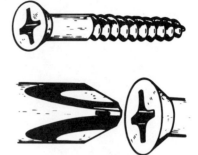

Fig. 14-4 Phillips screwdriver tip and head of phillips screw

Fig. 14-5 Package of wood screws with classification data on label

of boring a hole to recess the head of a screw is called *counterboring.*

The Phillips screw is used extensively in the woodworking and the metalworking industries. The head design of a Phillips screw prevents the Phillips screwdriver from slipping out of the screw slot, figure 14-4. This is especially true when using an electric screwdriver.

Screws are packed in pasteboard boxes containing 100 screws. The *1 1/4* on the label of the box, figure 14-5, indicates that the screw is 1 1/4 inches long. The type of head is indicated by the words *Flat Head* on the label. The number 12 indicates the screw gauge. *Screw gauge* is the diameter of the screw just below the head.

Other wood screws are shown in figure 14-6. The screw eye is often used for hanging picture frames and other objects requiring an anchor for wire, cord, and small ropes. It can also act as a door hook. The curved screw hook and the right-angled screw hook are used as an anchor on which articles are hung.

The lag screw, figure 14-6, is larger than the other wood screws. It has a square head and is driven in place with a wrench instead of a screwdriver. Lag screws are used to fasten heavy timbers in rough construction work and benches and machinery to the floor.

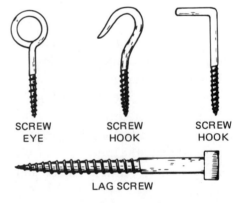

SCREW EYE   SCREW HOOK   SCREW HOOK

LAG SCREW

Fig. 14-6 Other wood screws

SIZES OF WOOD SCREWS

Screws used for general woodworking purposes range in sizes from No. 0 to No. 24, table 14-1. The number indicates the screw gauge, according to a standard screw

No. of Screw	0	1	2	3	4	5	6	7	8	9	10	11	12	14	16	18	20	24
Diameter of Head	1/8	5/32	11/64	13/64	15/64	1/4	9/32	5/16	11/32	23/64	25/64	27/64	7/16	1/2	9/16	5/8	21/32	3/4
*No. of Auger Bit			3	3	4	4	5	5	6	6	6	7	7	8	9	10	12	12
Diameter of the Shank of Screw	1/16	5/64	3/32	7/64	1/8	1/8	9/64	5/32	11/64	3/16	13/64	13/64	7/32	1/4	9/32	5/16	21/64	3/8
Size of Bit for Pilot Hole	1/16	5/64	3/32	7/64	1/8	1/8	9/64	5/32	11/64	3/16	13/64	13/64	7/32	1/4	9/32	5/16	21/64	3/8
Size of Bit for Anchor Hole { Hard Wood	1/32	1/32	1/32	1/16	1/16	5/64	5/64	3/32	3/32	7/64	7/64	1/8	1/8	9/64	5/32	3/16	13/64	1/4
Soft Wood	1/64	1/32	1/32	3/64	3/64	1/16	1/16	1/16	5/64	3/32	5/64	3/32	3/32	7/64	7/64	9/64	11/64	3/16

Note: The above chart shows the size bit that should be used to bore the pilot and the anchor holes for the size screws indicated in the chart.
*The number of auger bit given indicates the size of holes to bore for screwheads when a plug is to be used to cover them.

Table 14-1 Sizes of bits for boring

gauge (Brown & Sharpe). For example, a No. 3 screw has a 7/64-inch diameter, while a No. 18 screw has a 5/16-inch diameter.

In length, screws range from 1/4 inch to 1 inch with 1/8-inch increments and from 1 inch to 5 inches with 1/4-inch increments. The length of the flathead screw and the drive screw includes their overall measure. The length of the roundhead screw does not include the head, figure 14-2. The length of the ovalhead screw includes the bottom, tapered part of the head, as indicated in figure 14-2. This is because only the tapered part is set below the wood or metal surface.

Screws have many advantages as wood fasteners. They are more permanent than nails because they hold better. Screws can be tightened easily and the parts they hold together can be taken apart readily. However, much time and care is required to insert screws properly, and they are easily seen.

SCREWDRIVERS AND THEIR PROPER USE

Screwdrivers are available in a large variety of kinds and sizes. The most common is the standard screwdriver, figure 14-7. The two main parts are the handle, available in wood or plastic, and the blade. The size of the screwdriver is determined by the length of the blade. The smaller sizes range from 3

Fig. 14-7 Standard screwdriver

Fig. 14-8 Spiral screwdriver

Fig. 14-9 Screwdriver bit

inches to 6 inches in length. Screwdrivers used for large screws are from 6 inches to 12 inches long.

The spiral screwdriver is used to save time in driving screws. When pressure is put on the end of the handle, a spiral groove along the barrel causes the end of the screwdriver to turn and drive the screw in place. This screwdriver requires more skill to use than the standard screwdriver, figure 14-8.

The screwdriver bit, figure 14-9, is made for driving screws with the hand brace. It should be used with care. Much leverage is obtained and there is a danger of twisting off the screw. There is also the possibility of damaging the screwhead or the wood surface if the bit is allowed to twist out of the screw slot.

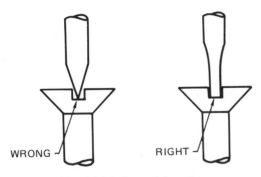

Fig. 14-10 Screwdriver tips

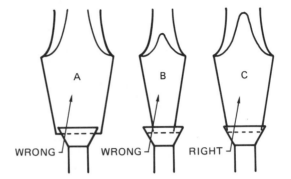

Fig. 14-11 Fitting screwdriver to screwhead

The efficiency of a screwdriver is determined by the condition and shape of its tip. Figure 14-10 shows the correct and incorrect shapes of the tip. If the tip is ground to a chisel edge, it has a tendency to twist out of the screw slot. The width of the tip is also important. The tip shown in figure 14-11A is too wide and can cause damage to the wood around the screw hole. Figure 14-11B shows a tip that is too narrow. This tip can twist out of the screw slot and damage both the tip and screwhead. The correct width of a screwdriver tip is shown in figure 14-11C.

The tip of a large screwdriver should never be ground to fit the head of a small screw. Instead, select a smaller screwdriver.

SELECTION OF BITS

The bit and screw chart, table 14-1, should be used to determine the bit size used in boring holes for screws. The number of the auger bit is the size used to bore the hole for a wood plug when it is desirable to set the screwhead below the surface and cover it.

FASTENING WITH SCREWS

When fastening hinges and other hardware in place, bore a hole slightly smaller than the screw shank. The depth should be equal to half of the screw length.

When two pieces of stock are fastened together with screws, it is necessary to drill two holes for the screw, figure 14-12. The

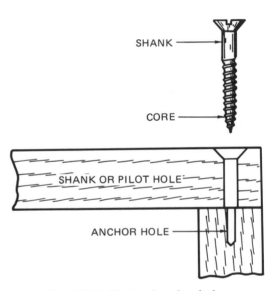

Fig. 14-12 Pilot and anchor holes

pilot hole is drilled through the first piece of stock. The anchor hole is drilled only far enough into the second piece to allow the screw core the necessary clearance to be driven its full length. The pilot hole is just large enough to fit the shank of the screw without binding.

Figure 14-13 shows a scratch awl in position for marking the center of the anchor hole after the pilot hole has been bored. If the anchor hole is drilled only large enough to allow clearance for the core of the screw, the threads of the screw will be anchored firmly in the sides of the hole. When the screw is to be anchored in end grain, the hole should be 1/32 inch smaller than when anchoring the screw in side grain.

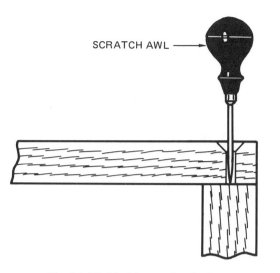

Fig. 14-13 Marking anchor hole

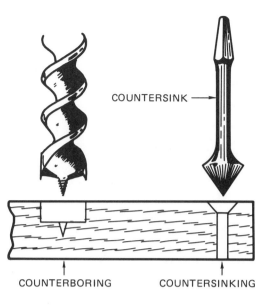

Fig. 14-14 Counterboring and countersinking

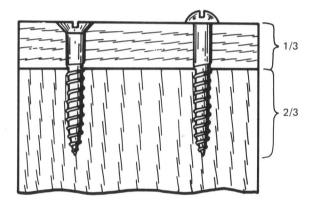

Fig. 14-15 Screws properly installed

If you wish to put a plug over the top of the screw, it is necessary to counterbore a hole as large as the screwhead. Table 14-1 gives the proper size of auger bit for counterboring various screw sizes. Always counterbore the hole before boring the pilot or anchor holes, figure 14-14.

When using brass screws, it is advisable to drive a steel screw of the same size into the hole first, remove it, and replace it with the brass screw. The chance of twisting off the brass screw is lessened. A countersink is used to bevel the top of the pilot hole when a flathead screw is used, figure 14-14. As indicated in figure 14-15, the flathead screw should be set flush or slightly below the surface. The roundhead screw is not countersunk.

PROCEDURE FOR FASTENING STOCK WITH SCREWS

1. Select a screw that is long enough to allow approximately 2/3 of its length to go into the second piece, figure 14-15.
2. Locate the centers for the screw holes.
3. Select the drill bit that is just large enough to take the shank of the screw, see table 14-1.
4. Place the point of the bit on the center mark and drill the pilot hole using a

hand drill or an electric drill, figure 14-16. Keep the bit perpendicular to the surface being bored.

5. Bore all other pilot holes.
6. Lay the stock in position on the piece to which it is to be fastened and clamp it in place.
7. Mark the centers of the anchor holes by inserting a nail or a scratch awl in the center of the pilot hole, figure 14-13. Tap it lightly with a mallet or hammer.
8. Select a bit the size of the screw core, according to the screw chart. Drill the anchor hole to a depth slightly less than

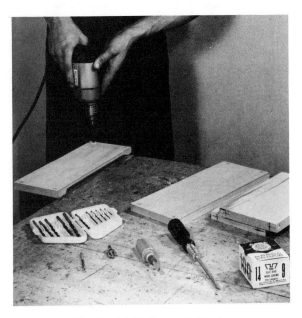

Fig. 14-16 Drilling pilot holes

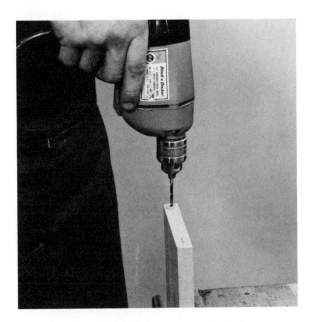

Fig. 14-17 Drilling an anchor hole

the distance the screw will enter the wood, figure 14-17.

9. If flathead screws are used, countersink the pilot hole, figure 14-18, until the head of the screw sinks flush with the wood surface, figure 14-15.

10. Place the stock in the final assembly position, figure 14-19.

11. Rub a little soap or paraffin wax on the threads of the screw. Insert the screw in the pilot hole.

12. Insert a screwdriver, figure 14-19, in the slot of the screwhead. Turn the screw in a clockwise direction until the pieces of stock are drawn together tightly.
    Keep enough pressure on the screwdriver with the palm of the hand. This prevents it from twisting out of the screw slot and marring the surface. *Caution*: Be very careful when checking the surface of a wood screw with your finger. Many times the screwdriver will turn up a small sharp burr on the screwhead that will cut your finger.

13. When fastening corners of frames together, it is sometimes advisable to

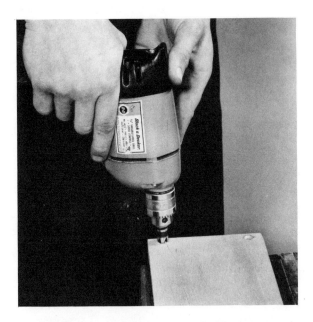

Fig. 14-18 Countersinking for flathead screws

insert one screw and then drill a second anchor hole as shown in figure 14-20.

14. Screws may also be driven with the electric drill and screwdriver attachment, figure 14-21.

15. After the final screw is driven, try all the other screws again to make sure they are tight and the slot in the screwhead is parallel with the grain direction.

Fig. 14-19 Driving first screw with standard screwdriver

Fig. 14-20 Drilling second anchor hole

Fig. 14-21 Driving screw with electric drill and screwdriver attachment

REVIEW QUESTIONS

A.   **Identification**

    1.   Name each of the following wood screwhead types.

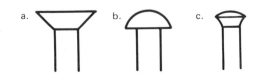

B.   **Multiple Choice**

2. Which of the following screwheads helps to prevent the screwdriver from slipping off of the screw?
    a. Slotted head   c. Ovalhead
    b. Phillips head   d. Counterhead

3. The number of a screw indicates the:
    a. screw length.   c. shank diameter.
    b. head diameter.   d. thread size.

4. A screw-type device that is driven in place with a wrench is:
    a. a lag screw.   c. a heavy-duty screw.
    b. a wrench screw.   d. a hex screw.

5. When selecting a screwdriver to drive a slotted-head screw, care should be taken to select one that:
    a. has a blade as wide as the shank of the screw.
    b. is as large as possible.
    c. is slightly smaller than the diameter of the head.
    d. has a plastic handle.

6. How long should screws be to attach 1/2-inch stock to 2-inch stock?
    a. 1 inch   c. 2 inches
    b. 1 1/2 inches   d. 2 1/2 inches

7. Which of the following is the correct order for installing flathead wood screws?
    a. Anchor hole, pilot hole, countersink hole
    b. Countersink hole, anchor hole, pilot hole
    c. Countersink hole, pilot hole, anchor hole
    d. Pilot hole, anchor hole, countersink hole

8. Which of the following will be the smallest hole bored when installing a wood screw?
    a. Counterbored hole   c. Anchor hole
    b. Pilot hole   d. Countersink hole

9. Which of the following is not an advantage of wood screws?
    a. Wood screws have better holding power.
    b. Wood screws are easily installed.
    c. The members can be taken apart easily.
    d. Wood screws can be tightened easily.

10. The length of a wood screw is measured from the screw point to:
    a. the top of the head.
    b. the bottom of the head.
    c. the start of the screw threads.
    d. the portion of the head that will be even with the wood surface when the screw is properly installed.

unit 15
nails and other wood fasteners

OBJECTIVES

After completing this unit, the student will be able to:

- describe the various types, sizes, and specific uses of nails.
- name and give the uses of special wood fasteners.
- properly drive and pull nails.

The nails frequently used in attaching wood are common, box, finish, casing, brads, and wire nails. Common, box, casing, and finishing nails are sized by a penny system of measure. The term *penny*, abbreviated *d*, is used when ordering nails. This penny system indicates the length of the nail, not the specific nail sizes. All 8d nails are approximately the same length. For example, and 8d finish nail is 2 1/2 inches long. An 8d box nail is also 2 1/2 inches long. Brads and wire nails are specified by length and gauge number.

COMMON NAILS

Common nails, figure 15-1, have a large, flat head and are used where it is acceptable for the heads to show. They are also used where more holding power is desired. The largest use of common nails is in home and building construction. They come in sizes from 2d (1 inch long) to 20d (4 inches long).

Fig. 15-1 Common nail

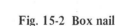

Fig. 15-2 Box nail

Larger sizes from 30d (4 1/2 inches long) to 100d (12 inches long) are available. These are called *spikes*.

BOX NAILS

The box nail is like the common nail except it is smaller in diameter and has a thinner head, figure 15-2. Since it is smaller, it may be used to nail thinner stock and stock that is likely to split when nailed with a common nail. Because the head is thinner, the holding power is less than the common nail. The nail itself is more likely to bend than a common nail. The box nail was originally made for nailing packing crates and boxes.

FINISHING NAILS

Finishing nails are used on finished surfaces where nailheads should not be visible, figure 15-3. Their small heads permit them to be driven below the surface with a nail set, figure 15-4. The hole left by the head is then filled with putty, plastic wood, or stick shellac.

The finishing nail is made from the same diameter wire as the box nail of the same size. Since this nail has a very small head, it does not have as much holding power as nails with larger heads.

CASING NAILS

Although similar to finishing nails, casing nails have a larger, cone-shaped head which gives them more holding power, figure 15-5. It is used for fastening door and window casings and for fastening interior trim.

WIRE BRADS

Wire brads are similar to finishing nails but are available in several combinations of lengths and wire sizes. For example, a 1-inch brad is available in wire sizes ranging from 16 gauge to 20 gauge. This allows one to select the diameter as well as the length. Standard lengths are from 1/2 inch to 1 1/2 inches, figure 15-6.

WIRE NAILS

Wire nails, figure 15-7, are similar to brads except the wire nail has a flat head. They are available in the same sizes as the brads. Wire nails are mainly used in the construction of small items where it is acceptable for the head to show.

COATINGS

All of the nails mentioned with the exception of the brads and wire nails are available as a standard steel nail or with a coating. If the nail is covered with a zinc or

Fig. 15-3 Finish nail

Fig. 15-4 Nail set

Fig. 15-5 Casing nail

Fig. 15-6 Wire brad

Fig. 15-7 Wire nail

Fig. 15-8 Corrugated fasteners

galvanized coating, it has more holding power and is corrosion resistant. This will not allow the nail to rust and stain the wood. Another available coating is a resinous material that gives the nail greater holding power. It may be used where the nature of the wood limits the nail size used.

CORRUGATED FASTENERS

Corrugated fasteners are used when a quick method of fastening butt or mitered joints is desired. They are suitable to use for wood screen frames and rough carpentry. Corrugated fasteners are not suitable for finished cabinetwork. Figure 15-8 shows two types of corrugated fasteners. One has a sawtooth edge, while the other has a plain edge. A butt joint is fastened with corrugated fasteners in figure 15-9. When installing this

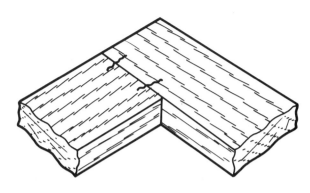

Fig. 15-9 Butt joint fastened with corrugated fasteners

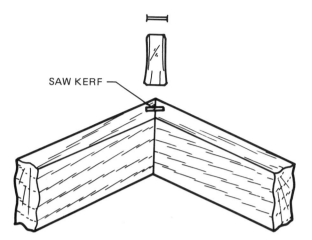

Fig. 15-10 Clamp nail

fastener, it is necessary to have the work on a very solid surface, otherwise the fastener will be difficult to install.

CLAMP NAILS

Figure 15-10 shows how clamp nails hold edge-mitered joints together. This wood fastener is available in lengths from 3/4 inch to 2 inches. As indicated in figure 15-10, the lower end of the clamp nail is flared slightly. The flared end should always be driven in first. This end acts to draw the joint together tightly.

To use clamp nails for holding edge-mitered joints together, thin, matched saw kerfs are first cut into each face of the joint, figure 15-10. The depth should be equal to one-half the width of the clamp nail. A 22-gauge saw blade is used for this purpose. The clamp nail is then driven into this slot the same way that a nail is driven.

CLAW HAMMERS

The claw hammer, figure 15-11, is used for driving and withdrawing nails. Claw hammer sizes are indicated by the weight of the head, which ranges from 7 ounces to 20 ounces. For most work, a 16-ounce hammer is the proper size. However, for fine bench-type work, use a 13-ounce hammer. For house framing, a 20-ounce hammer allows the nails to be driven faster and better. A claw hammer with straight claws, figure

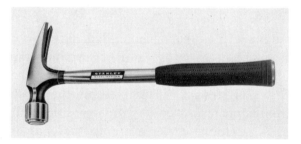

Fig. 15-11 Claw hammer

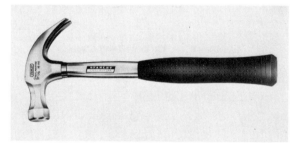

Fig. 15-12 Ripping hammer

15-12, is called a *ripping hammer*. The claws of the ripping hammer are straight and wedge-shaped. They are used for prying off boards.

Striking a blow with the hammer is a technique that must be mastered before the tool can be used skillfully. When driving small nails and brads, the wrist is used to deliver the blow. When driving large nails, the blow is delivered through the wrist, elbow, and shoulder. The face of the hammer, figure 15-13, which must meet the nailhead squarely,

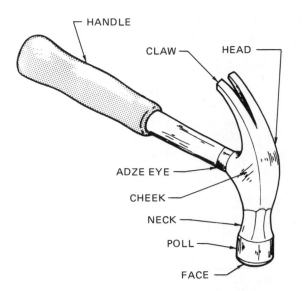

Fig. 15-13 Parts of a hammer

HANDLE

CLAW

HEAD

ADZE EYE

CHEEK

NECK

POLL

FACE

FIRST NAIL DRIVEN

Fig. 15-14 Driving nails at an angle

should always be kept clean. This prevents it from slipping off the nail.

Caution: Never use one hammer to strike another. The face of one hammer may chip, and the flying piece may hit someone.

DRIVING NAILS

Nails driven at an angle to the surface, figure 15-14, have more holding power than those driven at a right angle to the surface. However, it is advisable to drive the first nail straight. This prevents the stock from slipping out of its proper position. If nails are to be driven close to the ends or edges of hardwood stock, drill small holes where the nails are to be driven. This prevents the wood from splitting. A drill bit slightly smaller than the nail is used for this purpose. Another method is to place the nail on the bench stop and blunt the point of the nail with a hammer, figure 15-15. This allows the nail to partially cut its way into the wood and, therefore, reduces the chance of splitting the wood.

There is a chance that you might miss the nail while driving it, thus damaging the work surface. Therefore, it is helpful to make a nailing shield as shown in figure

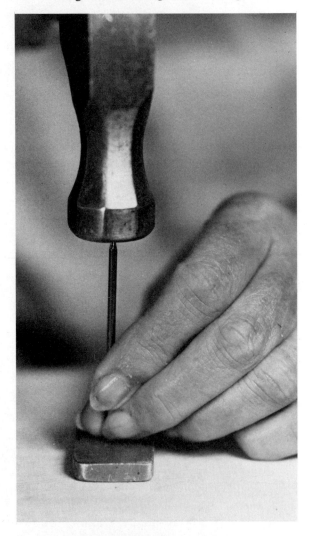

Fig. 15-15 Blunting the point of a nail to prevent splitting the wood

Fig. 15-16 Using a nailing shield

15-16. This device can be made from a small piece of thin wood scrap by cutting a slot into the center of the piece. The nail is first started and then the shield is slipped on the nail. If a hammer blow misses the nail, the shield board protects the project surface. When the nail is nearly driven, remove the board and complete the nailing with a nail set.

PROCEDURE FOR DRIVING NAILS

1. When driving large nails and striking a full blow with the hammer, grip the handle at the end, figure 15-17. If small nails are driven, the handle is gripped a short distance from the end and a shorter stroke is used.

2. Rest the face of the hammer on the nail, raise the hammer slightly, and give the nail a light tap to start it and determine the aim.

3. Hold the hammer so the handle is at a right angle to the nail when striking the blow, figure 15-17.

4. Drive the nail until the head is nearly level with the surface of the wood.

5. Finish driving the nail with light blows to prevent marring the wood surface.

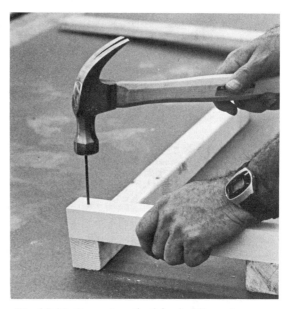

Fig. 15-17 Correct method for holding a hammer

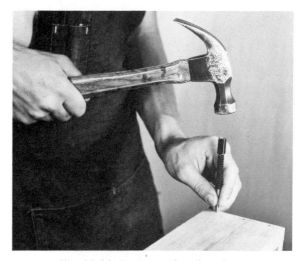

Fig. 15-18 Setting nail with nail set

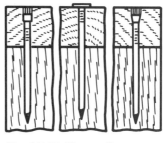

Fig. 15-19 How nails are set

6. If finishing nails are driven, use a nail set and a hammer to drive the nailhead below the surface, figure 15-18. Figure 15-19 shows how finishing and casing

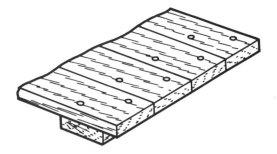

Fig. 15-20 How to nail cleats

Fig. 15-21 First step in drawing nails

nails are set below the surface of the wood. The finish nail should be set below the surface at a distance equal to the diameter of the head.

7. Where possible, drive the nails at a slight angle to the surface, figure 15-14.

8. Stagger the nails when nailing cleats, figure 15-20. This helps to prevent the cleat from splitting.

9. If the nail bends after it has been driven part of the way, withdraw it and start another nail. The nail often follows the grain of the wood and is led off its proper course. In this case, withdraw the nail and start a new nail in another place. Another method is to straighten the first hole with a small drill bit and drive a new nail.

PROCEDURE FOR WITHDRAWING NAILS

1. If the nail to be withdrawn has been driven until its head is near the wood surface, set the fork of the hammer claws firmly against the nail, just below the head, figure 15-21.

Fig. 15-22 Using block when drawing nails

2. Withdraw the nail by pulling the handle of the hammer toward you until it is nearly in a vertical position.

3. Tip the hammer handle forward and place a block of scrap wood under the hammer head, as shown in figure 15-22.

4. Withdraw the nail until the hammer handle is again in a vertical position.

5. If a long nail is withdrawn, it may be necessary to place a second block under the head of the hammer and repeat the operation in Step 4. Because finishing and casing nails are set below the wood surface when a nail set is used, they cannot be withdrawn successfully.

REVIEW QUESTIONS

A. Identification

1. Name each of the following wood fasteners.

a.

b.

c.

d.

e.

B. Multiple Choice

2. Which of the following nails is made from the largest size wire?
   a. Box nail
   b. Common nail
   c. Finish nail
   d. Casing nail

3. Which of the following nail sizes is the longest?
   a. 16d
   b. 6d
   c. 8d
   d. 10d

4. Which of the following nails has the greatest holding ability?
   a. Finish nail
   b. Casing nail
   c. Box nail
   d. Common nail

5. What is the one similarity between an 8d common nail and an 8d finish nail?
   a. They both have the same length.
   b. They are both made from the same size wire.
   c. They both have the same kind of head.
   d. There are no similarities.

6. A tool that is used with the hammer to place the head of a finish nail below the surface is a:
   a. nail punch.
   b. nail driver.
   c. nail set.
   d. nail pusher.

7. The wood fastener that requires you to cut a thin slot in each face of the joint is called:
   a. a corrugated fastener.
   b. a clamp nail.
   c. a drive nail.
   d. an uncommon nail.

8. Which one of the following hammer sizes is used for all-around general work?
   a. 12 ounce
   b. 14 ounce
   c. 16 ounce
   d. 20 ounce

9. Which of the following is used to help prevent the splitting of wood while driving a nail near the end of a piece of stock?
   a. Drill a hole for the nail first.
   c. Blunt the end of the nail.
   b. Drive the nail in very slowly.
   d. Both a and c

10. The difference between a brad and a wire nail is:
    a. the brad is smaller.
    b. the wire nail is smaller.
    c. the brad has a different head.
    d. they are different names for the same nail.

unit 16

common wood joints

OBJECTIVES

After completing this unit, the student will be able to:

- name the common woodworking joints.

- explain the uses of each common woodworking joint.

Joints are used to fasten various pieces of wood together. In every woodworking project at least one or more joints are used. These joints are usually glued to strengthen them.

The woodworker must consider such factors as strength, appearance, and construction time when selecting joints for a project. If the woodworker is familiar with each type of wood joint, the proper joint will be selected for the job. For example, a dovetail joint is better than a butt joint for holding the side of a drawer to the drawer front.

It is important that the parts of a joint be balanced according to strength. For instance, when a mortise-and-tenon joint is made, the tenon thickness on 3/4 or 1-inch stock should never be less than 3/8 inch or more than 1/2 inch.

END-BUTT JOINT

The end-butt joint is the easiest to construct. It is formed by butting the end of one board against the edge or face of

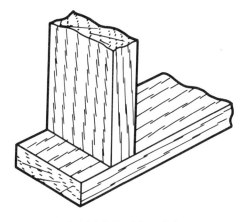

Fig. 16-1 End-butt joint

another, figure 16-1. The joint is held in place by the use of nails, screws, or corrugated fasteners. The end of the stock must be square before butting it against the other piece.

EDGE-BUTT JOINT (GLUE JOINT)

The edge-butt joint, figure 16-2, is used when it is necessary to glue several narrow boards together to form a large surface such as a tabletop. Due to the direction of the

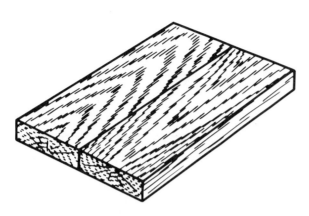

Fig. 16-2 Edge-butt joint

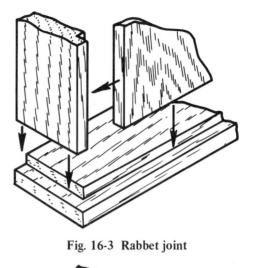

Fig. 16-3 Rabbet joint

grain in the edge joint, a properly made joint is stronger than the wood itself.

RABBET JOINT

A rabbet joint is cut on the end or edge of a board, figure 16-3. This joint is commonly used to attach the back and top of a cabinet to the sides. It is one of the simplest joints to use when attaching the sides of a drawer to its front.

DADO JOINT

The dado joint, figure 16-4, is similar to the rabbet joint. The difference is the recessed portion of the dado joint is made away from the end of the board. A groove, figure 16-5, is similar to the dado except that a groove runs with the grain and a dado runs across the grain. The dado joint is used for attaching the shelves to the sides in bookcases and the back to the sides in drawer construction. It is also used in places where it is important not to allow cabinet parts to be easily twisted apart or pushed out of place.

The stopped dado joint, or gain joint, is used for fastening shelves to the sides of a bookcase and installing supporting frames between drawers, figure 16-6. It is also used for producing similar types of construction where a through dado joint would show on the front edge of the cabinet.

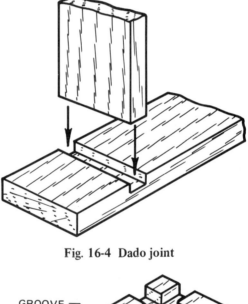

Fig. 16-4 Dado joint

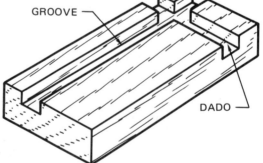

GROOVE

DADO

Fig. 16-5 Groove and dado joints

The combination dado, tongue, and rabbet joint, figure 16-7, is used for fastening corners of chests and boxes together. It may also be used for attaching the drawer front to the sides.

CROSS-LAP JOINT

Cross-lap joints, figures 16-8 and 16-9, are used for stretchers of tables and stands, bases of pedestal-type tables, and construction where two pieces of material are lapped across each other.

The middle lap, figure 16-10, and the half lap, figure 16-11, are similar to the cross-lap joint. In the construction of lap

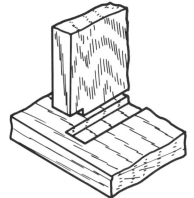

Fig. 16-6 Stopped dado joint

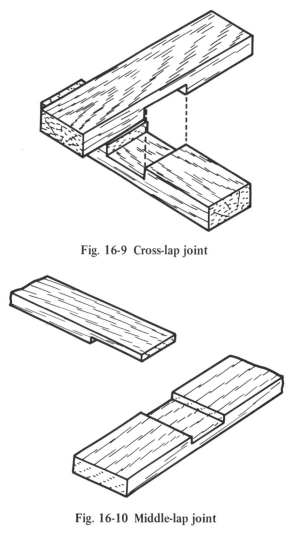

Fig. 16-9 Cross-lap joint

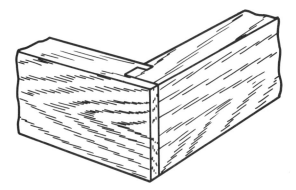

Fig. 16-7 The combination dado, tongue, and rabbet joint

Fig. 16-10 Middle-lap joint

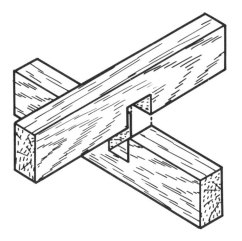

Fig. 16-8 Edge cross-lap joint

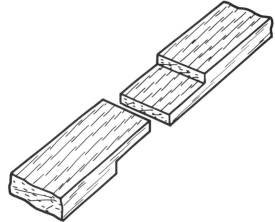

Fig. 16-11 Half-lap joint

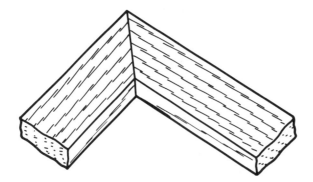

Fig. 16-12 Miter joint

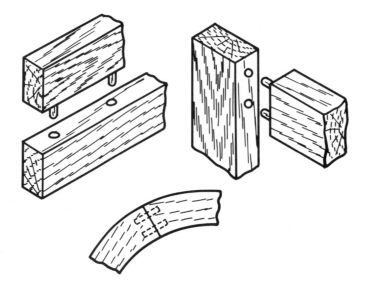

Fig. 16-13 Dowel joints

joints, half the thickness of each part is cut away where they are to be joined. Therefore, the assembled joint is only as thick as the stock.

MITER JOINT

The miter joint, figure 16-12, is used on picture frames and trim around doors, windows, and cabinet fronts. The miter joint allows the end grain to be hidden. This joint is not strong. Many times it is necessary to reinforce it with dowels, nails, or splines.

DOWEL JOINT

Dowels are often used where extra strength is needed in butt joints, dado joints, and miter joints. The dowel joint is also used for joining curved pieces of stock to each other or to flat surfaces, figure 16-13.

Dowels are usually made of birch and are available in diameters ranging from 1/8 inch to 1 inch with 1/8-inch increments. The 3/8-inch or 1/2-inch dowels are most commonly used for joints. Dowels are purchased in 3-foot lengths, although a special short-length, grooved dowel pin is available.

BLIND MORTISE-AND-TENON JOINT

Although this joint is difficult to make, it is used in cabinet construction more often than any other joint, figure 16-14. It is easier to fit the tenon (projection) to the mortise (slot). Therefore, the mortise is made first. When square stock, such as table legs, is

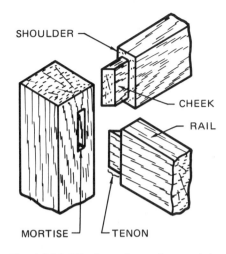

Fig. 16-14 Blind mortise-and-tenon joint

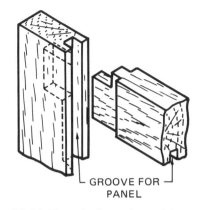

Fig. 16-15 Haunched mortise-and-tenon joint

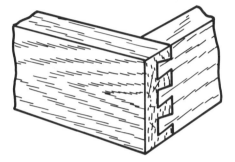

Fig. 16-16 Dovetail joint

mortised to receive a tenon, the mortise is placed near the outside surface, figure 16-14. This spreads the leg strength more evenly and prevents the stock between the mortise from splitting too easily.

The thickness of the tenon must be in proportion to the thickness of the rail and to the stock to be mortised. If the rail is made of stock 3/4 inch thick, the tenon should be 3/8 inch thick. Thus, when the 3/4-inch rail is used, the shoulder on one side of the tenon will be 3/16 inch. The outside of the rail should be set in 1/4 inch from the outside leg surface. This is the proper spacing for most table construction. The first side of the mortise is then marked 7/16 inch from the outside leg surface. Rails are often used to connect the legs that support a tabletop or the chair legs that support the seat.

THE HAUNCHED MORTISE-AND-TENON JOINT

This joint is used for doors and other flat frame construction where a panel must be fitted into the frame, figure 16-15. The haunch on the top edge of the rail fits into the end of the groove that has been cut for the panel. This construction allows the groove to be plowed the entire length of the stock. When 3/4-inch stock is used for the frame, a panel 1/4 inch or 3/8 inch thick is used. The tenon is made the same thickness as the panel.

DOVETAIL JOINT

The dovetail joint is used in high-quality drawer construction and in corners where much strength is needed, figure 16-16. It is a difficult joint to construct by hand but relatively easy to make with a router and a dovetail attachment.

REVIEW QUESTIONS

A. Identification

1. Name each of the following joints.

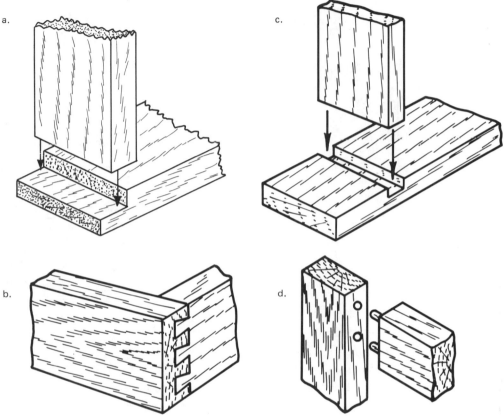

B. Multiple Choice

2. Which of the following joints is best for fastening the sides of a drawer to the front?
   - a. Butt joint
   - b. Rabbet joint
   - c. Dado joint
   - d. Dovetail joint

3. The thickness of a tenon on a 3/4-inch thick table rail should be:
   - a. 3/8 inch.
   - b. 1/2 inch.
   - c. 3/16 inch.
   - d. 1/4 inch.

4. Which of the following joints is best for fastening the back to the sides of a drawer?
   - a. Butt joint
   - b. Rabbet joint
   - c. Dado joint
   - d. Miter joint

5. Which of the following joints is used for stretchers on a flower stand?
   - a. Cross-lap joint
   - b. Middle-lap joint
   - c. Half-lap joint
   - d. Quarter-lap joint

6. Dowels are generally made from:
   - a. ash.
   - b. birch.
   - c. maple.
   - d. pine.

7. What diameter of dowel is used when fastening 3/4-inch stock together with an edge joint?
   a. 1/4 inch
   b. 3/8 inch
   c. 5/16 inch
   d. 1/2 inch

8. When fastening the legs to the rails on a table, which of the following joints would be the strongest?
   a. Butt joint
   b. Cross-lap joint
   c. Mortise-and-tenon joint
   d. Dowel joint

9. Which of the following joints is used to fasten picture frame corners together?
   a. Rabbet joint
   b. Dado joint
   c. End-lap joint
   d. Miter joint

C. Short Answer

10. What is the difference between a groove joint and a dado joint?

unit 17

how to make
common wood
joints

OBJECTIVES

After completing this unit, the student will be able to:

- properly lay out, cut, and fit stock to make common wood joints.

- assemble common wood joints.

When building any project that uses more than a single, flat piece of wood, it becomes necessary to assemble the pieces with joints. The appearance of the finished product greatly depends on how well the pieces are assembled. The completed joint should be as unnoticed as possible. This is done by matching grain patterns in each piece and making sure there are no gaps or spaces where the two pieces meet.

PROCEDURE FOR MAKING THE EDGE JOINT

1. Place the boards to be joined on the bench top with the best face up.

2. Arrange the boards in different combinations until the best grain match for the boards is obtained.

3. Place location marks across each joint to be made, as shown in figure 17-1. If there is more than one joint, use one mark on the first joint, two marks on the second, etc. This allows you to return

Fig. 17-1 Location marks on boards

the boards to their original position later.

4. Fold the boards along the joint so they are side by side with the edge to be jointed facing up. Clamp them in the vise, figure 17-2.

130

Fig. 17-2 Clamping boards in a vise

Fig. 17-3 Planing both boards at the same time

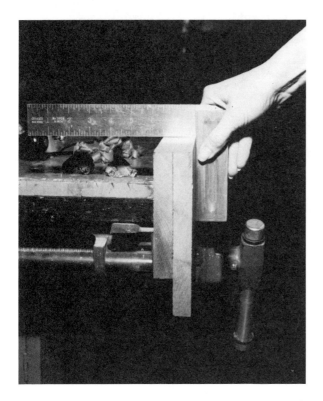

Fig. 17-4 Checking squareness

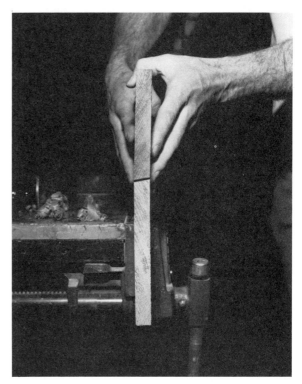

Fig. 17-5 Flat surface obtained even when slight
bevel is planed on both boards

5. Plane both edges at the same time until they are straight, figure 17-3, and as nearly square as possible, figure 17-4. If the planed edges are not perfectly square with the face, a flat surface will be obtained due to planing them both at the same time, figure 17-5.

6. Remove the boards from the vise and test for proper fit. Do this by holding them up in front of you. Observe how well the planed surfaces meet. Edge joints are planed so there is a slight opening in the center. This provides for additional tension on the ends where the joint is most likely to fail.

7. If the joint does not fit properly, return the boards to the vise and plane them again. A final test before gluing should be made. Place the boards in the clamps to make sure they fit properly. A poorly fitted joint will eventually fail and ruin the project appearance.

PROCEDURE FOR REINFORCING JOINTS WITH DOWELS

1. Complete the joint to be doweled as described in the previous section.

2. Place the pieces to be doweled face side up and correctly aligned on the bench. Locate the positions of the desired dowels with the try square and a pencil, figure 17-6.

3. Square a line across the edge on both pieces from the marks indicated in Step 2, figure 17-7.

4. Determine the proper dowel size needed for the joint. The dowel size should be one-half the thickness of the wood.

5. Select the same size of bit guide as the dowel. Place the guide in the dowel jig with the bevel end up and the bottom of the guide flush with the underside of the jig, figure 17-8.

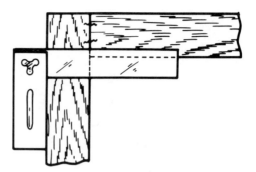

Fig. 17-6 Locating dowels

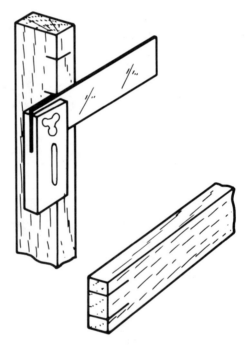

Fig. 17-7 Squaring a line across the edge

Fig. 17-8 Locking bit guide in place

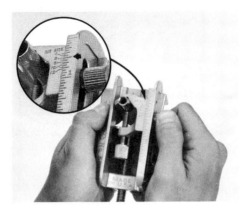

Fig. 17-9 Aligning index line

Fig. 17-10 Attaching and aligning the doweling jig

6. Adjust the slide, aligning the index line for the guide selected with the distance the dowel center will be placed from the face of the work, figure 17-9.

7. Place the dowel jig on one of the pieces of stock with the fence next to the face side of the workpiece. Line up the mark on the fence of the dowel jig with the mark placed on the stock in Step 2. Clamp the jig securely, figure 17-10.

8. Secure the proper size auger bit in the brace. Place the bit stop on the auger bit and adjust it to the desired depth.

9. Carefully place the bit into the bit guide of the dowel jig. Make sure not to strike the bit on the guide. Proceed to bore until the bit stop contacts the bit guide. If desired, select a piece of scrap stock to check for the proper hole size and depth before proceeding on the workpiece.

10. Cut the dowels 1/8 inch shorter than the combined hole depths. Make a trial assembly to see that the joints fit properly before gluing.

With another type of dowel jig, figure 17-11, the centering of the dowel is automatic when you clamp the jig on the stock. The procedure for using this jig is the same as the one described above except that Steps 5 and 6 may be eliminated.

Fig. 17-11 Using self-centered dowel jig to bore holes for dowels

Procedure for Using Dowel Centers

A third method of locating holes for dowels is to use dowel centers, figure 17-12. The following is the procedure for using them.

1. Bore the desired holes in one of the pieces of stock. Insert the dowel centers.

2. Carefully align the two pieces to be doweled. When satisfied, push or tap the

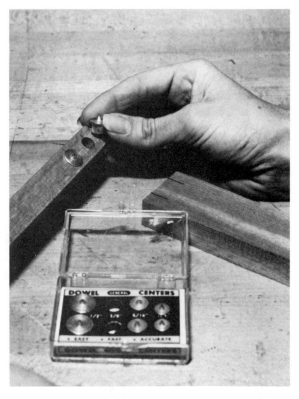

Fig. 17-12 Using dowel centers to locate holes

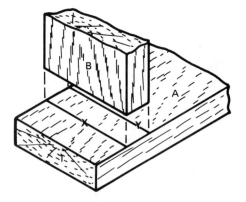

Fig. 17-13 Marking for width of dado

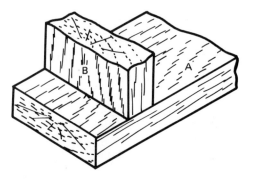

Fig. 17-14 Checking layout

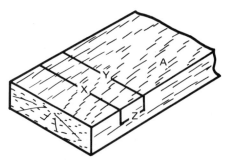

Fig. 17-15 Marking for depth of dado

pieces together. This marks the centers of the second piece.

PROCEDURE FOR MAKING A DADO JOINT

1. Be sure the pieces to be joined are squared to the given dimensions.

2. Select the piece to be dadoed, piece A in figure 17-13. Locate one edge of the dado by measuring from the end of the stock.

3. With a try square and knife, square a line across the face through this point, line X in figure 17-13.

4. Measure the exact thickness of piece B. Lay off this measurement on piece A from line X. Square line Y through this point.

5. Check the accuracy of these lines by placing piece B in position, figure 17-14.

6. Extend the knife lines from the face of piece A across the edges using a try square and sharp pencil.

7. Gauge the depth of the dado on the edges between the pencil lines, line Z in figure 17-15. This depth is half the thickness of the stock.

8. With the try square as a guide, deepen the knife lines X and Y across the face of piece A, figure 17-15.

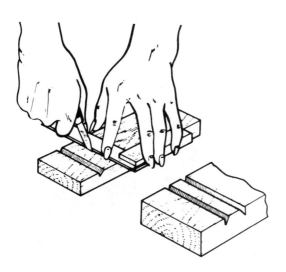

Fig. 17-16 Making V cuts

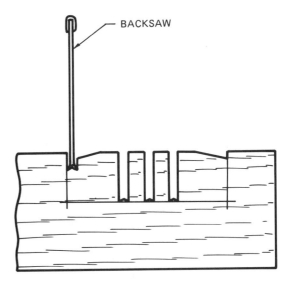

Fig. 17-17 Using V cuts for starting saw

9. Make a slanting cut on the inside of these lines with a knife or chisel, figure 17-16.

10. Place the backsaw in these cuts and saw until the gauge lines are touched on both sides, figure 17-17.

11. Make an extra saw cut between these cuts as an aid in removing surplus wood.

12. Remove the wood between the outside cuts with a wood chisel slightly narrower than the width of the dado being cut. Turn the bevel up and cut from the edges of the stock toward the center. This prevents the edges from splitting off below the gauge lines.
If a router plane is available, it may be used to remove surplus stock and smooth the bottom of the cut, figure 17-18.

Fig. 17-18 Using router plane

13. If the joint is too tight, carefully pare the edges of the dado with a sharp inch chisel. The pieces should fit together snugly without driving them into place.
If preferred, the thickness of piece B, figure 17-13, may be slightly reduced with a plane until a proper fit is obtained.

Fig. 17-19 Assembling dado joint for drawer

14. Fasten the joint together with nails and glue as shown in figure 17-19. Notice that the piece which fits into the dado is clamped in the vise.

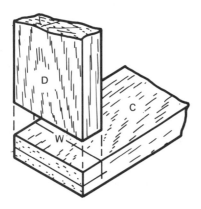

Fig. 17-20 Marking rabbet

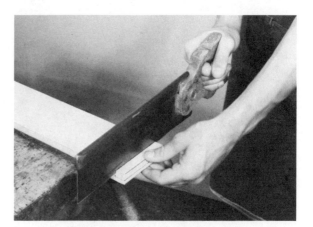

Fig. 17-21 Making shoulder cut

PROCEDURE FOR MAKING A RABBET JOINT

The rabbet joint is similar to the dado joint except that the members join each other at their ends.

An edge rabbet joint, discussed in Unit 16, has the cut on the edge instead of on the end.

1. Be sure the pieces to be joined are squared to the given dimensions.

2. Select the piece C to be rabbeted. Measure from the end the distance equal to the thickness of piece D, figure 17-20.

3. With a knife or sharp pencil and a try square, square the line W through this point across the face of piece C.

4. Check the accuracy of line W by placing piece D in position, figure 17-20.

5. Using a try square and a sharp pencil, extend the knife or pencil line W across both edges of piece C.

6. Set a marking gauge to the required depth of the rabbet. Mark across the end and on the edges to the pencil lines just marked. Keep the head of the marking gauge against the face of C.

7. Clamp piece C in a vise.

8. If desired, clamp a block on piece C to act as a guide.

Fig. 17-22 Making end cut

Fig. 17-23 Assembling rabbet joint

9. With a backsaw, saw just outside of line W until the depth gauge lines have been reached on both edges, figure 17-21.

10. Clamp the stock upright in the vise as shown in figure 17-22.

11. Saw on the waste side of the gauge line with a backsaw until the other saw cut is reached.

12. If necessary, smooth the joint with a wood chisel or router plane. When a rabbet joint is assembled, it is advisable to hold the stock in place with a cabinet clamp while the nails or screws are driven, figure 17-23.

PROCEDURE FOR MAKING THE CROSS-LAP JOINT

1. Square two pieces of stock to the dimensions desired. Be careful to get them the same width and thickness.

2. Lay the pieces on a bench, edge to edge. Have the working face turned up on one piece. On the other, have the opposite face turned up, figure 17-24.

3. Determine where the two pieces are to cross and square a centerline, point W, across each piece.

4. Align the centerline of one piece with the centerline of the other piece. Measure and mark half the width of one piece of stock on each side of this line and square lines through these points A and B, figure 17-24.

5. With a try square and a sharp pencil, extend these lines about half the distance across both edges of the stock.

6. Set the marking gauge to half the thickness of the stock. With the head of the marking gauge against the working face, mark line C on the edges between the lines that have been extended.

7. Place these pieces as shown in figure 17-25 and check the accuracy of the marking.

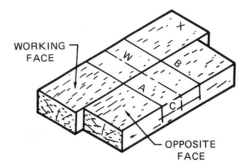

Fig. 17-24 Laying out a cross-lap joint

Fig. 17-25 Checking layout

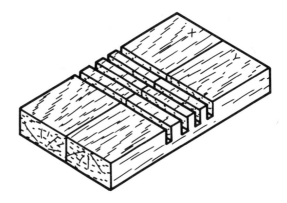

Fig. 17-26 Making saw cuts

8. With a backsaw, saw just inside the lines marked on surfaces X and Y to the depth of gauge line C.

9. Make a few extra saw cuts to the same depth between these outside cuts, figure 17-26. This aids in removing surplus stock.

10. Use a chisel to remove the waste stock by paring from the edges toward the center until the depth line is reached,

Fig. 17-27 Paring to depth with chisel

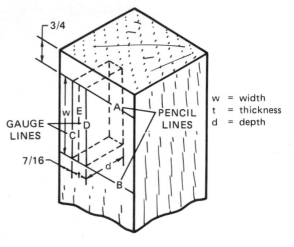

Fig. 17-28 Cross-lap joint fastened with flathead
screws from bottom

figure 17-27. The router plane may also
be used to smooth the bottom of this
cut. If the joint fits too tightly, the
edges of pieces X and Y may be planed
lightly until a snug fit is obtained.

A good joint slips together snugly,
leaving no cracks where surfaces join
each other. Cross-lap joints are often
fastened together with flathead screws,
figure 17-28.

PROCEDURE FOR LAYING OUT
AND CUTTING A MORTISE

1. To locate a mortise in the legs of a table
    or footstool, measure 1/2 inch to 3/4
    inch from the top of the leg on one of
    the surfaces to be mortised. Square line
    A, figure 17-29, using a try square and
    pencil.

2. Measure the desired width of the mortise
    and square a second line B at this point.
    The width of the mortise is generally no
    more than six times the thickness. See
    Step 9 for desired thickness.

3. With a try square and pencil, extend
    lines A and B across the adjoining sur-
    face to be mortised, figure 17-30.

4. Lay the four legs together on the bench
    and line up their top ends with a square,

Fig. 17-29 Laying out mortise

w = width
t = thickness
d = depth

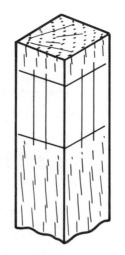

Fig. 17-30 Marking adjoining surface

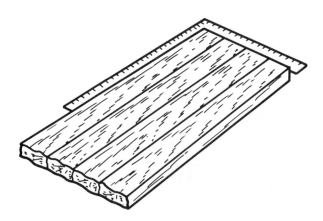

Fig. 17-31 Lining up four legs

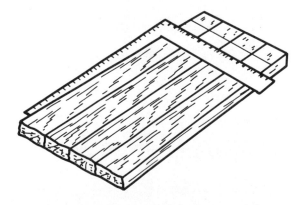

Fig. 17-32 Extending pencil lines across other legs

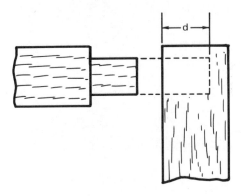

Fig. 17-33 Determining depth (d) of mortise

Fig. 17-34 Drilling holes for mortise

figure 17-31. It may be necessary to clamp the legs together to maintain proper alignment.

5. With a square, extend the lines marked on the first leg across the other three surfaces, figure 17-32.

6. On each leg, mark the second surface to be mortised by extending the lines from the first surface marked, figure 17-29.

7. Measure the desired distance from the outside leg surface to the edge of the mortise, figure 17-29. Set a marking gauge to this measurement.

8. With the head of the marking gauge against the outside leg surface, mark line C between the mortise width lines A and B, figure 17-29.

9. Measure the desired thickness of the mortise from line C and mark line D with the head of the marking gauge. Use the same position as before. The thickness of the mortise is generally from one-third to one-half the thickness of the thinner piece to be joined.

10. Mark line E through the center of the mortise.

11. Select an auger bit slightly smaller than the width of the mortise. The depth of the mortise depends on the width of the rail to be fitted, figure 17-33. The holes

should be no deeper than two-thirds the width of the thicker piece to be joined. Bore a series of holes in the mortise by placing the bit screw on the centerline just drawn, figure 17-34. Use a depth gauge on the bit to insure uniform depth of the mortise, figure 17-35.

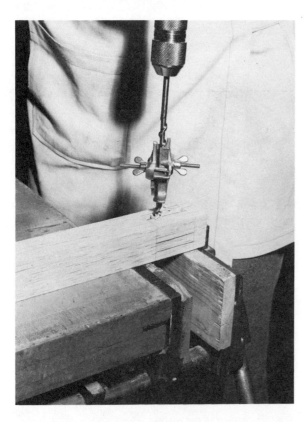

Fig. 17-35 Using depth gauge in boring for mortise

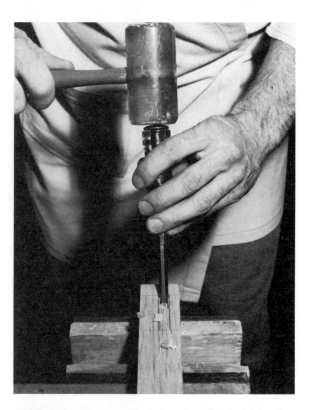

Fig. 17-36 Cutting mortise with a chisel and mallet

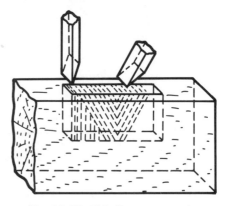

Fig. 17-37 Chiseling out mortise

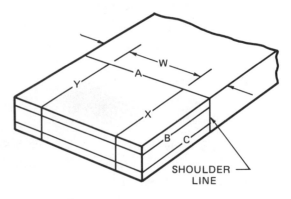

Fig. 17-38 Laying out tenon

12. Pare the sides of the mortise to the gauge lines with a wood chisel.

13. Use a narrow mortise chisel to pare ends of the mortise and remove surplus stock.

   When the mortise is entirely cut with a chisel, the chisel should be about the thickness of the mortise, figure 17-36. Start a V cut in the middle of the mortise. Remove the wood by cutting alternately toward both ends of the mortise, figure 17-37.

PROCEDURE FOR LAYING OUT AND CUTTING A TENON

1. Cut the stock for the rails to the length required including the tenon.

2. Measure the depth of the tenon from the ends of the stock. With a try square, square line A completely around the stock through this point, figure 17-38.

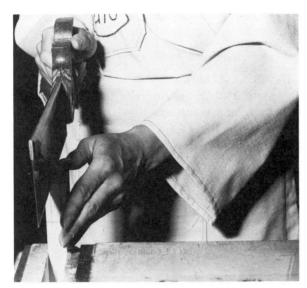

Fig. 17-39 Cutting cheeks of tenon

This line locates the shoulder of the tenon.

3. Deduct the thickness of the tenon from the thickness of the stock. Set a marking gauge to half of the remaining thickness.

4. Place the head of the gauge firmly against the face of the stock. Mark line B across the end and down both edges to the shoulder line, figure 17-38.

5. Reset the marking gauge to include the thickness of the tenon in addition to the original setting. Place the head of the gauge against the same face and mark line C in the same manner as line B, figure 17-38.

6. From the top edge of the rail, measure down the required distance about 3/4 of an inch.

7. Place the head of the marking gauge against the top edge of the rail. Mark line X, figure 17-38, from the shoulder line on one face, continuing the line across the end, to the shoulder line on the opposite face.

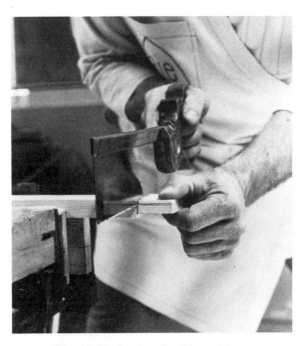

Fig. 17-40 Cutting shoulders of tenon

8. From line X, measure the required width W of the tenon. Mark line Y with the head of the marking gauge against the lower edge of the rail, figure 17-38.

9. Clamp the stock in a vise as shown in figure 17-39.

10. With the backsaw, saw just outside the gauge lines to the depth of the shoulder line, figure 17-39.

11. While holding the stock in the vise or with a bench hook, saw on the shoulder line entirely around the stock, figure 17-40.

If extreme accuracy is desired, the shoulders are marked with a knife and V cuts made as shown in figure 17-16.

12. Try the tenon in the mortise. If it is too large, pare the cheeks of the tenon with a sharp chisel or rabbet plane until a proper fit is obtained.

REVIEW QUESTIONS

Multiple Choice

1. The proper order for making an edge joint is:
   a. to mark boards, plane boards, match grain, and test joint.
   b. to match grain, mark boards, plane boards, and test joint.
   c. to plane boards, match grain, mark boards, and test joint.
   d. to plane boards, mark boards, match grain, and test joint.

2. A properly made edge joint will be slightly open at:
   a. the ends.   c. the center.
   b. one end.   d. the edge.

3. A dowel jig is used:
   a. to make dowels the proper size.
   b. to make dowels the proper length.
   c. to locate a hole in a dowel.
   d. to locate dowel holes in stock.

4. The proper dowel length for a dowel joint is:
   a. the total length of the holes in both pieces.
   b. 1/8 inch longer than the combined hole lengths.
   c. 1/8 inch shorter than the combined hole depths.
   d. 1/2 inch shorter than the combined hole depths.

5. When cutting on the dado joint, the kerf should be on the:
   a. waste side of the stock.   c. right side of the stock.
   b. left side of the stock.   d. underside of the stock.

6. To aid in removing surplus wood from a dado joint:
   a. use a wide chisel.
   b. make extra cuts between the two outside cuts.
   c. use a chisel and a large hammer.
   d. use a knife to cut it out.

7. To smooth the bottom of dadoes and cross-lap joints, use a:
   a. small chisel.   c. router plane.
   b. sharp saw.   d. dado plane.

8. When laying out the mortises for a table, they should be:
   a. layed out one at a time.
   b. layed out in a clockwise manner.
   c. layed out from the top only.
   d. clamped and layed out together.

9. When making a mortise, you should select a bit that is:
   a. slightly smaller than the width of the mortise.
   b. the same size as the mortise.
   c. the same length as the mortise.
   d. 2/3 the width of the mortise.

10. When making a tenon in 3/4-inch stock to fit a 3/8 inch mortise, the
    amount of stock to be removed from each side of the tenon is:
    a. 1/4 in.   c. 3/16 in.
    b. 3/8 in.   d. none of the above.

unit 18
clamping and holding tools

OBJECTIVES

After completing this unit, the student will be able to:

- name the common wood clamps.
- describe the uses of different clamps.
- properly hold stock with clamps.

Clamps are used in woodworking to hold pieces of wood together while glue is drying. They are also used to hold stock in position and to hold special jigs which aid in the cutting or construction of an item. Some clamps are operated by means of screws. Others apply pressure with springs. To hold stock securely, the proper clamp must be selected for the job and applied correctly.

VISE

The woodworking vise, figure 18-1, is usually attached to the work bench. It is used to hold stock while working on it. The vise may also be used to clamp stock while the glue is drying. Two of the most common woodworking vises are the continuous-screw and rapid-action vises. The handle on the continuous-screw vise must be turned around

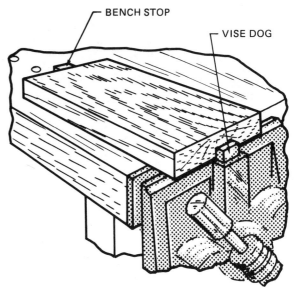

Fig. 18-2 Clamping stock between vise dog and bench stop

Fig. 18-1 Vise

several times to move the jaw in or out. The rapid-action vise allows the jaw to move in or out with only a partial handle turn. The capacity of the vise may be increased through the use of the vise dog and the bench stop, figure 18-2.

Fig. 18-3 Bar clamp

BAR CLAMPS

Bar clamps, or cabinet clamps, are used for clamping stock, gluing narrow pieces of stock edge to edge to create large surfaces, and for assembling cabinets and other large furniture, figure 18-3. The clamp is usually made from a heavy steel bar and ranges in length from 24 inches to 10 feet. The clamp consists of a screw device on one end and a sliding stop on the other end.

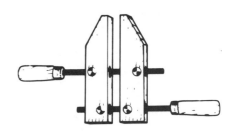

Fig. 18-4 Hand screw

HAND SCREW

The hand screw is used for holding stock under pressure (especially for gluing built-up or laminated stock) and in different positions for work convenience, figure 18-4. The jaws are made of wood with metal inserts that receive the metal adjusting screws for the jaws. Hand screws range from size 5-0 with a jaw opening of 2 inches to size 7 with a jaw opening of 17 inches.

Fig. 18-5 C clamp

C OR CARRIAGE CLAMPS

The C clamp, figure 18-5, is used for clamping irregularly shaped wood while it is being glued and for holding stock securely on the workbench. The opening sizes of the C clamp range from 2 inches to 12 inches. They are also available in a deep-throat model. This model allows greater distance from the screw to the back of the clamp.

Fig. 18-6 Spring clamp

SPRING CLAMPS

The spring clamp is a special-purpose clamp that applies its pressure through a heavy-steel spring, figure 18-6. These clamps are useful for holding small items while

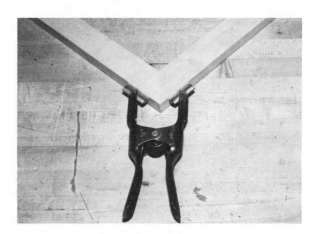

Fig. 18-7 Spring clamp

gluing. Some spring clamps are equipped with movable jaws that allow miter joints to be clamped, figure 18-7.

MITER CLAMP

The miter clamp, figure 18-8, is used for clamping mitered joints such as picture

Fig. 18-8 Miter clamp

frames. The clamp holds the joint securely and does not obstruct the corner so that nails and other metal fasteners can be applied.

BENCH HOOK

The bench hook is a wooden holding device that may be constructed as shown in figure 18-9. When in use, one end is hooked over the bench, while the other end is used to hold the stock while cutting. The bench hook helps support the stock and also protects the bench top.

SAWHORSE

The sawhorse is used to hold long pieces of stock while cutting it to size, figure 18-10.

Fig. 18-9 Bench hook

Fig. 18-10 Sawhorse

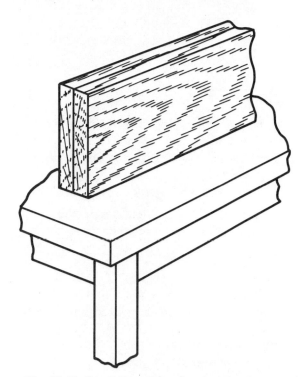

Fig. 18-11 Stock in position for clamping face to
face

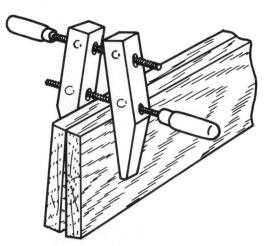

Fig. 18-12 First step in adjusting the hand screw

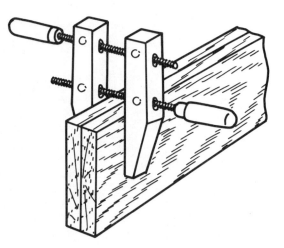

Fig. 18-13 Final step in adjusting the hand screw

Fig. 18-14 Stock clamped face to face for gluing

Sawhorses are made in pairs and are about 20 inches to 22 inches high. They are also handy for supporting large cabinets that are too high to work on if placed on the workbench.

CLAMPING STOCK FOR ASSEMBLING AND GLUING

The three types of clamps used most frequently for woodworking are the bar clamp, the hand screw, and the C clamp. The main purpose of these clamps is to hold glued stock until the glue dries.

The beginning woodworker often applies excessive pressure with clamps to make a poorly made joint fit properly. The joints must be made to fit properly. Otherwise, they will pull apart. It is necessary to apply only enough pressure to hold the joints together firmly while the glue is drying.

Procedure For Clamping Stock Face To Face

1. Place the stock on a bench or glue table in the position shown in figure 18-11. Do not apply glue at this time.

2. Place the hand screws in position on the stock. Adjust the screw nearest the stock until the jaws are clamped firmly against it, figure 18-12.

3. Adjust the outside screw until the jaws of the clamp are parallel and enough pressure has been applied, figure 18-13. More pressure or leverage can be applied when the outside screw is adjusted last.

4. On the first edge, space hand screws 12 inches to 18 inches apart, depending upon the stock length and thickness.

5. Turn the stock over with the hand screws resting on the table. Fit and adjust the clamps on the second edge, placing them between the clamps installed on the first edge, figure 18-14.

6. Remove the clamps and apply the glue quickly. Replace and tighten the clamps in their former positions.

Procedure For Clamping Stock Edge To Edge

The proper method of arranging and marking stock to be used for a tabletop is shown in figure 18-15.

1. Arrange the boards so that the annular rings are reversed in every other board. This equalizes the warping of the stock.

2. To aid in planing and smoothing the surface, arrange the stock so the grain runs in the same direction. The grain direction should be marked with arrowheads. Place face marks across the adjoining edges to aid in matching the edges of the stock.

3. To prevent buckling, place clamps on both sides of the stock, figure 18-16, and spaced approximately 18 inches apart. Stock 24 inches or less in length still requires three clamps, two on the

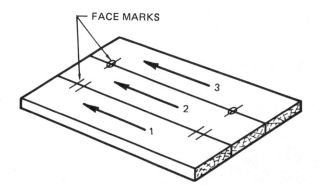

Fig. 18-15 Stock marked for clamping edge to edge

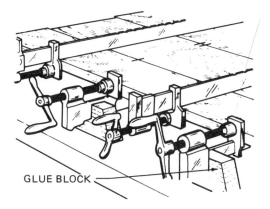

Fig. 18-16 Clamping stock edge to edge

bottom and one in the middle on the top side.

4. Place the bar clamps used for the underside of the stock on the bench or glue table. Each end of the clamp should rest in a glue block that holds it securely in a level position.

5. Place the stock on the clamps in the final position in which it is to be glued.

6. Test the boards to make sure that they lie flat on the clamps. If the end of one clamp is higher or lower than the other ends, the wood surface will not be level after gluing.

7. Place the clamps on the top side to alternate with those on the bottom side, figure 18-17.

Fig. 18-17 Stock glued and clamped

8. Try the clamps in place before applying glue. When all joints fit properly, apply the glue with a squeeze bottle or brush, figure 18-18.

9. Clamp with even pressure and allow to dry.

Procedure for Clamping Frame Assemblies

Figure 18-19 shows a cabinet frame clamped for gluing. This particular frame is for a chest of drawers. Other cabinet types fitted with drawers are glued and clamped in a similar manner.

1. If the drawers are to fit easily and properly, the frames between the drawers must be squared carefully and to exact size. Place heavy scrap stock horizontally across the case ends opposite the frame ends. This keeps the case ends flat when pressure is applied with the clamps.

2. Cut thick pieces of scrap stock to a length equal to the width of the case sides.

3. With the aid of an assistant, assemble and clamp the frames and ends of the case together. Use only enough pressure on the clamps to pull the ends of the

Fig. 18-18 Applying glue

Fig. 18-19 Clamping framework for cabinet

frames into the blind dadoes, figure 18-19.

4. Test with a try square or foot square. Make sure the front and back faces of the frames are square with the sides.

5. If the frames are not square, raise or lower one end of a center clamp on the front and back sides to pull the frames square.

6. Remove the clamps and apply glue to the ends of the frames and in the dadoes.

7. Reassemble the framework. Replace and tighten the clamps. Test as in Steps 2, 3, and 4.

REVIEW QUESTIONS

A.   Identification

1. Name each of the following clamps.

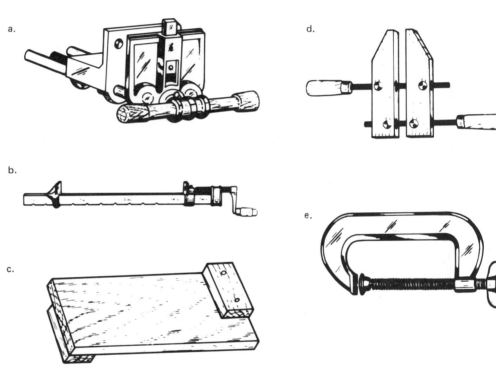

a.

b.

c.

d.

e.

B.   Multiple Choice

2. The _____ clamp is most useful for holding stock that is being glued edge to edge.
   a. vise
   b. bar clamp
   c. hand screw
   d. spring clamp

3. The clamp that has two adjusting screws is called a:
   a. spring clamp.
   b. bar clamp.
   c. hand screw.
   d. vise.

4. The clamp that holds miter joints while allowing the joint to be nailed is called a:
   a. bar clamp.
   b. spring clamp.
   c. hand screw.
   d. miter clamp.

5. When using the hand screw, the outside screw is adjusted:
    a. first.
    b. last.
    c. both screws should be adjusted at the same time.
    d. it makes no difference when it is adjusted.

6. Bar clamps should be placed approximately _____ inches apart when gluing stock edge to edge.
    a. 10   c. 18
    b. 14   d. 24

7. When clamping a cabinet frame with bar clamps and the frame is not square, it may be squared by:
    a. moving one end of the clamp so it is not parallel to the edge.
    b. moving both ends of the clamp.
    c. moving the clamp near the frame edge.
    d. placing more clamps on the frame.

8. When gluing an edge joint, the arrangement of clamps should be:
    a. all of the clamps on the bottom.
    b. all of the clamps on the top.
    c. two clamps on the bottom and one on top.
    d. all of the above are correct.

9. When gluing stock for a 20″ x 30″ tabletop, how many cabinet clamps are needed?
    a. 1   c. 5
    b. 4   d. 3

10. The sawhorse is approximately _____ inches high.
    a. 20 to 22   c. 27 to 30
    b. 23 to 26   d. 31 to 32

unit 19
glues and adhesives

OBJECTIVES

After completing this unit, the student will be able to:

- discuss the uses of different glues.
- list the safety precautions to follow when working with glues.

Glue is an adhesive material used for fastening pieces of wood together. Commercial glues in the woodworking industry can be grouped by their composition as:

- starch or vegetable glue.

- protein, which includes animal, casein, soybean, blood, and liquid fish glue.

- synthetic glues, which include urea resin, phenol resin, melamine resin, resorcinol resin, and resin emulsions.
  Glues may also be grouped according to their resistance to moisture.

- The cured glue line of waterproof glue can withstand the severest conditions. Because of this durable characteristic, Marine plywood is assembled with a waterproof adhesive.

- In the water-resistant glue group, the cured glue line continues to hold under repeated soaking and drying conditions. These glues are used where there is exterior exposure but some protection from the elements.

- Low water-resistant glue cannot withstand high humidity or frequent contact and saturation with water.

Refer to table 19-1 for additional information on each of the following glues.

LIQUID HIDE GLUE

Liquid hide glue is obtained from bones and other animal parts with a high gelatin content. It is one of the best glues to use for interior furniture. This glue gives the best results when the moisture content of the wood does not exceed 10 percent. Cold liquid-hide glue is relatively easy to use, although it is less sensitive than hot liquid-hide glue.

POLYVINYL OR WHITE LIQUID GLUE

White liquid glues require no mixing. They are easily applied from a dispenser or with a brush. The glue line is colorless and cures rapidly at room temperature, but this type of glue is easily affected by temperature

Glue Type	Room Temperature	How to Prepare	How to Apply	Clamping Time
Liquid Hide	Sets best above 70°. Can be used in temperature 33° and above. Moisture resistant.	Ready to use.	Apply thin coat on both surfaces; let it get tacky before joining.	70° – 2 hrs. strength in 24 hrs.
Liquid Polyvinyl Resin	Any temperature above 60°. Not good above 110°. Softens at 160°.	Ready to use.	Spread on and clamp at once.	70° – 1 hr. cure – 24 hrs.
Resorcinol Resin	Must be 70° or warmer. Will set faster at 90°. Completely waterproof.	Mix 3 parts powder to 4 parts liquid catalyst.	Apply thin coat to both surfaces. Use within 8 hrs. after mixing.	70° – 10 hrs. 80° – 6 hrs. 90° – 3 1/2 hrs.
Powdered Casein Glue	Any temperature above freezing. The warmer the better. Moisture resistant.	Stir together equal parts by volume of glue and water. Wait 10-15 minutes and stir again.	Apply thin coat to both surfaces. Use within 8 hrs. after mixing.	70° – 2 to 4 hrs.
Plastic Resin	Must be 70° or warmer. Will set faster at 90°. Water resistant.	Mix 2 parts powder with 1/2 to 1 part water.	Apply thin coat to both surfaces. Use within 8 hrs. after mixing.	70° – 12 hrs. 80° – 8 hrs. 90° – 5 hrs.
Contact Cement	70° or warmer. Solvent-water resistant. H_2O mix type is not water resistant. Rubber base is water resistant.	Ready to use.	Brush on a thin coat. Dry for 20-25 min. Apply second coat.	No clamping, bonds instantly.
Epoxy Cement	Any temperature. Water resistant.	Resin and hardener mixed in amounts stated on container.	Apply with stick or brush.	No clamping. Dries faster with heat.
Aliphatic Resin	Temperature 50° to 110°.	Ready to use.	Apply same as Polyvinyl Resin.	70° – 1 hr. cure – 24 hrs.

Table 19-1

and moisture. White liquid glue is strong and fills gaps well.

RESORCINOL GLUE

These glues can stand the most extreme exposure to moisture and form an excellent bond. Resorcinol glues require the adding of a powder catalyst, which changes the curing and assembly time. Resorcinol glues are excellent for exterior work because they are waterproof. The main disadvantage is that resorcinol glue leaves a dark glue line.

PLASTIC RESIN GLUE

Plastic resin glues are cold-setting adhesives and are purchased as a powder. Plastic resin glues are used in woodworking because they produce a strong, hard, water-resistant bond. They are also easy to use.

CASEIN GLUE

Casein glue is made from milk curd and can be used on woods with up to 20 percent moisture content. It is purchased in powder form and is mixed with water to form a thick glue. Casein glues set very hard which makes it difficult to stain and extremely hard on cutting tools. Casein glue works well on oily woods such as teak.

CONTACT CEMENT

Contact cement is a synthetic, rubber-type resin adhesive which is applied to both surfaces to be glued. The cement should be allowed to dry according to directions before the surfaces are brought into contact. There is no need for clamping or holding because the bond is immediate. This bond is especially useful for plastic laminates and veneers to wood or plywood.

EPOXY RESIN

Epoxy resins are made from an exact mixture of resin and hardener. The combin-ing of the two ingredients causes a chemical reaction which provides a strong adhesive material. Epoxy glue can be used to join wood to metal or other materials.

ALIPHATIC RESIN

Aliphatic resin glue is an extremely strong glue that is used extensively by cabinetmakers. This glue lacks moisture resistance and is, therefore, only good for interior work. *Caution*: Some glues are very toxic to the skin and eyes. They should only be used in well-ventilated areas and with care. Some are also very explosive and should not be used in an area where sparks or open flames could light the adhesive.

GLUING TIPS

The durability of a project depends largely on the strength of its glue joints. Therefore, it is important to use the proper glue. It is equally important to have well-fitted joints and to use wood with the proper moisture content. The moisture content of the wood should not exceed 15 percent.

Check the following points to assure a good glue joint.

- Does the wood have the proper moisture content?

- Are the surfaces to be glued smooth and free of irregularities?

- Do the joints fit properly?

- Has the proper glue been selected to give the desired results?

- Has the glue been stored and mixed according to directions?

- Have the wood and the room been kept at the right temperature for gluing? 70 to 80 degrees is the average ideal temperature.

- Has sufficient glue been applied evenly to the joint?

- Has the proper pressure been applied evenly and continuously throughout the drying period?

- Has the glue dried without bonding at the glue line? If so, the joint will be dry and weak.

- Has the excess glue been removed from the surface before machining?

REVIEW QUESTIONS

Multiple Choice

1. Which of the following glues does not require clamping?
   - a. Liquid hide glue
   - b. White liquid glue
   - c. Contact cement
   - d. Powdered resin glue

2. When applying most glues, the temperature should be _____ degrees or above.
   - a. 50
   - b. 70
   - c. 80
   - d. 60

3. A properly constructed glue joint is:
   - a. very weak before it is attached with screws.
   - b. stronger than the wood itself.
   - c. very strong but not as strong as the wood.
   - d. weak but strong enough to hold the wood together.

4. Care should be taken when working with glues because some are:
   - a. very hard to work with.
   - b. very toxic to the skin.
   - c. explosive.
   - d. both b and c.

5. The proper procedure to assure a strong joint if the two pieces do not fit properly is to:
   - a. construct the joint again so it fits properly.
   - b. put a large amount of glue on the joint.
   - c. apply more pressure to pull the joint together.
   - d. bend the wood with water to make it fit properly.

unit 20
cabinet
hardware

OBJECTIVES

After completing this unit, the student will be able to:

- identify and give the uses of three types of hinges and three pieces of cabinet hardware other than hinges and pulls.

- install a surface hinge, butt hinge, and combination chest hinge.

Cabinet hardware is used to make the cabinet or furniture stronger and more functional. In producing quality cabinetwork, proper selection of hardware and careful installation are essential. Hardware suitable for woodworking is available in many styles and finishes. Cabinet hardware usually serves two purposes. The first purpose is the function for which it is applied. The second purpose is as surface decoration. The following are descriptions of common cabinet hardware.

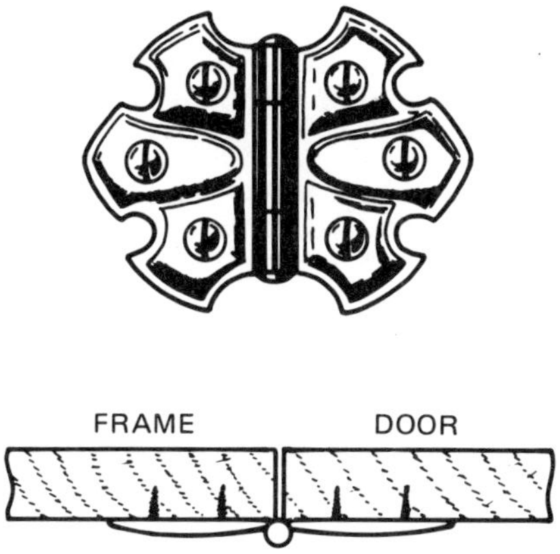

HINGES

Hinges are mechanical devices made of two metal plates fastened together with a pin fitted through the joints of the plates. They are used to provide a pivotal motion to chest lids, doors, and gates.

Surface Hinges

Surface hinges are designed to fit on the face of flat surfaces with the hinge visible.

Fig. 20-1 Surface hinge

These hinges are available in plain or ornamental styles. Surface hinges are the easiest to install, figure 20-1.

Offset Hinges

Figures 20-2 and 20-3 show two different offset hinges. These hinges are used with the lip or rabbeted doors. Only a small portion of the hinges show when they are fastened in place.

Fig. 20-2 Partially hidden offset hinge

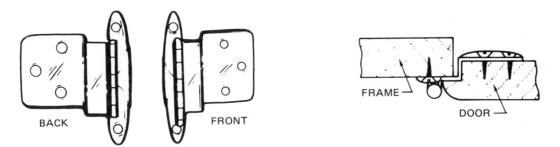

Fig. 20-3 Ornamental offset hinge

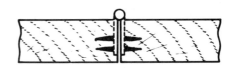

Fig. 20-4 Butt hinge

Fig. 20-5 Nonmortise butt hinge

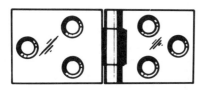

Fig. 20-6 Drop-leaf hinge

Butt Hinges

Butt hinges, figure 20-4, have both leaves gained into the wood, one half into the door edge and the other half into the door frame. A *gain* is the notch or mortise made to receive a hinge or other hardware.

The nonmortise butt hinge is shown in figure 20-5. The thin, overlapping leaves make it possible to install the hinge without cutting gains for it.

Drop-Leaf Table Hinges

Figure 20-6 shows the drop-leaf table hinge. It is used to hinge drop leaves to the center section of the table. One leaf of

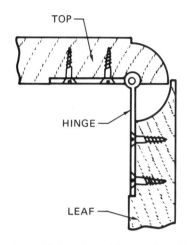

Fig. 20-7 Rule joint with drop-leaf hinge

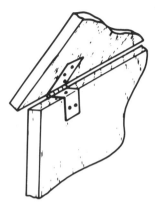

Fig. 20-8 Offset chest hinge

the hinge is lower than the other. This allows for a rule joint to be used, figure 20-7.

Other Hinges

The offset chest hinge, figure 20-8, is used to hinge chest lids in place. The combination hinge, figure 20-9, is also used for this purpose since it also has a built-in lid stop. The invisible hinge, figure 20-10, is mortised into the door edge and the door frame. It is quite difficult to install but is entirely concealed from the face of the door and frame. The concealed hinge, figure 20-11, is designed for doors that completely cover the cabinet frame. Only a small portion of the hinge shows when the cabinet door is closed.

FURNITURE TRIM

The appearance of furniture is improved by the use of appropriate knobs, drawer pulls, and hinges selected to go with the furniture finish and style. Materials used for trim include steel, copper, brass, plastics, and porcelain. They are available in antique brass, antique copper, dull brass, chrome, and rustic-black finish.

Trim Styles

Figure 20-12 shows a pull and knob that is often used on French Provincial furniture. The pull and knob, shown in figure 20-13, is available in various finishes and goes well with contemporary furniture. The trim in figure

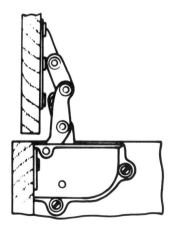

Fig. 20-9 Combination hinge

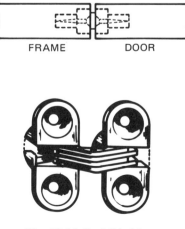

FRAME   DOOR

Fig. 20-10 Invisible hinge

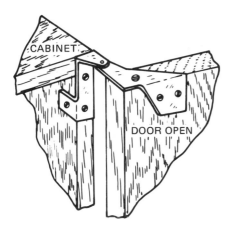

Fig. 20-12 French provincial pull and knob

Fig. 20-13 Modern, brushed brass trim

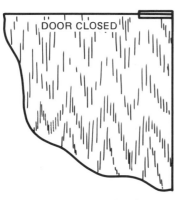

Fig. 20-11 Concealed hinge

Fig. 20-14 Pierced design pull and knob

Fig. 20-15 Colonial drawer pull

20-14 has a pierced design that is suitable for use on Mediterranean-style furniture. Figure 20-15 shows an antique brass, bail-type pull that goes well with Colonial-style furniture. Pendant pulls, figure 20-16, are made of cast metal and frequently used on Mediterranean-style furniture. Examples of Early American furniture and cabinet trim are shown in figure 20-17. The pull on the left and the surface hinge in the middle are usually finished in antique copper or rustic black.

Trim Placement

Pulls and knobs must be properly spaced on the drawer front. A good rule to follow is to place the pulls 3/4 inch to 1 inch above center on the lower drawers and in the center on the top row of drawers.

When two pulls are placed on a drawer front, the distance that each pull is located from the end of the drawer should be equal to

Fig. 20-16 Pendant pull

from one-third to one-fourth the space left between the pulls. Most pulls are fastened with machine screws. These are inserted into a hole through the door or drawer front and fastened in place from the inside.

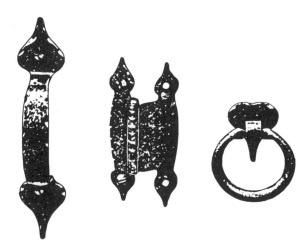

Fig. 20-17 Early American pulls and hinges

Doorknobs are usually spaced so that three-fifths of the door length is left below the knob.

CATCHES

The ball-type friction catch is used on the edges of light doors to keep them closed, figure 20-18. Magnetic catches, figure 20-19, have two parts. The first part has a permanent magnet. This is installed on the bottom face of a shelf or on the inside cabinet surface. The second part is a metal plate that is fastened to the inside door surface to make contact with the magnet when the door is closed.

CASTERS AND GLIDES

Casters are sometimes used on the base or legs of heavy furniture where frequent moving is necessary. The caster wheels are made of materials such as hard rubber and plastic that will not mar the floor easily. Smooth steel glides with rubber cushions are used on lighter types of furniture. These glides are fastened to the furniture by a center point that is driven into place. Or, they may have an adjustable screw that fits into a sleeve, figure 20-20. The latter furniture glide makes it possible to level furniture that stands on an uneven floor.

Fig. 20-18 Ball-type friction catch

Fig. 20-19 Magnetic catch

Fig. 20-20 Adjustable furniture glide

Fig. 20-21 Hanger bolt and angle plate

LEG FASTENERS

Figure 20-21 shows a 10-degree angle plate and hanger bolt. These are used for fastening short, turned legs on desks, dressers, chests, and other furniture. The plate fastens firmly to the bottom of the case while the

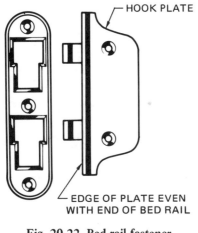

Fig. 20-22 Bed rail fastener

Fig. 20-23 Tabletop fastener

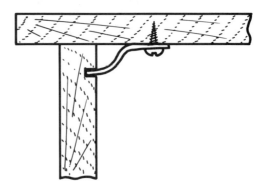

Fig. 20-24 Tabletop fastener installed

hanger bolt is screwed into the top end of the leg. The other threaded end is then screwed into a tapped hole in the plate center.

BED FASTENERS

Bed fasteners, figure 20-22, are used to fasten the bed rails between the head and foot of the bed. The plates are mortised into the legs so that they are flush with the leg surface. The hook plates are fastened on the inside of the rails with the edge of the plate even with the end of the bed rail.

TABLETOP FASTENERS

The tabletop fastener, figure 20-23, allows for slight movement of the tabletop due to changes in moisture. This still allows the top to be firmly fastened to the desk or table frame. The tabletop fastener is installed by cutting a groove on the inside of the rails for the fastener tongue to hook into, figure 20-24.

DRAWER GUIDES

Drawer guides are often used in the construction of cabinets because they are easy to install and durable. Figure 20-25 shows a guide that supports the drawer on two rollers that are mounted on the cabinet frame and a third roller that travels

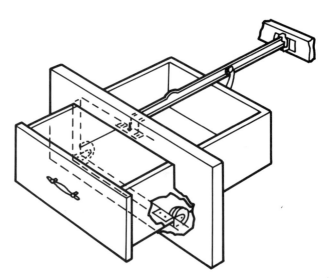

Fig. 20-25 Drawer guide

in the metal track. One advantage of this drawer-guide system is the drawer is supported on three points. This allows for ease of operation even if the drawer is warped or twisted.

DRAWER LOCKS

It is often necessary to install locks on drawers, doors, and chest lids for various

Fig. 20-26 Drawer lock

security reasons. This is especially true with gun cabinets. The drawer lock, figure 20-26, is installed on the inside surface of the drawer by boring a hole through the drawer front to accommodate the diameter of the barrel of the lock.

SHELF BRACKETS

Shelf brackets allow for the easy movement of shelves to accommodate various size books or other items. Figure 20-27 shows a shelf bracket that is commonly used. Adjustable shelf brackets come in several types and styles. Follow the manufacturers' instructions when installing them.

PROCEDURE FOR INSTALLING SURFACE HINGES

1. Place the door in the position it is to be hinged, figure 20-28.

2. Mark the location for the center of the hinge on the door and frame, figure 20-28.

3. Lay the lid or door on the workbench and fasten the hinge to it. Be careful to line up the center of the hinge with the located centerline, figure 20-29.

4. Place the door or lid in the same position as in Step 1.

5. On the frame, mark the screw holes of the stationary side of the hinge, figure 20-29.

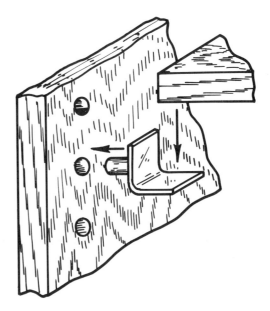

Fig. 20-27 Shelf bracket

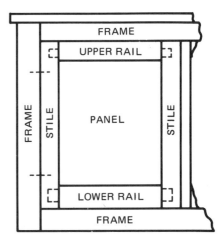

Fig. 20-28 Door and frame construction

Fig. 20-29 Installing surface hinge

6. With a hand drill, bore one hole for each hinge and fasten the hinges in place.

7. Swing the door to make sure it works freely.

Fig. 20-30 Cutting gain for hinge

Fig. 20-31 Placement of hinge in gain

8. If the door works properly, bore the remaining holes and insert the screws.

9. If it does not work properly, remove the screws in the frame and adjust the door to the desired position. Mark a different hole for each hinge. If the hole first bored is out of line, plug it with a piece of hardwood and restore the hole. Repeat Steps 6, 7, and 8.

PROCEDURE FOR INSTALLING BUTT HINGES

1. Lay the door, with the outside face up, on the bench and mark the required distance that the top hinge is from the door top.

2. Lay the hinge in place with the top of the hinge even with the mark.

3. Mark a second line determining the length of the hinge.

4. Mark the location of the bottom hinge in the same manner.

5. Turn the door up on edge. With a try square and sharp pencil, extend the lines on the face across the edge.

6. Place the door in the position it is to be hinged. On the frame, mark the location of the stationary side of the hinge.

7. After removing the door, extend these marks to the inside edge of the frame. Use a try square and sharp pencil.

8. Set a marking gauge equal to the thickness of the hinge. Place the head of the gauge against the back edge of the door. Gauge a line on the face of the door between those marks indicating the hinge length.

9. Measure the width of the hinge leaf, not including the joint. Set a marking gauge equal to this measurement.

10. Place the head of the marking gauge against the face of the door. Gauge a line on the edge of the door between those marks indicating the hinge length.

11. Clamp the door, with the edge up, in a vise. Chisel out the gain in the edge of the door to the width, length, and depth lines, figure 20-30.

12. Place the leaf of the hinge in the gain, figure 20-31, and mark the holes for the screws.

13. Bore the holes and fasten the hinge in place with flathead screws.

14. Place the door in the position it is to be hinged. Mark a line on the frame even with the face of the door.

15. Remove the door and pull the pin from the hinge, figure 20-32.

16. Place the loose leaf of the hinge in the installed position with the inside edge of

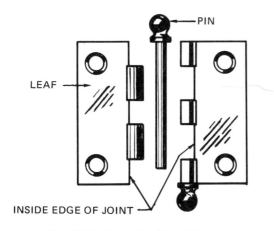

Fig. 20-32 Loose-leaf butt hinge

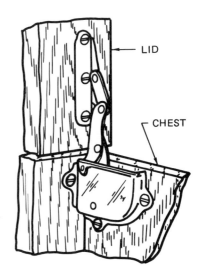

Fig. 20-33 Combination hinge installed

the joint even with the line marking the outside face of the door.

17. Scribe a line around the edges of the loose leaf with a sharp pencil.

18. With a chisel and mallet, cut a gain for the loose leaf slightly deeper than the thickness of the leaf.

19. Fasten the leaf in place with screws.

20. Install the door and insert the pins in the hinges. Check to see that the door swings properly. If the door binds on the hinge side when it is closed, it may be necessary to add thin wood shims under one leaf of the hinge.

PROCEDURE FOR INSTALLING COMBINATION CHEST HINGES

1. Select the side to be used as the back of the chest.

2. Select a pair of right-and-left combination hinges.

3. Place the hinge, figure 20-33, in the back corner of the chest with the top edge of the hinge even with the top edge of the chest. To accomplish this, a flat board is placed diagonally across the top edge of the back corners, and the hinge is raised against it.

4. While the hinge is held in place, mark the screw holes with a pencil.

5. Remove the hinge and drill anchor holes to receive the screws.

6. Place the hinge back in position and fasten with the screws.

7. Place the chest lid on the chest in a closed position with the overhang spaced evenly.

8. With the aid of an assistant, hold the back edge of the lid down firmly on the back edge of the chest. Then, raise the front edge of the lid just enough to allow screw holes to be marked through the holes in the hinges.

9. Drill one hole for each hinge and fasten the lid to the hinges.

10. Test the lid to see that it fits correctly on the chest. If properly fitted, drill the remainder of the screw holes and set the screws. If the top does not fit correctly, remove the screws and repeat Step 8 using two new holes.

REVIEW QUESTIONS

A. **Multiple Choice**

1. The hinge that is attached to the face of a cabinet and door is called a:
    a. face hinge.   c. leaf hinge.
    b. surface hinge.   d. butt hinge.

2. The hinge that fits in a rabbet of a door is called:
    a. a surface hinge.   c. an offset hinge.
    b. a butt hinge.   d. an invisible hinge.

3. The device used to attach the tabletop to the rails is a:
    a. hanger bolt.   c. tabletop lock.
    b. hook plate.   d. tabletop fastener.

4. The cut placed in a door edge to receive the leaf of a butt hinge is called a:
    a. mortise.   c. leaf cut.
    b. gain.   d. hinge cut.

5. A good rule to follow when locating the pull on the top drawer of a cabinet is to locate the pull:
    a. 1/5 of the way down from the top.
    b. one inch above the center of the drawer.
    c. in the center of the drawer.
    d. 2/3 of the way up from the drawer bottom.

6. The parts of a hinge fastened together by a pin are called:
    a. wings.   c. leaves.
    b. plates.   d. gates.

B. **Short Answer**

7. Which is the easiest to install, a surface hinge or a butt hinge?

section 2

machine woodworking

common woodworking machines and general safety precautions

OBJECTIVES

After completing this unit, the student will be able to:

- identify seven common stationary woodworking machines.
- identify five common portable power woodworking tools.
- list the general safety precautions to follow when working with stationary woodworking machines and portable power tools.

There are numerous types of special machines and power tools used in the woodworking industry. However, only the more common woodworking machines are found in school and home shops.

Stationary woodworking machines are classified as those machines permanently fastened to the floor or a bench. The following are examples of the machines often found in school and home shops:

- Jointer
- Surfacer
- Table saw
- Radial arm saw
- Band saw
- Drill press
- Mortiser
- Jigsaw
- Wood lathe

- Spindle shaper
- Stationary belt and disk sanders

Portable power woodworking tools are considered the light, portable types of equipment held in the hands. Examples of these common portable power tools follow:

- Saber saw
- Circular saw
- Power hand plane
- Portable electric drill
- Hand drill
- Router
- Portable belt and finish sanders

GENERAL SAFETY PRECAUTIONS

Stationary woodworking machines and portable power tools must operate at high speeds to function efficiently. Therefore, it is important to learn how to use these machines and tools safely and correctly.

It is difficult to design a guard that gives full protection to the operator. For special operations, it may be necessary to remove the guard. A power tool or machine should not be used until the correct operation and dangers of the operation involved are presented. The following are general safety rules to follow:

- Keep the machine or tool in good repair and properly adjusted. Cutting edges must also be kept sharp.

- Do not attempt to operate the machine until its correct use has been thoroughly demonstrated.

- Keep the guards in place when possible. For special operations where it may be necessary to remove the guard, get the instructor's permission.

- Never wear loose clothing or sweater. Keep sleeves rolled up and remove neckties.

- Keep the floor around the machines free of scrap wood and other obstacles. Keep the machine table free of tools, scraps, and extra wood stock.

- Hold the stock firmly. Keep the fingers and hands where they are not in line with the cutting edge and where they cannot slip against the cutting edge.

- Be sure that the stock is large enough to be safely worked on the machine.

- Always stop the machine before making adjustments.

- Avoid conversation while operating a machine - divided attention may cause an accident. Remember that safe work habits develop safe operators.

- Safety glasses should be worn at all times while operating portable and stationary woodworking equipment.

- Never machine stock that contains loose knots, nails, paint, varnish, or other finishes.

REVIEW QUESTIONS

A. Identification

1. List seven stationary power woodworking machines commonly used in home and school shops.

2. List five portable power woodworking tools commonly used in home and school shops.

3. List seven general safety precautions to follow when working with power woodworking equipment.

B. Multiple Choice

4. The clothing worn while operating woodworking equipment:
    a. is not considered part of general safety.
    b. is considered part of general safety.
    c. is totally up to the equipment operator.
    d. is of little importance if guards are kept in place.

5. Tools should be kept sharp and in good repair because:
   a. they use less power.
   b. they do a better job of cutting.
   c. they are safer to use.
   d. all of the above.

6. While another person is operating a power tool, you should:
   a. read him the safety rules for that particular tool.
   b. caution him as to the general safety rules for machines.
   c. not do anything to distract him from concentrating.
   d. stand by the machine switch so you can shut it off if the operator gets into trouble.

7. Adjustments should be made on the machine:
   a. only while it is running.
   b. just before you start to feed the stock into the machine.
   c. only while the machine is stopped.
   d. only after the machine has come up to full operating speed.

unit 22
machining stock

OBJECTIVE

After completing this unit, the student will be able to:

- demonstrate the correct procedure for squaring post or leg stock and rectangular-shaped stock.

When squaring stock on power woodworking machines, the operator must understand the correct order of procedure. For the project parts to fit together accurately, all surfaces must be square and true. When the required woodworking machines are available, the following procedure is suggested, figures 22-1 and 22-2.

PROCEDURE FOR MACHINING STOCK FOR TABLETOPS AND OTHER WIDE SURFACES

It is often necessary and desirable to glue stock edge to edge to provide pieces with enough width to construct a project. It is not necessary to square each piece of stock completely before they are glued together. The steps listed below may be followed:

1. Cut enough stock to rough length to provide at least 3 inches over the finished width.

2. Joint a working face and edge of each piece on the jointer.

3. Plane the stock to rough thickness on the surfacer. Allow about 1/8 inch over the finished thickness desired.

Step	Surface Squared	Operation	Machine Used
1	Working face	Joint working face	Jointer
2	Adjoining face	Joint adjoining face	Jointer
3	3rd surface	Plane to thickness	Surfacer
4	4th surface	Plane to thickness	Surfacer
5	1st end	Square first end	Table saw or radial arm saw
6	2nd end	Cut to length	Table saw or radial arm saw

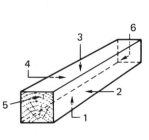

Fig. 22-1 Order of procedure for squaring post stock.

Step	Surface Squared	Operation	Machine Used
1	Working face	Plane working face	Jointer
2	Working edge	Joint working edge	Jointer
3	2nd face	Plane to thickness (allow 1/16 inch over finished thickness)	Surfacer
4	2nd edge	Rip to width (plus 1/8 inch)	Table saw
5	1st end	Square first end	Table saw or radial arm saw
6	2nd end	Cut to length	Table saw or radial arm saw
7	2nd edge	Joint to finished width	Jointer

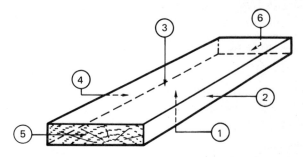

Fig. 22-2 Order of procedure for squaring rectangular-shaped stock

4. Rip each piece to rough width on the table saw.

5. Joint the ripped edge on the jointer.

6. Place the pieces on the workbench. Arrange them so the grain pattern and color of the boards match to the best advantage. The grain direction should be the same in all boards.

7. Mark identifying lines across each joint with chalk.

8. Without gluing, place the pieces in clamps, to see that all joints fit properly.

9. Joints not fitting tightly should be rejointed.

10. If dowels are used, mark and drill holes for them.

11. Apply glue to the dowels and edges. Draw the joints together with cabinet clamps. If the total glued sections are wider than the surfacer, glue two separate sections. Then, glue the sections together after they are run through the surfacer.

12. After the glue is dry, remove the clamps. Remove the surface glue with a glue scraper.

13. Run both faces of the glued sections through the surfacer. Leave 1/16 inch of stock over the finished thickness desired. This allows for planing, scraping, and sanding.

14. Joint one edge. Rip the piece to a rough width, allowing 1/8 inch for jointing.

15. Joint the ripped edge.

16. Square one end of the glued sections on the table or radial arm saw.

17. Mark to length and square the second end.

18. Prepare the visible surfaces for finishing. See Step 13.

PROCEDURE TO FOLLOW
IF A SURFACER IS NOT AVAILABLE

If a surfacer is not available, it is best to buy the hardwood lumber S2S (lumber surfaced on two sides).

For surfaced stock that is slightly warped, proceed as follows:

1. If the boards are 6 inches or less in width, joint both faces lightly on the jointer.

2. If the boards are more than 6 inches wide, rip each piece down the center.

3. Joint the ripped edges and glue the two pieces together.

The following method may also be used to get rough stock to uniform thickness:

1. Joint one edge of the stock and rip it into widths of 6 inches or less.

2. Joint the first face with the concave side of the stock down on the jointer table.

3. On the table saw, set the space between the saw and the ripping fence to a width equal to the rough thickness desired.

4. Raise the saw blade a distance above the table equal to one-half the board width.

5. Place the stock on the saw table with the jointed face held firmly against the ripping fence. Push the stock through the saw.

6. Reverse the stock. Repeat Step 5 with the opposite edge of the stock resting on the table.

7. Joint the ripped face lightly on the jointer.

REVIEW QUESTIONS

Identification

1. List the proper order of procedure and each machine used when machining a rough piece of stock that measures 1" x 6" x 20" to the finished dimensions of 3/4" x 5" x 18".

unit 23
the jointer

OBJECTIVES

After completing this unit, the student will be able to:

• identify the major parts of the jointer.

• list nine safety precautions to follow when using the jointer.

• properly use the jointer for surfacing the face of stock, squaring stock, jointing end grain, and jointing a bevel or chamfer.

The jointer, figure 23-1, is used to plane the face and the edge of stock straight and true. It is the first piece of equipment used when squaring stock on machines. The jointer is also used to plane chamfers, bevels, rabbets, and tapers.

The machine size is determined by the length of the cutting knives that are clamped

in the cutterhead. The 8-, 10-, and 12-inch sizes are commonly used in school shops. The 6-inch and 8-inch sizes are often used in home workshops.

To do accurate work, the rear (outfeed) table must be exactly level with the cutting edge of the knives at their highest point, figure 23-2. It is important to feed the stock across the jointer tables so the rotating knives are cutting with the wood grain. If the stock is run against the wood grain, wood fibers are torn from the surface leaving it rough.

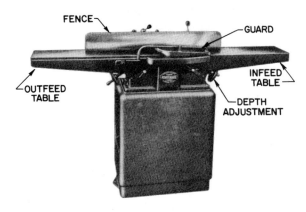

Fig. 23-1 8-inch wood jointer *(Courtesy of Power-matic Houdaille, Inc.)*

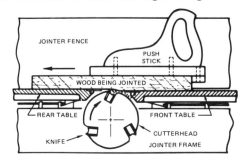

Fig. 23-2 Cross section of a jointer in operation

SAFETY PRECAUTIONS

- Check spring tension on the guard so the guard is kept tightly against the wood being jointed.

- Check the depth adjustment before starting the machine. A cut 1/16 inch deep is usually enough.

- Stock to be planed should not be less than 10 inches long, 2 inches wide, and 1/2 inch thick.

- Feed the stock with the grain.

- Always use a push stick when planing the face of stock.

- If the stock is warped, turn the concave face down on the jointer table.

- Never allow the fingers to pass over the cutterhead while pushing down on the stock.

- Hold the stock firmly and stand where the stock can be controlled as it is fed on the outfeed table.

- When jointing the edges of stock, keep the hands high on the stock.

- Follow the other general safety precautions in Unit 21.

PROCEDURE FOR SQUARING A WORKING FACE OF STOCK

1. With a try square, test the jointer fence to see that it is square with the face of the rear (outfeed) table, figure 23-3.

2. Set the depth adjustment to give a cut of approximately 1/16 inch.

3. Examine the edge of the stock to determine the grain direction, figure 23-5.

4. Place the stock on the front (infeed) table. If the stock is warped, place the concave side down.

Fig. 23-3 Testing jointer fence for squareness

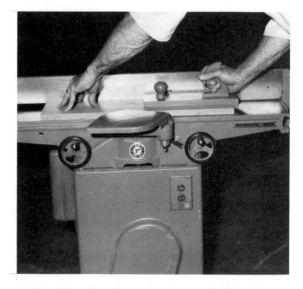

Fig. 23-4 Jointing edge of stock

5. Hold the stock firmly and feed it slowly across the cutterhead. Use a push stick, as shown in figure 23-4.

   Caution: Never joint the face of stock without a push stick.

6. Stand to the left of the jointer and even with the center of the infeed table. Move forward slowly as the stock is fed on the outfeed table.

7. While the planed face is fed on the outfeed table, hold it down firmly to insure a true face cut.

8. Inspect the planed surface. If necessary, take a second, light cut to complete the squaring process.

PROCEDURE FOR SQUARING AN EDGE ON A JOINTER

1. Place the planed surface tightly against the jointer fence.
2. Keeping your hands in the position shown in figure 23-5, push the stock slowly across the cutterhead. Keep the stock firmly down on the infeed table and against the jointer fence.
3. As the stock is fed across the jointer, shift the pressure of the hands from the infeed table to the outfeed table. This insures a straight edge which is at a 90-degree angle to the working face.

PROCEDURE FOR GETTING STOCK TO ROUGH THICKNESS

The following procedure is to be used when a surfacer is not available.

1. After the face and edge of the stock have been squared on the jointer, rip the stock to a width of approximately 6 inches. Be sure to place the planed face against the rip fence of the table saw and the jointed edge against the face of the saw table.
2. Adjust the rip fence of the table saw so that the distance between the saw and the fence is 1/8 inch more than the desired stock thickness.
3. Adjust the blade to a height of 3 inches.
4. Place the stock back on the table of the saw and hold the planed face firmly against the rip fence.
5. Before proceeding, a *feather board* is required, figure 23-6. This is made from stock 3/4 inch thick by 6 inches wide and 18 inches long. At one end of this stock, rip saw kerfs 1/8 inch apart to a length of 8 inches. Cut a bevel in the slotted end.
6. Clamp the feather board to the top of the saw table so that the bevel end

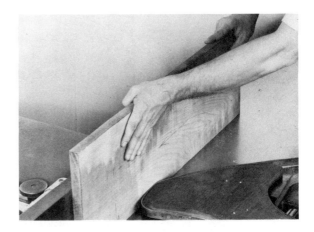

Fig. 23-5 Using a push stick when jointing the face of stock

Fig. 23-6 Ripping stock to thickness

provides tension against the face to be ripped.

7. Feed the stock slowly between the fence and the feather board. Ask an assistant to support the front end of the stock as it leaves the saw table.
8. Reverse the ends of the stock. Make the second cut with the opposite edge of the stock turned down.
9. Smooth the ripped face and edge by planing lightly on the jointer.

PROCEDURE FOR PLANING CHAMFERS AND BEVELS

1. Set the jointer fence to the angle desired. Chamfers are usually 45 degrees.

Fig. 23-7 Jointing a bevel or chamfer

2. If possible, tip the fence to the left so it makes a *V* between the table and the fence. This makes it easier to support the stock at the proper angle.

3. Feed the stock across the jointer, the same as when planing edges, figure 23-7.

4. Take as many cuts as necessary to get the desired chamfer width.

5. If the end grain is to be chamfered or beveled, it is planed before the edges are planed.

PROCEDURE FOR PLANING END GRAIN

Use the jointer for planing the end grain of stock only if the piece is at least 14 inches across each end.

1. Set the jointer to a 1/16-inch depth.

Fig. 23-8 Jointing end grain

2. Start the motor. Feed the end of the stock about 2 inches across the knives.

3. Pull the stock back carefully and reverse the edges of the stock, figure 23-8.

4. Complete jointing the end grain by feeding the stock across the jointer. Cutting towards the center of the stock prevents the stock from being splintered on the edge as the cut is completed.

Fig. 23-9 Portable power plane
(Courtesy of Millers Falls Co.)

THE PORTABLE POWER PLANE

The portable power plane, figure 23-9, may be used for straightedge planing and beveling. It is useful for fitting doors, windows, and other stock where a straight, smooth edge is needed. The motor unit may also be used for edge shaping, routing, and other molding work.

REVIEW QUESTIONS

A.   Multiple Choice

1. The maximum depth of cut that should normally be used on the jointer is:
   a. 1/16-inch.   c. 3/16-inch.
   b. 1/8-inch.   d. 1/4-inch.

2. What is the shortest length of stock that should be planed on the jointer?
   a. 6 inches.   c. 10 inches.
   b. 8 inches.   d. 12 inches.

3. The size of the jointer is determined by:
   a. the horsepower of the motor.
   b. the length of the table.
   c. the width of the table.
   d. the length of the knives.

4. The thinnest stock that should be surfaced on the jointer is:
   a. 1/4 inch.   c. 1/2 inch.
   b. 3/8 inch.   d. 3/4 inch.

5. Which direction should the edge of the board in the illustration be jointed?
   a. A
   b. B
   c. Neither A or B.
   d. It depends on what it will be used for.

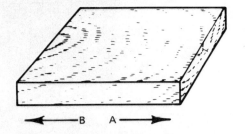

6. Adjust the jointer to the proper depth:
   a. before the machine is started.
   b. while the machine is running.
   c. while the board is being jointed.
   d. before the board is jointed, but after the machine is turned on.

7. While operating the jointer, it is best to:
   a. have a fellow student help you.
   b. operate the machine alone.
   c. have two other friends help you.
   d. hold the board while another student turns the machine on.

8. The guard on the jointer is designed to:
   a. hold the work.
   b. prevent accidents for only those who do not know how to use the machine.
   c. be used at all times.
   d. prevent all accidents.

B. **Completion**

9. The _____ (concave, convex) side of the board should be turned down while jointing the face of stock.

10. The name of the device used to help move the wood safely across the jointer is called a _____.

11. _____ protection should be worn at all times while operating the jointer.

12. The hands should never be allowed to pass over the _____ while any pressure is being applied to the board.

unit 24
the surfacer

OBJECTIVES

After completing this unit, the student will be able to:

- identify the major parts of the surfacer and explain how the size of the surfacer is determined.

- list eight safety precautions to follow when using the surfacer.

- surface a board to a thickness of both 1/4 inch and 3/4 inch with a surfacer.

The surfacer, sometimes called a thickness planer, is used to plane stock to a desired thickness after one face has been planed true on the jointer, figure 24-1.

The size of the surfacer is determined by the length of the knives in the cutterhead and by the maximum stock thickness it can plane. The 12-, 18-, and 24-inch widths are most frequently used in school shops.

The surfacer frame supports a fixed overhead cylindrical cutterhead which contains the cutting knives. The feed table below the cutterhead may be raised or lowered to give the desired stock thickness. A cross section of the surfacer and how it operates is shown in figure 24-2.

SAFETY PRECAUTIONS

- Set the depth adjustment so that it takes light cuts.

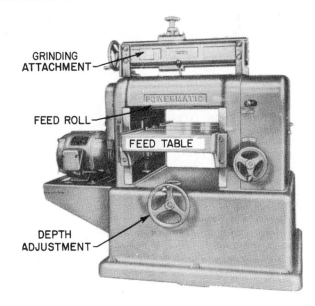

GRINDING ATTACHMENT

FEED ROLL

FEED TABLE

DEPTH ADJUSTMENT

Fig. 24-1 Surfacer

- Feed the stock so that the cutterhead knives are cutting with the grain, figure 24-2.

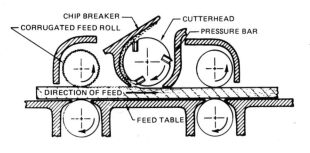

Fig. 24-2   How the surfacer operates

Fig. 24-3   Planing stock to thickness on surfacer

- Keep fingers and loose clothing away from the table and the feed mechanism.

- Do not stand directly behind the stock. Stand to one side of the stock as it is fed through the surfacer.

- Unless the surfacer is equipped with sectional feed rolls, feed only one piece of stock through the machine at one time.

- Do not look into the throat of the surfacer while it is running. If loose slivers and knots are thrown from the machine, they may cause eye injury.

- The surfacer planes the second face parallel to the opposite face of the stock. Do not attempt to surface stock unless the lower face has been planed true on the jointer.

- Stock shorter than 12 inches should not be fed through the surfacer unless it is butted end to end.

- Follow the other general safety precautions in Unit 21.

PROCEDURE FOR PLANING STOCK TO THICKNESS

1. After truing one face of the stock on the jointer, measure the stock at its thickest point.

2. Turn the depth adjustment until the thickness gauge reads 1/16 inch less than the thickest part of the stock.

3. Examine the jointed edge of the stock to determine the grain direction.

4. Start the machine. Place the stock on the feed table with the trued face turned down.

5. While feeding the stock through the surfacer, make sure the correct end is fed first according to the grain direction of the wood, figure 24-2.

6. If necessary, feed the stock through the surfacer again to get the desired thickness, figure 24-3. The final cut should leave an extra thickness of 1/32 inch to 1/16 inch for hand planing and sanding.

7. After squaring two adjoining faces of square posts or legs on the jointer, plane the other two faces true on the surfacer. Turn the jointed faces down on the table. Plane to square size by making two or more cuts for thickness.

PROCEDURE FOR PLANING THIN STOCK

1. When planing stock to a thickness less than 3/8 inch, obtain a piece of stock that has been planed about 3/4 inch thick and larger in width and length than the thin stock to be planed. This piece is called a *back-up board*.

2. Place the thin stock on top of the back-up board and measure the combined thickness of the two pieces. Set the planer to a thickness of 1/16 inch less than this measurement.

3. Feed the two pieces through the surfacer as many times as necessary to get the desired thickness.

PROCEDURE FOR PLANING SHORT STOCK

1. If pieces of thin stock shorter than 12 inches are planed to thickness, first plane a large back-up board to uniform thickness.

2. Set the thickness gauge of the planer to 1/16 inch less than the combined stock and back-up board thickness.

3. Place the pieces of short stock end to end on top of the back-up board, figure 24-4.

Fig. 24-4 Planing short, thin stock to thickness

4. Feed the stock through the surfacer. If necessary, repeat the operation to get the desired thickness.

REVIEW QUESTIONS

A. Multiple Choice

1. The minimum safe length of a single piece of stock to be run through the surfacer is:
   a. 6 inches.
   b. 12 inches.
   c. 18 inches.
   d. 24 inches.

2. Planing may be done as soon as:
   a. power is turned on.
   b. the machine has warmed up to room temperature.
   c. the motor has reached full speed.
   d. none of the above.

3. Stock should always be planed:
   a. with the grain.
   b. across the grain.
   c. either with or across the grain but never diagonal.
   d. none of the above.

4. When planing hardwoods, the depth adjustment should be set so the planer will remove _____ inch at a time.
   a. 1/64
   b. 1/16
   c. 1/8
   d. 1/4

5. If the wood sticks in the machines, you should:
   a. look into the machine from either end to determine what is wrong.
   b. press the reverse button to back out the stock.
   c. stop the machine, release pressure on the feed rolls, and remove the work.
   d. none of the above.

6. Before stock can be planed to thickness, one face should be trued by which of the following?
   a. Table saw   c. Planer
   b. Jointer   d. Planed by hand

7. To plane thin stock less than 3/8 inch thick, it is necessary to use:
   a. a back-up board.
   b. long boards.
   c. a feather board.
   d. a surfacer that will adapt to this thickness.

8. To plane short pieces of stock in the surfacer, it is necessary to use:
   a. the infeed roll.   c. a back-up board.
   b. heavy cuts.   d. the pressure bar.

9. In which direction, A or B, should this board be run through the surfacer to plane the top of the board?

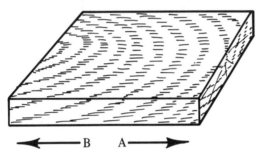

10. How is the size of the surfacer determined?

unit 25
the table saw

OBJECTIVES

After completing this unit, the student will be able to:

- identify a combination blade, a dado head, and a molding head.
- list eleven safety precautions to follow when using the table saw.
- properly use the table saw for: crosscutting stock; ripping stock; cutting duplicate pieces to length; cutting miters, tenons, dadoes, grooves, and rabbets; and shaping stock with the molding head.

The table saw, figure 25-1, is also called a variety saw, a circular saw, or a bench saw. The table saw is used for ripping and crosscutting stock, bevel ripping, mitering, and cutting dadoes and grooves. Several joints may be made on the table saw: cross-lap and half-lap joints, tenons for the mortise-and-tenon joint, rabbet, and tongue-and-groove joints. A molding head cutter is also used on the table saw to cut moldings and shapes on edges of stock.

The size of the table saw is determined by the maximum saw-blade diameter that can be used on it. Home shops usually use the 8-, 9-, and 10-inch sizes. School shops use the 10-, 12-, and 14-inch sizes. Small-size table saws are mounted on benches or stands. The larger sizes rest on the floor.

Most table saws have an arbor that can be tilted to various angles for mitering, chamfering, and beveling. The combination

Fig. 25-1 Parts of the table saw

blade, figure 25-2, is used for both crosscutting and ripping thick stock. Figure 25-3 shows a combination-type, hollow-ground saw blade that is used for both light crosscutting and ripping operations. Dado heads, figure

Fig. 25-2 Combination blade for heavy-duty work

Fig. 25-3 Combination-type, hollow-ground blade

25-4, have two blades and several cutters. They can bc built up to various thicknesses, from 1/4 inch to 1 1/2 inches or more. The assembly is used to cut dadoes, grooves, rabbets, and tenons. The molding head cutter has insert blades that are changed for different edge or molding cuts, figure 25-5.

SAFETY PRECAUTIONS

- Keep the guards in place when possible. When the guard cannot be used, get the instructor's permission before removing it. Use extreme care to avoid accidents.

- When ripping stock, keep the straight edge firmly against the rip fence. The *rip fence* is a guide clamped on the table and parallel to the blade. Use the splitter guard to prevent wood from binding on the blade and to prevent kickback.

- When crosscutting stock, hold it firmly against the sliding cutoff fence.

- Use a push stick when ripping stock less than 4 inches wide.

- Adjust the height of the saw blade so it projects through the wood not more than 1/8 inch.

- When cutting duplicate pieces of stock to length, always use a clearance block to prevent kickback, figure 25-9.

- Stand slightly to the left of the ripping fence. Never stand directly in line with the saw blade.

Fig. 25-4 Dado head assembly

Fig. 25-5 Molding head cutter
(Courtesy of Rockwell International)

- Never reach over the saw blade. Never allow the left hand to move past the side of the saw blade.

- Never attempt to rip stock unless it rests flat on the saw table and has a straight edge against the ripping fence.

- Do not remove scrap wood from the saw table until the motor has stopped.

- Stop the motor before making any adjustments.

- Follow the other general precautions in Unit 21.

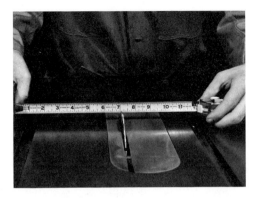

Fig. 25-6 Setting rip fence to desired width

PROCEDURE FOR RIPPING STOCK

1. Adjust the rip fence to the desired width of the finished stock plus 1/8 inch, as in figure 25-6.

2. Adjust the height of the saw blade so it projects through the table a distance equal to the stock thickness plus 1/8 inch.

3. Make sure the cover guard and the splitter guard are in place, figure 25-7.

4. Turn on the motor. Hold the straight edge of the stock tightly against the rip fence with the left hand. Push the stock forward with the right hand.

5. Do not allow the left hand to move along with the stock past the side of the saw.

6. If long, heavy stock is ripped, ask an assistant to hold up the front end of the stock. This is done so the stock remains level with the table after passing through the saw.

7. When stock is ripped to narrow widths, use the push stick to feed the tail end of the stock past the saw.

8. For narrow stock, rip half the length from one end. Lift the stock carefully from the saw and reverse the ends to complete the cut.

Fig. 25-7 Guard in place and ready for ripping operation

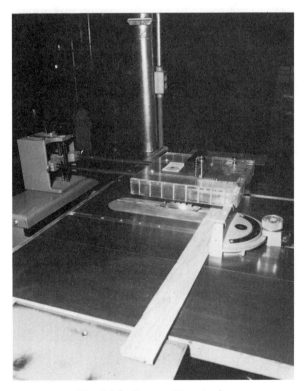

Fig. 25-8 Crosscutting stock

PROCEDURE FOR CROSSCUTTING STOCK

1. Install a crosscut or combination blade.

2. Adjust to the proper height.

3. Remove the ripping fence or slide it back out of the way.

4. Place the miter- gauge cutoff fence in the tabletop groove on the left side of the saw.

5. Square a line across the face and across the front edge of the stock.

6. Hold the edge firmly against the miter cutoff fence. Turn on the motor.

7. Line up the saw blade to cut just outside of the line previously marked.

8. Feed the stock slowly against the blade until the cut is completed, figure 25-8.

9. When extra-wide stock is cut on the crosscut saw, the miter fence may be placed in the groove in a reverse position, and the stock is held firmly against the fence as it is fed across the saw.

PROCEDURE FOR CUTTING DUPLICATE PIECES TO LENGTH — FIRST METHOD

1. Clamp a stop block to the rip fence in front of the saw blade, figure 25-9.

2. Adjust the space between the face of the stop block and the saw teeth a distance equal to the length of the pieces to be cut.

3. Feed the stock through the saw.

PROCEDURE FOR CUTTING DUPLICATE PIECES TO LENGTH — SECOND METHOD

1. Screw a piece of stock 3/4 inch thick and 2 inches wide to the face of the miter cutoff fence, figure 25-10.

2. Move the fence up even with the face of the saw blade.

3. Measure from a saw tooth set to the left of the saw a distance equal to the desired length. At this point, square a line across the face of the stock fastened to the miter cutoff fence.

Fig. 25-9 Cutting short, duplicate pieces to length
(Guard removed for photo)

Fig. 25-10 Cutting long, duplicate pieces to length
(Guard removed for photo)

4. Clamp a small hand screw to the stock with the edge of the jaw even with the squared line.

5. Remove the ripping fence from the table.

6. Place the end of the stock to be cut against the hand screw and move the miter cutoff fence past the saw, figure 25-10.

PROCEDURE FOR CUTTING REGULAR MITERS

1. Place the crosscut or combination blade on the saw arbor.

2. Adjust the miter gauge to a 45-degree angle.

3. Hold the stock firmly against the miter gauge and cut one end of the stock, figure 25-11.

Fig. 25-11 Cutting miters on table saw
(Guard removed for photo)

4. Measure the inside length required. Square a line across the inside edge at this point.

5. Reverse the ends of the stock and miter the second end as in Step 3.

PROCEDURE FOR CUTTING TENONS - FIRST METHOD

1. Square the pieces to be tenoned to the correct size.

2. Lay out the length, width, and thickness of the tenon on one end of the stock.

3. Adjust the height of the saw blade to equal the length of the tenon.

4. Stand the stock on end with one face of the stock flat against the fence.

5. Adjust the ripping fence so the saw lines up outside the marking-gauge line farthest from the rip fence, figure 25-12.

6. With the end of the stock flat on the saw table, hold the stock firmly against the rip fence. Use the feather board for cutting cheeks of tenons. The feather board minimizes the danger of this operation, figure 25-12.

7. After the first cut is made, place the opposite face of the stock against the rip fence and rip the opposite cheek.

8. Rip all cheeks of the tenons.

9. Lower the height of the saw until it projects through the table to a height equal to the depth of the shoulder cuts.

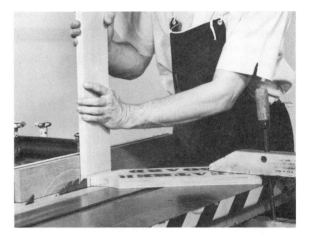

Fig. 25-12 Using feather board when ripping cheeks of tenon (Guard removed for photo)

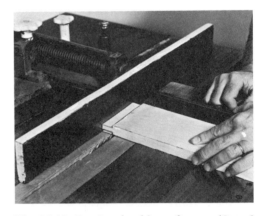

Fig. 25-13 Cutting shoulders of tenon (Guard removed for photo)

10. Clamp a clearance block against the face of the rip fence.

11. Adjust the rip fence so the distance from the face of the clearance block and the outside edge of the saw teeth is equal to the length of the tenon.

12. Test the depth of the cut on a scrap piece of stock.

13. With the edges of the stock against the miter cutoff fence, make all of the shoulder cuts, figure 25-13.

14. Remove waste on the edges of the tenon by making repeated saw cuts close together until the tenon is reduced to the correct width.

PROCEDURE FOR CUTTING TENONS - SECOND METHOD

1. Place the dado head on the saw arbor.

2. If the tenon is to be 1 inch to 1 1/4 inches long, make the dado head 3/4 inch wide.

3. Raise the cutting edge of the dado head a distance equal to the depth of the shoulder cuts of the tenon.

4. Set the rip fence so the distance from the outside edge of the dado head is equal to the length of the tenon, figure 25-14.

5. Make test cuts on both faces of a scrap piece that is the same thickness as the stock on which the tenons are to be cut. Hold the stock firmly against the face of the table and the edge of the miter cutoff fence.

6. After the test cuts have been properly adjusted, make the first cut with the end of the stock held against the rip fence, figure 25-14.

7. Move the stock a short distance away from the rip fence and make a second cut to remove the surplus stock on the end of the tenon.

8. After all cheeks of tenons have been cut, adjust the dado head to the height of the edge cuts.

9. Place the stock on edge and make shoulder cuts on the edges.

PROCEDURE FOR CUTTING DADOES AND GROOVES

1. Place the dado head on the saw arbor. Make the dado head width equal to the width of the dado desired.

2. Adjust to the depth desired.

3. Mark the exact dado location on the edge of the stock.

4. Make trial cuts on a scrap piece to get the correct depth adjustment.

Fig. 25-14 Cutting tenons with dado head
(Guard removed for photo)

Fig. 25-15 Cutting dadoes on face of stock
(Guard removed for photo)

5. Place the stock against the miter cutoff fence and adjust until the dado head fits between the width marks.

6. Feed the stock slowly over the dado head and hold it firmly against the miter cutoff fence, figure 25-15.

7. After all cuts are made, the bottom of the dado may be smoothed with a router plane.

8. Grooves are plowed lengthwise with the grain by using the dado head and keeping the edge of the stock against the rip fence, figure 25-16.

Blind dadoes or gains are cut the same way as dadoes, but the cut does not go completely across the face of the stock. A stop block or a hand screw is clamped to

Fig. 25-16 Plowing grooves in face of stock
(Guard removed for photo)

Fig. 25-17 Cutting cross-lap joint (Guard
removed for photo)

the table to stop the stock feed at the desired place. The radial arm saw is ideal for cutting dadoes and blind dadoes.

PROCEDURE FOR CUTTING CROSS-LAP JOINTS

1. Mark the joint location and size of the edges and faces of the stock.

2. Place the pieces of stock in their final assembled position. Check the accuracy of the layout.

3. Install a 3/4-inch or 1-inch dado head. Adjust to a depth equal to one-half the thickness of the stock.

4. Test the depth on a scrap piece that is the same thickness as the stock to be jointed.

5. Place the stock against the miter cutoff fence and cut out the surplus stock between the lines marked on the edges, figure 25-17.

PROCEDURE FOR CUTTING RABBETS

1. Mark the width and depth of the rabbet on the end of the stock to be rabbeted.

2. Install the 3/4-inch dado head on the saw arbor.

Fig. 25-18 Cutting rabbet on dado head
(Guard removed for photo)

3. Place the stock on edge with a face of the stock against the ripping fence.

4. Adjust the fence until the space between the dado head and the fence is equal to the stock to be left beside the rabbet, figure 25-18.

5. Adjust the height of the dado head to cut the correct depth of the dado.

6. Test the depth on a scrap piece of stock.

7. Feed the stock over the dado head. Be careful to hold the face of the stock firmly against the fence and the edge flat on the table.

The rip saw may also be used for cutting rabbets by making two right-angle cuts to rip out the corner of the stock.

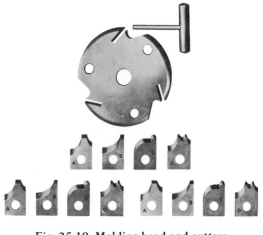

Fig. 25-19 Molding head and cutters

PROCEDURE FOR CUTTING MOLDINGS WITH THE MOLDING HEAD CUTTER

A variety of cutters can be installed in the molding head. This makes it possible to produce many molding shapes that can be cut on the faces and edges of stock, figure 25-19.

1. Select the cutters to be used and clamp them securely in the molding head. Check to see that they are properly lined up and securely tightened.

2. If the edge of the stock is to be shaped, adjust the ripping fence and make trial cuts on a scrap piece until the desired depth and shape are obtained.

3. Feed the stock slowly to obtain a smooth cut.

4. If necessary, screw or clamp a scrap piece to the ripping fence so that a cut may be made across the entire edge of the stock, figure 25-20.

5. Beads and other cuts are made on the face of the stock or molding, as shown in figure 25-21.

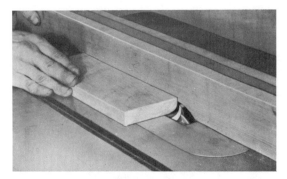

Fig. 25-20 Shaping edge of stock with molding head cutter (Guard removed for photo)

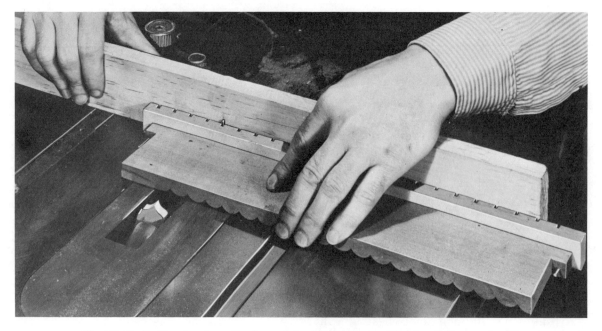

Fig. 25-21 Cutting beads on the face of stock *(Courtesy of Rockwell International)*

REVIEW QUESTIONS

A. **Multiple Choice**

1. When sawing, the circular saw blade should not project through the stock more than:
   a. 1 inch.
   b. 1/2 inch.
   c. 1/4 inch.
   d. 1/8 inch.

2. When should a push stick be used?
   a. When removing scrap
   b. When ripping narrow stock
   c. When turning the switch on or off
   d. When making adjustments

3. Freehand cutting (cutting without the aid of a rip fence or crosscut guide) is:
   a. permitted when stock is too large for the table.
   b. permitted if the operator has assistance.
   c. never permitted because it is dangerous.
   d. a generally accepted practice because it is fast.

4. Assistants who help with ripping stock should remember:
   a. to support the work from underneath but not to grasp it.
   b. to pick up all scraps which might cause an accident.
   c. to hold the stock firmly and gently pull it through the saw.
   d. to hold the two pieces of stock close together as you pull.

5. Never back work out of the saw without:
   a. making sure chips and sawdust behind the wood have been cleared away.
   b. turning off the power and waiting for the saw to stop turning.
   c. removing the fence or crosscut guide.
   d. giving a signal for assistance.

6. When you crosscut short pieces of equal length:
   a. a clearance block must be fastened to the rip fence.
   b. use care to insure all pieces are of equal length.
   c. use the crosscut guide and the fence to guide the stock.
   d. measure and mark each piece individually and cut separately.

7. When using the table saw, the operator should never stand:
   a. to the rear of the saw.
   b. to the right of the saw.
   c. to the left of the saw.
   d. directly behind the blade.

8. If it is necessary to clear the table of lumber scraps, you should:
   a. use the brush.
   b. use your hand.
   c. use the push stick.
   d. first stop the saw.

9. When ripping, the stock used should be between the:
   a. blade and miter gauge.
   b. miter gauge and fence.
   c. fence and blade.
   d. blade and table edge.

10. A push stick should be used if the stock is less than:

    a. 4 inches wide.   c. 2 inches wide.

    b. 3 inches wide.   d. 1 1/2 inches wide.

B.   Short Answer

11. Explain how the size of a table saw is determined.

12. When ripping stock on the table saw, you must always have a _____ edge against the rip fence.

unit 26
the radial arm saw

OBJECTIVES

After completing this unit, the student will be able to:

- list ten safety precautions to follow when using the radial arm saw.

- demonstrate the proper procedure on the radial arm saw for cutting stock to length, cutting dadoes, ripping stock to width, and cutting bevels and miters.

The greatest advantage of using a radial arm saw is for crosscutting long boards to length, figure 26-1. This is because the board is held flat on the table and the saw is moved into it. Another advantage is that all

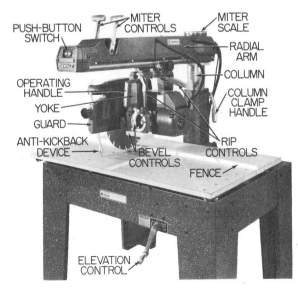

PUSH-BUTTON SWITCH — MITER CONTROLS — MITER SCALE — RADIAL ARM — OPERATING HANDLE — COLUMN — YOKE — COLUMN CLAMP HANDLE — GUARD — ANTI-KICKBACK DEVICE — BEVEL CONTROLS — RIP CONTROLS — FENCE — ELEVATION CONTROL

Fig. 26-1 Parts of the radial arm saw

cutting is done on top of the board. This allows the saw to be in full view of the operator while the cut is taking place. The radial arm saw is also used for cutting duplicate parts at the same time to the correct length, cutting straight and angle dadoes, ripping stock to width, and cutting miters and bevels.

The size of the radial arm saw is determined by the diameter of the largest blade that it will hold. The blades on the radial arm saw are similar to those used on the table saw.

SAFETY PRECAUTIONS

- Install the saw blade so the teeth at the top of the blade point toward the operator. An arrow on the motor unit indicates the direction of rotation.

- Set the lower edge of the saw blade even with the tabletop surface. If the blade is

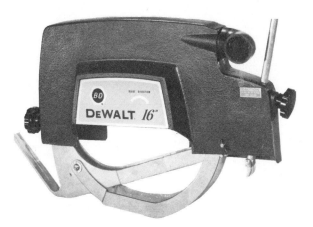

Fig. 26-2 Saw guard used on later models

lowered below this level, it will damage the tabletop.

- Before turning on the motor, push the saw unit back as far as it can go toward the pivot post (column).

- Be sure the stock is held firmly against the table fence.

- If it is necessary to rip stock on the radial arm saw, the antikickback device must be in contact with the surface of the stock.

- When ripping stock, ask an assistant to hold up the tail end of the stock.

- Always keep the guard in place.

- Keep your hands and arms away from the path of the saw.

- Be sure the stock has a straight edge. Place it against the table fence.

- For added safety, the saw guard shown in figure 26-2 is used on several late-model radial arm saws.

- Follow the other general safety precautions in Unit 21.

PROCEDURE FOR CROSSCUTTING STOCK

1. Place the stock on the table with a straight edge against the fence.

2. Adjust the board for proper length.

Fig. 26-3 Crosscutting stock with radial arm saw

3. Push the saw-blade unit back past the table fence. Grasp the saw handle tightly with the left hand and turn on the saw with the right hand, figure 26-3.

4. Pull the saw slowly across the face of the stock. Check the cut ends of the stock frequently with a framing square to make sure the saw is in proper adjustment.

5. To cut long stock, ask an assistant to hold each end level with the tabletop.

6. Return the saw to the back position on the radial arm. Turn off the switch.

PROCEDURE FOR CUTTING DADOES AND GAINS

1. Install the dado head of correct width.

2. Make sure the teeth of the blades and the points of the inside cutters are directed toward the operator when they are on the top of the blade.

3. Mark the location and width of the dadoes.

4. Obtain scrap stock of the same thickness as the stock to be dadoed.

5. Using the scrap stock for testing, make the desired width and depth adjustment.

Fig. 26-4 Crosscutting dadoes with radial arm saw

Fig. 26-5 Ripping stock with antikickback guard in place

6. Place the good stock in position against the table fence. Move the stock until the dado head lines up between the marked lines.

7. Hold the stock down firmly on the table. Pull the dado head the desired distance across the face of the stock, figure 26-4.

8. Push the saw back to its original position before moving the stock for the next cut.

PROCEDURE FOR RIPPING STOCK

It is better to rip stock on a table saw and use the radial saw for other operations. If the radial saw is used, however, proceed with extreme care.

1. If the saw blade has previously been set for crosscutting stock, lift the locking pin at the top of the yoke assembly. Also, loosen the locking lever and rotate the yoke assembly 90 degrees counterclockwise. Make sure the locking pin is in the 90-degree hole used for ripping and then tighten the locking lever.
   Use the combination blade for light ripping. Use the ripsaw blade for hardwood that is over 1 inch thick.

2. Move the yoke assembly sideways on the radial arm until the space between the saw teeth and the table fence is equal to the width desired for ripping. A scale is

usually located on the radial arm for setting the width of the cut.

3. Lock the yoke assembly in place by tightening the clamp screw located on the right side of the radial arm.

4. Adjust the antikickback guard so that its teeth will drag on the face of the stock, figure 26-5.

5. Check the direction of saw rotation. Make sure the points of the teeth at the bottom of the saw blade point toward the operator when in the position for ripping.

6. Start the motor. Hold the edge of the stock firmly against the fence. Feed the stock slowly across the table, figure 26-5. Do not feed from the antikickback side of the guard.

7. When ripping long stock, ask an assistant to hold the tail end of the stock level with the table.

PROCEDURE FOR RIPPING BEVEL CUTS

1. If bevel ripping is required, raise the radial arm assembly by using the crank below the front edge of the table.

2. Release the bevel clamp handle below the yoke. Lift the bevel latch handle. Swing the motor to the desired bevel angle as indicated on the bevel scale.

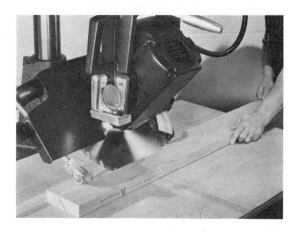

Fig. 26-6 Ripping bevel cuts

3. Adjust the blade depth and lock the yoke to the desired width on the radial arm saw.

4. Proceed in ripping as shown in figure 26-6.

PROCEDURE FOR CUTTING MITERS

1. Pull the miter latch handle and the arm clamp handle forward. These are located near the front on the top of the radial arm.

2. Move the radial arm assembly to the right or left. Check the miter-gauge

Fig. 26-7 Cutting a miter with a radial arm saw

scale on top of the column post. When the dial gauge pointer indicates the desired angle, push both levers back to lock the arm in place.

3. Place the stock in position on the table and hold it tightly against the table fence.

4. Start the motor and pull the saw slowly across the stock being mitered, figure 26-7.

REVIEW QUESTIONS

A.   Multiple Choice

1. When crosscutting, the stock should be held tightly against the:
   a. back stop.
   b. table fence.
   c. stop block.
   d. column.

2. Before ripping on the radial arm saw, always check to see that the stock will be fed:
   a. against the blade rotation.
   b. with the blade rotation.
   c. under the blade rotation.
   d. over the blade rotation.

3. The radial arm saw is primarily intended for:
   a. crosscutting short stock.
   b. crosscutting long stock.
   c. crosscutting both long and short stock.
   d. none of the above.

4. When installing a new blade on the radial arm saw, make sure that the teeth at the top of the blade point:
   a. toward the operator.
   b. away from the operator.
   c. toward the fence.
   d. toward the motor.

5. When ripping stock on the radial arm saw, the antikickback fingers should:
   a. clear the stock by 1/4 inch.
   b. clear the stock by 1/8 inch.
   c. be in contact with the stock.
   d. be removed to allow for ripping.

B. **Short Answer**

6. How is the size of the radial arm saw determined?

unit 27
the band saw

OBJECTIVES

After completing this unit, the student will be able to:

- identify the major parts of the band saw.
- list eight safety precautions to follow when using the band saw.
- demonstrate the correct procedure for cutting curves and ripping stock with the band saw.

The band saw is primarily used for cutting curves or irregular shapes on the edges of stock. It is also used for all kinds of straight sawing and for resawing medium and narrow widths of stock. Crosscutting may also be done on the band saw.

Figure 27-1 shows the principal parts of the band saw. The cutting blade, which is a flexible band of steel with teeth filed or ground on one edge, operates under tension between two rubber-faced wheels.

Two guide units, located above and below the table, have slots to prevent the blade from twisting. The two ball bearing supports prevent the blade from being forced out of alignment when wood is fed against it, figure 27-2.

When the blade is properly adjusted, the ball bearing support guides rub lightly against the back edge of the blade only when stock is fed against the blade. However, if the back

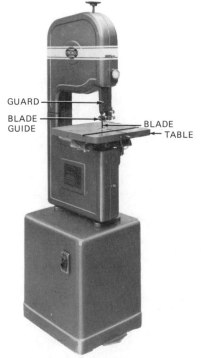

GUARD
BLADE GUIDE
BLADE
TABLE

Fig. 27-1 The band saw *(Courtesy Powermatic Houdaille, Inc.)*

edge rubs hard against the guide at all times, the blade has a tendency to break.

Careful attention to the correct blade alignment and tension increases blade life and makes accurate work possible. High-tempered, skip-tooth saw blades produce the best results. They stay sharp longer and cut faster.

SAFETY PRECAUTIONS

The band saw is a safe woodworking machine to use. If all safety precautions are observed, the band saw can be easily used by the beginning woodworker.

- Stand to the left of an imaginary line through the cutting edge of the saw.

- Keep the upper guide within 1/2 inch of the wood surface being sawed.

- If small curves are cut, use a narrow blade or make close, radial cuts on the waste side of the curved line, figure 27-3. This allows the wood to chip out and prevents the saw from binding.

- Keep the fingers at least 2 inches away from the cutting edge of the saw blade.

- Always stop the machine before making adjustments.

- If it is necessary to back out of a cut, first stop the machine. Then, back the

stock out. This prevents the blade from being pulled off the wheels.

- Use a saw blade that is sharp and has sufficient set.

- Use an assistant to handle long stock.

- Follow the other general safety precautions in Unit 21.

PROCEDURE FOR CUTTING CURVES

1. Lay out the curves to be cut on the stock.

2. If the design has short curves, install a blade 3/16 inch or 1/4 inch wide on the machine.

3. If necessary, make a few short cuts to the curved line. This allows the surplus wood to fall off as the saw follows the curve, figure 27-3.

4. Feed the stock slowly against the saw blade and cut 1/16 inch outside the marked line.

5. When possible, cut the longer curves first and finish with the smaller ones.

6. If the saw blade binds due to making too short a turn, back up in the kerf a short distance and saw through the scrap stock outside the line.

PROCEDURE FOR RIPPING STOCK

1. If the freehand method is used, draw a straight line with the grain with a straight-edge and a sharp pencil.

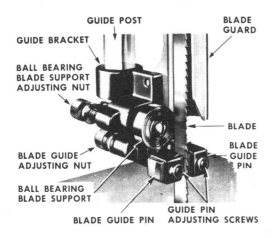

Fig. 27-2 Ball bearing blade support and guides
(Courtesy of Rockwell International)

Fig. 27-3 Sawing small curves on the band saw

Fig. 27-4 Freehand method of ripping on band saw *(Courtesy of Rockwell International)*

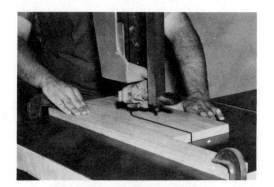

Fig. 27-5 Using a straight piece of stock as a ripping guide

2. Place the stock on the table and saw 1/8 inch outside the line, figure 27-4.

3. Joint the sawed edge on the jointer until the pencil line is reached.

4. If a guide is required, use the rip fence or clamp a straight piece of stock to the face of the table, figure 27-5. The edge of the stock should be to the right of the saw blade at a distance equal to the desired stock width.

5. Make sure the edge of the stock is at a 90-degree angle to the front edge of the saw table.

6. Start the saw. Feed the stock slowly past the blade with the working edge of the stock against the rip guide.

7. If the blade leads off of the marked line, it may be necessary to adjust the fence to make up for the uneven set of the saw teeth.

REVIEW QUESTIONS

Multiple Choice

1. When using the band saw, the upper guide should be within _____ inch(es) of the wood surface being sawed.
   a. 1   c. 2
   b. 1/4   d. 1/2

2. To avoid possible injury if a blade breaks, the operator should stand:
   a. to the right of the saw.   c. directly behind the saw.
   b. to the left of the saw.   d. none of the above.

3. What is the procedure for backing out of a saw cut?
   a. Stop the saw and then remove the stock.
   b. Saw forward making an arc and proceed outward by cutting forward.
   c. Back out slowly with the saw in motion.
   d. None of the above.

4. The best blade to use on the band saw for cutting wood is a:
   a. wave tooth.   c. skip tooth.
   b. cross-set tooth.   d. fine tooth.

5. While operating the band saw, your fingers should not get within _____ inch(es) of the blade.
   a. 1   c. 3
   b. 2   d. 4

unit 28
the jigsaw

OBJECTIVES

After completing this unit, the student will be able to:

- explain how the size of the jigsaw is determined.
- list seven safety precautions to follow when using the jigsaw.
- demonstrate the proper procedure on the jigsaw for cutting curves, replacing blades, and cutting out internal sections.

The jigsaw, or scroll saw, is used for cutting irregular curves and making internal cuts in soft wood, soft metal, plastics, layers of paper, and other materials. Its size is determined by the distance from the blade to the over arm (the C-shaped frame), figure 28-1. The 24-inch size is ideal for most work. Various blade widths are available to fit special curves. The saber blade, fastened only in the lower chuck, is also used in the jigsaw for special work. This blade saves time in cutting out the waste stock of pierced designs.

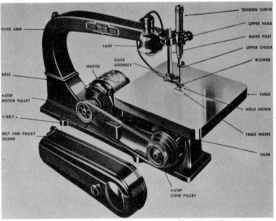

Fig. 28-1 Parts of a jig saw or scroll saw *(Courtesy of Rockwell International*

SAFETY PRECAUTIONS

- The hold-down must be in contact with the work to help hold it down.
- Make adjustments only while the machine is stopped.
- Check for clearance by first rotating the jigsaw through one complete cycle.
- Do not push fingers towards the blade.
- Support all material against the downward thrust of the blade.
- When installing a new blade, make certain that the teeth are pointing down.
- Use a V block for supporting all round stock.

- Follow the other general safety precautions in Unit 21.

PROCEDURE FOR REPLACING THE JIGSAW BLADE

1. Remove the throat plate.

2. Remove the old blade by loosening the thumbscrew or Allen screws in the upper and lower chucks.

3. Select a blade that will have a minimum of 3 teeth in contact with the stock at all times. Determine the direction the teeth point.

4. Place the new blade in the lower chuck with the teeth pointing down. Tighten the lower chuck.

5. Loosen the blade tension device on the upper head, figure 28-1.

6. Fasten the upper end of the blade in the upper chuck and tighten.

7. Adjust for proper tension on the blade. Do this by raising the tension sleeve so it just clears the upper blade chuck.

8. Adjust the blade guide to the proper slot size. Adjust the back-up roller so it just clears the rear of the blade.

9. Replace the throat plate.

10. Rotate the machine through one complete cycle by turning the knob on the motor shaft while checking for proper setup.

11. Adjust the jigsaw speed for the material being cut. Use slow speeds with heavy blades and thick cuts. Select a higher speed for fine cuts in thin material.

PROCEDURE FOR CUTTING CURVES ON THE EDGES OF STOCK

1. Lay out the design on the stock.

2. If the design has many sharp curves, install a blade 1/8 inch wide.

Fig. 28-2 Cutting edge of stock to shape

Fig. 28-3 Making internal cuts on wood surface

3. Place the stock against the side of the blade and adjust the hold-down device against the stock surface. Rotate the jigsaw through one complete cycle by hand.

4. Start the motor. Make saw kerfs in from the stock edges to points on the design where sharp turns must be made.

5. Saw carefully just outside the marked lines, figure 28-2.

PROCEDURE FOR MAKING INTERNAL CUTS IN STOCK

1. Lay out the design on the stock.

2. Bore 3/16-inch starting holes in the waste stock.

3. Release the clamp on the upper end of the jigsaw blade.

4. Move the top end of the blade slightly to one side. Thread the blade through the holes drilled in the stock.

5. Place the stock flat on the table. Clamp the top end of the blade into the upper chuck.

6. Lower the hold-down device until it is in contact with the face of the stock and clamp it in place. Rotate the jigsaw through one complete cycle by hand. Start the motor.

7. Saw close to the marked line on the waste side, figure 28-3.

8. Stop the motor. Follow the same procedure for each area of the design.

REVIEW QUESTIONS

A.   Multiple Choice

1. When installing a new blade, always make certain that the teeth are pointing:
   a. up.
   b. down.
   c. up or down.
   d. to one side.

2. The hold-down should:
   a. rest firmly on the work.
   b. be 1/8 inch away from the workpiece.
   c. be 1/4 inch away from the workpiece.
   d. be used only in special cases.

3. When cutting dowels on the jigsaw, you should:
   a. use the miter gauge.
   b. use the fence.
   c. use a V block.
   d. not attempt this operation.

4. Before turning on the jigsaw, you should first:
   a. ask for assistance.
   b. clear away any scraps on the hold-down.
   c. replace the blade.
   d. rotate the machine through one complete cycle.

B.   Short Answer

5. When should adjustments be made on the jigsaw?

6. The cutting action of the jigsaw blade is _____.

7. Be extremely careful not to push the fingers _____ the blade.

unit 29
the saber saw

OBJECTIVES

After completing this unit, the student will be able to:

- list five safety precautions to follow when using the saber saw.

- demonstrate the proper procedure on the saber saw for cutting curves and cutting pierced designs.

The saber saw is small, portable, and held in the hand, figure 29-1. It is used for cutting internal and external curves and is often substituted for the jigsaw. One advantage of the saber saw is it can be used for cutting out designs in panels that have already been assembled.

SAFETY PRECAUTIONS

- Always start the saw before the blade is in contact with the work.

- Make sure the saw is turned off before plugging in the power cord.

- Support the workpiece before beginning to saw.

- Select a blade that will have at least 3 teeth in contact with the stock at all times.

- Provide for blade clearance underneath the stock.

- Follow the other general safety precautions in Unit 21.

PROCEDURE FOR CUTTING OUT PIERCED DESIGNS

1. Bore a starting hole in the waste stock if a pierced design is required.

2. Install a fine-toothed, narrow blade in the saw.

3. Clamp the stock so that it projects far enough over the workbench edge to

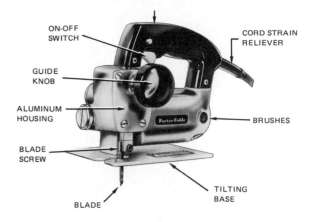

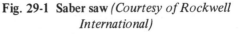

Fig. 29-1 Saber saw *(Courtesy of Rockwell International)*

Fig. 29-2 Sawing out pierced design with saber saw

Fig. 29-3 Starting cut with saber saw

provide clearance for the blade. The stock may also be held with a hand screw which is clamped in the vise.

4. Insert the saber blade in the starting hole. Start the motor and saw carefully on the waste side of the design outline, figure 29-2.

PROCEDURE FOR MAKING STARTING CUTS

Where straight, internal cutting in the face of thin stock is required, it may not be necessary to bore a starting hole.

1. Hold the saber saw in a forward, tilted position, as shown in figure 29-3.
2. Before turning on the motor switch, make sure the tip of the saw blade is not in contact with the surface to be cut.
3. Turn on the switch and gradually lower the back end of the saw until the blade comes in contact with the wood.

Fig. 29-4 Crosscutting stock with aid of guide

4. When the sole of the saber saw is brought in full contact with the wood surface, move the saw forward on the line to be cut.

When near the end of stock, a rip fence may be used as a guide for crosscutting, figure 29-4. Otherwise, a straightedge guide or the freehand method may be used.

REVIEW QUESTIONS

Multiple Choice

1. When selecting a blade to use in the saber saw, select one that will have at least _____ in contact with the stock at all times.

   a. 1 tooth   c. 3 teeth
   b. 2 teeth   d. 4 teeth

2. The saber saw should be turned on:

   a. just before the teeth come into contact with the work.
   b. while the stock is being repositioned.
   c. only after the teeth are in contact with the work.
   d. either a or c, depending on how hard the wood is.

3. When operating the saber saw, care should be taken to:

   a. always use a rip fence.
   b. never start a cut without first boring a hole.
   c. hold the saw in both hands.
   d. provide for blade clearance under the stock.

unit 30
the drill
press

OBJECTIVES

After completing this unit, the student will be able to:

- describe how the size of a drill press is determined.
- list five safety precautions to follow when using the drill press.
- properly set up the drill press for boring holes in wood.

The drill press, figure 30-1, is most frequently used for drilling and boring holes and comes in either a floor or bench model. Other drill press operations include drum sanding, plug cutting, grinding, mortising, and countersinking. Most drill presses provide a means of changing how fast the drill rotates. When drilling holes up to 1/4 inch in diameter, the faster speeds should be used. When boring holes 3/4 inch or larger, the slower speeds should be used.

The size of the drill press is determined by measuring twice the distance from the center of the chuck to the front of the vertical column. For example, if a drill press measures 7 1/2 inches from the center of the chuck to the column, it is a 15-inch drill press.

SAFETY PRECAUTIONS

- Never leave the chuck key in the drill press chuck.

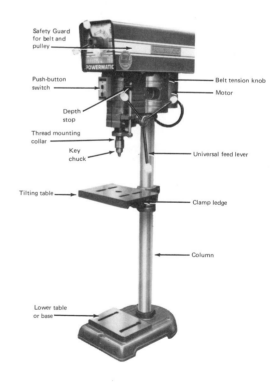

Fig. 30-1 The drill press *(Courtesy of Powermatic Houdaille, Inc.)*

- Always support round stock in a V block or vise.

- When drilling small pieces of stock, always secure the material in a vise or with clamps.

- Place a scrap piece of stock under the workpiece.

- Make sure the speed setting is correct for the work.

- Follow the other general safety precautions in Unit 21.

PROCEDURE FOR USING THE DRILL PRESS

1. Select the bit to be used and fasten it securely in the drill chuck. Never attempt to fasten a bit with a square shank in the drill press chuck.

2. Select the proper speed. For the slowest speed, place the belt on the smallest motor pulley and the largest spindle pulley. Use slow speeds for large holes and high speeds for small holes.

3. Place a flat piece of scrap stock on the drill press table.

4. Place the stock to be drilled on top of the scrap stock and clamp both to the table with C clamps.

5. Set the depth stop to allow the bit to cut to the desired depth.

6. Line up the bit center with the center of the hole to be drilled. Feed the bit into the wood slowly, figure 30-2.

Hole Saws

Hole saws are sometimes used in the drill press for cutting large holes or circular discs. For example, wheels for toys are often cut this way, figure 30-3.

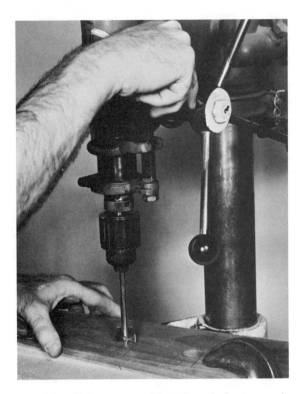

Fig. 30-2 Using a power bit to bore holes in wood

Fig. 30-3 Sawing discs with a hole saw

PROCEDURE FOR CUTTING
WOOD PLUGS

It is often desirable to use wooden plugs for covering countersunk screwheads and defects such as knots.

1. Bore a hole in the wood surface where the plug is to be used.

2. Install a plug cutter in the drill chuck. The cutter size must be the same size as the bit used to bore the hole in Step 1.

3. Select a piece of wood stock with characteristics (such as color and grain pattern) similar to the wood where the plug is to be inserted.

4. After clamping a scrap piece to the face of the drill press table, figure 30-4, place the stock selected in Step 3 on the scrap piece of stock.

5. Set the depth gauge of the drill press. Start the drill and feed the plug cutter slowly to cut the number of plugs needed.

6. Glue the plugs in place with the direction of the grain matching the board surface, figure 30-5.

Fig. 30-4 Cutting wood plugs with plug cutter

Fig. 30-5 Fitting plug in place

PROCEDURE FOR USING THE
DRUM RASP

1. Select a piece of 3/4-inch scrap stock the approximate size of the drill table. Cut a hole in the center of it slightly larger than the diameter of the drum rasp.

2. Clamp the rasp in the drill chuck. Lower the drill spindle until the bottom edge of the rasp extends about 1/8 inch into the hole of the scrap stock.

3. Lock the drill spindle into this position and clamp the scrap stock in place.

4. Start the drill and feed the curved edge of the stock against the rotating drum

Fig. 30-6 Smoothing curved edge with a drum rasp

rasp, figure 30-6. Use light, even pressure as the stock is moved against the rotating rasp.

REVIEW QUESTIONS

Multiple Choice

1. After removing a drill from the chuck, the chuck key should be:
   a. left in the chuck so it is not lost.
   b. removed from the chuck and put in the proper place.
   c. used to tighten the chuck.
   d. rotated to the left 1/2 of a turn.

2. A general rule to follow when boring a large hole is to:
   a. increase the speed of the drill press.
   b. drill a small hole first and gradually make the hole larger.
   c. reduce the drill press speed.
   d. drill the hole very slowly.

3. When boring holes in small pieces, which of the following is a good practice?
   a. Clamp the piece with a hand screw.
   b. Have a friend help to hold the piece.
   c. Hold the piece in a vise.
   d. Either a or c

4. When boring holes in round stock, the stock should be supported:
   a. in a V block.
   b. on another board.
   c. this operation is too dangerous and should not be attempted.
   d. on the drill press table.

5. If a drill press measures ten inches from the center of the drill to the column, the drill press size is:
   a. 5 inches.   c. 15 inches.
   b. 10 inches.   d. 20 inches.

OBJECTIVES

After completing this unit, the student will be able to:

- explain how the size of the portable electric drill is determined.
- list three safety precautions to follow when using the portable electric drill.
- properly use the portable electric drill.

The portable electric drill allows the worker to drill holes in a variety of places and positions not possible with any other power tool, figure 31-1.

The size of the portable electric drill is determined by the largest drill diameter the chuck will hold. The 1/4-inch drill is proba- bly the most common power tool found in workshops.

A recent development with the portable electric drill is a variable speed control. This allows the operator to select the proper speed for a job. Another development in some drills is the rechargeable batteries which allow the

A.

B.

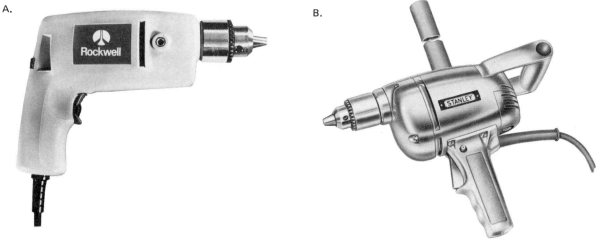

Fig. 31-1 Two portable electric drills: (A) light-weight 1/4-inch drill, and (B) a heavy-duty 1/2-inch drill

drill to operate without being connected to a power outlet.

SAFETY PRECAUTIONS

- Remove the power cord when installing or removing drill bits.
- Do not operate portable electric tools while standing in water or on damp surfaces.
- Make sure the power cord will not be cut by the drill.
- Follow the other general safety precautions in Unit 21.

PROCEDURE FOR USING THE PORTABLE ELECTRIC DRILL

1. Select the proper size drill bit and make sure the material to be drilled is securely fastened.

2. Place the drill bit in the chuck of the drill. Hand tighten the chuck. Make sure the bit is held by all 3 drill chuck jaws. Complete the tightening process with the chuck key and remove the key from the chuck, figure 31-2.

3. Connect the drill to the power outlet.

Fig. 31-2 Tightening the key chuck

4. Place the drill bit on locating marks on wood, press lightly, and start the drill. Make sure that pressure is properly applied so the drill is not bent.

5. Continue to drill the hole. With deep holes, pull the bit out of the hole occasionally to remove the wood chips.

6. Just as the drill begins to break through the material, ease off the pressure on the drill.

REVIEW QUESTIONS

A. Multiple Choice

1. When a drill is being installed or removed, the drill should be:
   a. secured in a vise.
   b. placed on the floor so it does not drop.
   c. held with a wrench.
   d. unplugged.

2. While operating the electric drill, the cord should be:
   a. located where it will not be cut by the drill.
   b. unplugged.
   c. wrapped around the handle of the drill.
   d. held in one hand so it may be pulled from the wall socket if there is trouble.

3. When drilling a hole completely through a piece of wood, the pressure on the drill should be:
   a. the same through all parts of the drilling operation.
   b. reduced as the drill breaks through the backside.
   c. as hard as you can push at all times.
   d. very light when the hole is started and gradually heavier as the hole progresses.

4. After tightening a drill, the chuck key is:
   a. left in the chuck so you can find it again.
   b. removed from the chuck.
   c. put in your pocket so you know where to find it.
   d. none of the above.

B. Short Answer

5. How is the size of the portable electric drill determined?

unit 32
the mortiser

OBJECTIVES

After completing this unit, the student will be able to:

- list four safety precautions to follow when using the mortiser.
- explain the correct method of marking stock to locate mortises.
- demonstrate the proper procedure for mortising stock.

A mortiser is used to cut the opening for a mortise-and-tenon joint. The hollow-chisel mortiser is used in most shops. The combination mortiser and drill press is also used, figure 32-1. It has interchangeable attachments that are useful for mortising, as well as drilling holes in wood and metal.

SAFETY PRECAUTIONS

- Make sure the stock is securely clamped.
- Make all adjustments with the power off.
- Feed only as fast as the machine will easily cut.
- Keep hands away from the chisel while the machine is on.

Fig. 32-1 Drill press with mortising attachment

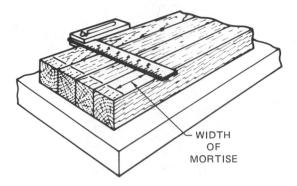

WIDTH OF MORTISE

Fig. 32-2 Marking width of mortise

Fig. 32-3 Testing the mortising chisel for depth

- Follow the other general safety precautions in Unit 21.

PROCEDURE FOR MORTISING STOCK

1. If several duplicate mortises are to be cut, place the stock on a bench and line up the ends with a square, figure 32-2.

2. Square lines across the faces or edges of the stock to indicate the width of the mortise, figure 32-2.

3. Mark the location and thickness of one mortise with a marking gauge.

4. Place one piece of stock on the mortiser table and clamp in place.

5. Adjust the table and the stock horizontally until the chisel is positioned between the lines indicating the thickness of the mortise.

6. Adjust the mortising chisel to the depth of the cut desired, figure 32-3.

7. Move the stock back into position for cutting the mortise.

8. Force the chisel into the wood with the feed lever. Make the first cut only about one-half as deep as the full depth of the mortise. This helps prevent the chisel from binding in the wood, figure 32-4.

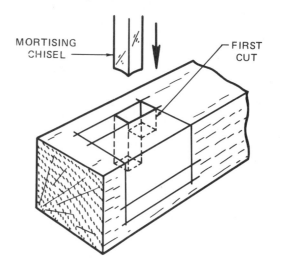

Fig. 32-4 Making first cut shallow to prevent the chisel from binding

Fig. 32-5 Completing the final cuts for mortise

9. Make a second cut to the full depth of the mortise. Then recut the first cut to the full depth.

10. Continue cutting to the side of the former cut until the mortise is completed, figure 32-5.

11. Cut all duplicate mortises while the machine is set.

12. Feed the mortising chisel into the wood as fast as it can cut.

    Caution: Do not use excessive pressure. Feeding either too slowly or too fast may cause extreme heating of the mortising chisel.

REVIEW QUESTIONS

Multiple Choice

1. When using the mortiser, make sure the stock:
   a. is square.
   b. is securely clamped.
   c. is soft pine.
   d. will not rotate.

2. To help prevent the chisel from binding in the wood, the first cut should:
   a. be made very slowly.
   b. be made very fast.
   c. be made only 1/2 the full depth.
   d. be drilled by hand.

3. The _____ is easily fitted with a mortising attachment.
   a. table saw
   b. lathe
   c. band saw
   d. drill press

4. While cutting mortises, the chisel should be fed into the stock:
   a. as fast as it will cut but without excessive pressure.
   b. as slowly as possible.
   c. within one minute.
   d. so you can just see a small amount of blue smoke coming from the chisel.

5. When making mortises on several pieces of duplicate stock, it is best to:
   a. mark each piece separately.
   b. line up the ends and square lines across all pieces.
   c. not waste time to mark the stock; the machine will do this.
   d. use a ball-point pen.

unit 33
the router

OBJECTIVES

After completing this unit, the student will be able to:

- list six safety precautions to follow when using the router.
- properly install and remove a router bit.
- explain the proper procedure for shaping a decorative edge on stock, cutting dadoes, and making surface designs with the router.

The portable router, figure 33-1, is used to make decorative cuts on the edges of boards and cut grooves, rabbets, and dadoes. It is also used for routing surface designs, making signs, and cutting designs on other parts of furniture.

The router has a high-speed motor, a chuck to hold the bit, and a base that allows

the operator to control the depth of cut. A large number of shapes and sizes of bits are available. Some bits have a round pilot on the end. These are used to control how far

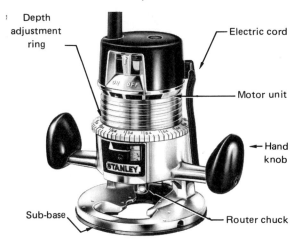

Fig. 33-1 Portable router

Depth adjustment ring

Electric cord

Motor unit

Hand knob

Sub-base

Router chuck

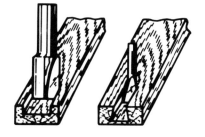

Fig. 33-2 Router bits with a pilot (top) and router bits without a pilot (bottom)

the bit can enter the wood. Other bits do not have the pilot and must be controlled by the use of a fence, figure 33-2.

SAFETY PRECAUTIONS

- Make sure the tool is unplugged when installing or removing bits.

- Make sure the router is turned off before you plug it into the electrical outlet.

- Make sure the bit is properly installed before operating the router.

- Hold the machine firmly before you turn on the machine.

- Turn off the router when it is not in use.

- Move the router against the rotation of the bit, see figure 33-3.

- Follow the other general safety precautions in Unit 21.

HOW TO SHAPE A DECORATIVE EDGE WITH THE ROUTER

1. Select a router bit with a pilot. Place it in the router chuck as far as it will go and tighten the locking nut.

2. Adjust the router to the desired depth of cut. Most routers have a locking device that must be loosened before the motor assembly can be moved up or down in the router base, figure 33-4.

3. Clamp a scrap piece of stock in the vise. Make sure the router bit will not cut the bench top.

4. Carefully set the router base on the workpiece. Make sure the router bit is not touching the wood.

5. Grasp the router firmly and turn it on.

6. Slide the router into the stock until the pilot on the bit makes contact with the wood. Immediately begin to move the router from left to right. This should be against the rotation of the router bit, figure 33-3. Be careful to keep the

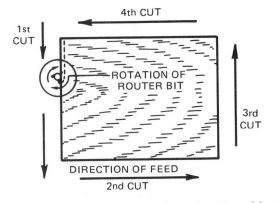

Fig. 33-3 Correct order of cuts and direction of feed

Fig. 33-4 Router base locking wing nut

router base resting firmly on the face of the stock. The feed should be continuous but not fast enough to overload the motor.

7. Shut off the router. When it has stopped, place it on the bench on its side.

8. Inspect your work. If the cut is not even, reshape the edge with the router. Make sure the base is resting on the face of the work and the pilot is against the edge.

9. Remove the router bit by loosening the nut. Tap the nut lightly to remove the bit from the chuck.

PROCEDURE FOR CUTTING DADOES WITH THE ROUTER

1. Select a straight router bit with the same width as the dado you wish to make. Place it in the chuck as far as it will go and tighten the locking nut.

Fig. 33-5 Cutting dadoes with router

Fig. 33-6 Routing letters of a sign

2. Adjust the router to the desired depth.

3. Clamp a scrap piece of stock in the vise.

4. Set the router guide to the desired position, figure 33-5.

5. Place the router on the stock. Make sure the bit does not touch the workpiece. Hold the router firmly and turn it on.

6. Move the router into the stock while holding the base firmly on the face and the fence tightly against the edge of the board.

7. After completing the cut, shut off the router. When the router has stopped, place it on the bench.

8. Check the cut for proper size.

9. If the desired width of the dado is wider than the bit diameter, readjust the guide and make a second pass.

10. To cut dadoes a distance from the ends of the stock, clamp a straight piece of wood across the face of the stock. This piece of wood serves as a fence and it allows you to cut a straight dado.

HOW TO MAKE SURFACE DESIGNS AND LETTERS WITH THE ROUTER

1. Install a veining bit or core-box bit in the router.

2. Lay out the outline of the letters or design.

3. Adjust the bit for proper depth.

4. Lower the router bit between the lines outlining the letters. Follow the lines carefully while cutting, figure 33-6.

5. After completing the work, shut off the machine and inspect your work.

6. Remove the bit from the router.

REVIEW QUESTIONS

Multiple Choice

1. When removing or installing router bits, check to see if:
   a. the router is on its side.
   b. the router is unplugged.
   c. the machine switch is off.
   d. the router is right side up.

2. Before plugging the router into an electrical outlet, make sure the router:
   a. switch is off.
   b. is turned on its side.
   c. is held by another student.
   d. is held in one hand.

3. Before turning the router on, make sure the machine is held:
   a. on the bench.
   b. firmly.
   c. in a vise.
   d. on the floor.

4. A properly installed router bit will be inserted _____ in the chuck.
   a. 1/4 inch
   b. 1/2 inch
   c. 5/8 inch
   d. as far as it will go

5. The proper direction of feed for the router:
   a. is against the direction of rotation.
   b. is with the direction of rotation.
   c. depends on the type of wood being cut.
   d. depends on the bit being used.

6. The part of a router bit that controls how far the bit can enter the wood is called:
   a. a ring.
   b. a pilot.
   c. a collar.
   d. a stop.

7. To adjust the depth of cut of a router bit,:
   a. slide the bit up or down in the chuck before tightening.
   b. move the router motor up or down in the router base.
   c. both a and b.
   d. do not make any adjustments.

8. When making surface designs in wood such as letters, control the router:
   a. with a fence.
   b. with a pilot.
   c. with a friend.
   d. by hand.

9. The device used to guide the router when making a dado is called:
   a. a fence.
   b. a guide.
   c. a pilot.
   d. an edge tool.

10. When removing a bit from the router, loosen the nut and if the bit will not slide out,:
    a. pry it out with a screwdriver.
    b. have your instructor remove the bit for you.
    c. tap the nut lightly to loosen the bit.
    d. twist it out with a wrench.

unit 34
the spindle shaper

OBJECTIVES

After completing this unit, the student will be able to:

- list eleven safety precautions to follow when using the shaper.
- list two methods for controlling the depth of cut on the shaper.
- explain the proper procedure for shaping a straightedge and a curved edge with the spindle shaper.

The spindle shaper is used for cutting designs on the edges of stock, cutting moldings, and cutting certain wood joints. Due to its high speed and the difficulty of guarding it adequately, the shaper should be used with extreme care.

SAFETY PRECAUTIONS

- Unplug the machine when changing bits.
- Feed the stock against the direction of cutter rotation, figure 34-1.

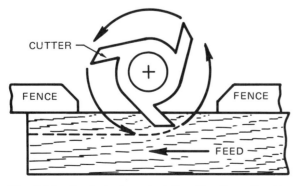

Fig. 34-1 **Feed stock against the direction of cutter**

- Feed the stock with the grain direction of the wood, figure 34-2.
- When possible, install the cutter next to the shoulder of the spindle.
- When possible, install the cutter so the bottom of the stock will be machined.
- Use the fence for all straight cuts.
- Check for the proper direction of rotation by turning the machine on and off rapidly and watching the shaper bit.
- Never shape stock that has large knots or splits.
- Use a depth collar and guide pin for all irregular cuts.

Fig. 34-2 **Shape stock with the grain**

221

- Never attempt to shape stock that is less than 10 inches unless it is held in a special jig.
- Use guards whenever possible.
- Follow the other general safety precautions in Unit 21.

PROCEDURE FOR SHAPING STRAIGHT EDGES

1. Install the desired cutter shape on the shaper spindle so the cut takes place on the lower part of the stock, figure 34-1.

2. Adjust the fence to give the proper shape and desired depth, figure 34-3.

3. Check the rotation of the cutter. Make necessary adjustments so the shaper cutter rotates against the direction of feed.

4. Feed a piece of scrap stock into the shaper to determine proper depth adjustments.

5. Feed the stock slowly. Hold it firmly against the shaper fence to prevent kickback.

PROCEDURE FOR SHAPING IRREGULAR EDGES

1. Remove the shaper fence. Install the cutter on the spindle so that the cut is made, if possible, on the lower side of the stock, figure 34-1.

2. Place a depth collar on the cutter. The collar size depends on the shape and depth of the desired cut, figure 34-4.

3. Install a safety pin in the shaper table on the side of the spindle from which the stock is fed, figure 34-5.

4. Place a scrap piece of stock on the table with the end against the cutter.

5. Adjust the height of the cutter to give the desired shape. A minimum of 3/16 inch must be left on the edge of the stock to rub against the depth collar.

Fig. 34-3 Using fence to control depth of cut

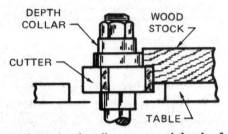

Fig. 34-4 Using depth collar to control depth of cut

Fig. 34-5 Using safety pin when starting cut

6. Start the shaper and check for proper rotation. Check for proper cut by feeding the piece of scrap stock against the cutter.

7. Feed the stock at moderate speed, shaping the end grain first. Too much pressure against the depth collar causes the collar to burn into the stock. This results in a poor job of shaping.

8. If an intricate design is shaped on the stock, change cutters and follow the same procedure above.

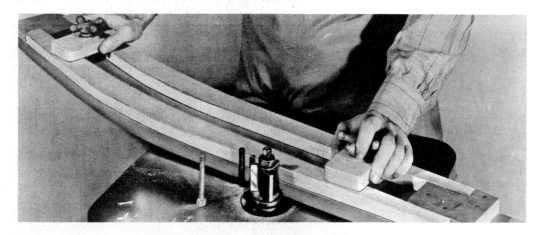

Fig. 34-6 Using jib to shape back legs of chair to size

PROCEDURE FOR SHAPING WITH PATTERNS

Although similar to the preceding operation, this procedure uses a pattern which runs against the shaper collar instead of the stock itself.

1. Make a pattern out of plywood or particleboard with its edge the exact size and shape of the pieces to be cut.

2. Cut the stock to a size 1/8 inch to 1/4 inch larger than the finished pattern size.

3. Fasten the stock on top of the pattern. To do this, use short, steel-pointed pins or clamps in the surface of the pattern, as shown in figure 34-6.

4. Adjust the cutter to make the desired cut when the collar rubs against the pattern.

REVIEW QUESTIONS

A. Multiple Choice

1. Always use a _____ when shaping irregular edges of stock on the spindle shaper.
   a. helper
   b. depth collar
   c. fence
   d. miter gauge

2. When shaping the edge on a straight piece of stock, use a _____ to control the depth of cut.
   a. helper
   b. depth collar
   c. fence
   d. hold-down

3. If at all possible, the cut should take place on the _____ side of the stock.
   a. upper
   b. lower
   c. inward
   d. outward

4. The cutter on the spindle shaper:
   a. rotates against the workpiece.
   b. rotates with the workpiece.
   c. parallel to the workpiece.
   d. perpendicular to the workpiece.

5. The shortest piece that should be shaped without the use of a special jig is:

   a. 6 inches.   c. 10 inches

   b. 8 inches.   d. 14 inches.

B. Short Answer

6. How do you check for the proper direction of rotation on a shaper?

unit 35
the wood lathe

OBJECTIVES

After completing this unit, the student will be able to:

- list eight safety precautions to follow when using the lathe.

- explain what each turning tool contained in a set of wood-turning chisels is used for.

- explain the difference between the cutting method and the scraping method used to turn.

- properly use the lathe for spindle and faceplate turning.

The wood lathe, figure 35-1, is used to spin stock so it can be cut to various shapes with turning tools. These turning tools are applied to the stock surface. The stock is held either between two centers (spindle turning), screwed to a plate which is attached to the headstock spindle (faceplate turning), or held in a chuck which is fastened to the faceplate and headstock.

The size of the wood lathe is determined by the largest diameter that can be turned. A common size of wood lathe is 12 inches.

TURNING TOOLS

Common turning chisels used with the wood lathe are shown in figure 35-2. The *gouge* is used for turning stock from square to cylindrical shape, shaping stock to various curved designs, and cutting coves. The *skew chisel* is used to cut beads, shoulders, cylinders, and V cuts. The skew chisel is difficult to use and requires much practice. The *round-nose chisel* is a scraping tool used for shaping stock fastened to the faceplate and shaping coves in spindle turning. The *parting-tool blade* is used to cut shoulders or ledges and square ends of spindle turnings. The *diamond-point* or *spear-point chisel* is a scraping tool used mostly for faceplate turning. It may also be used for shaping shoulders and beads in spindle turnings.

SAFETY PRECAUTIONS

- Never wear loose clothing.

- Be sure all stock to be turned has no defects.

- Fasten stock securely between centers. Check the tailstock to make sure the

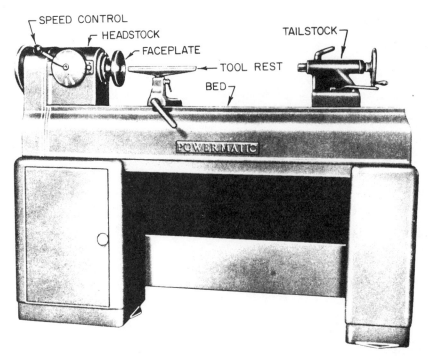

Fig. 35-1 Wood lathe *(Courtesy of Powermatic Houdaille, Inc.)*

stock is locked before turning the power on.

• Start turning at slow speed. The spindle speed may be increased after the wood is rounded.

• Small-diameter stock is turned at higher speeds than large-diameter stock.

• Keep the tool rest 1/8 inch from the stock being turned. Keep the top edge of the rest 1/8 inch above the lathe centers. Revolve the stock by hand to make sure it clears the tool rest.

• Hold turning tools firmly and in the correct position.

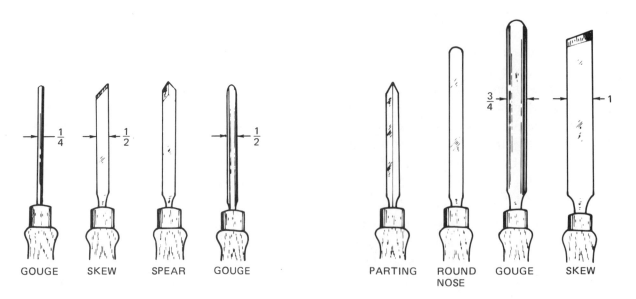

Fig. 35-2 Standard set of turning chisels *(Courtesy of Rockwell International)*

- Always stop the lathe before making any adjustments.

- Use moderate speed when turning stock on the faceplate or in a chuck.

- Follow the other general safety precautions in Unit 21.

PROCEDURE FOR FASTENING AND CENTERING STOCK IN THE LATHE

1. Select stock that is slightly larger than the largest diameter needed and at least 1 inch longer.

2. When turning legs that are to have square parts left on them, the stock is squared to finish size before mounting it on the lathe.

3. Draw diagonal lines across the ends of the stock.

4. Use a small drill bit or prick punch to make a small hole on both ends of the stock where the lines cross.

5. Remove the spur center from the lathe, place it in the hole, and drive it into the end of the wood with a mallet, figure 35-3.

6. Place the spur center back in the headstock.

7. Place a few drops of oil in the hole on the other end of the stock. Or, if preferred, rub beeswax or paraffin wax on the end of the dead center for lubrication purposes.

8. Place the stock in the lathe and clamp it tightly between centers, figure 35-4.

9. Adjust the tool rest until it is about 1/8 inch from the corners of the stock.

10. Turn the stock by hand to see that it clears the tool rest.

11. Start the lathe on slow speed. After it has run a minute or two, tighten the tailstock slightly.

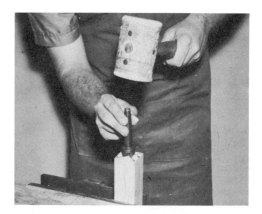

Fig. 35-3 Driving spur center into stock to be turned

Fig. 35-4 Turning cylinder with gouge

Fig. 35-5 Slipstone

PROCEDURE FOR TURNING A CYLINDER

1. Select a large gouge. If necessary, whet it with a slipstone until the edge is sharp, figure 35-5.

2. Start the lathe on low speed. Grasp the gouge as shown in figure 35-4.

3. Place the gouge on the tool rest. Guide the edge of the leading hand against the tool rest to act as a depth gauge.

4. Take a shearing cut with the heel of the gouge and cut from the tailstock toward the headstock.

5. Both right- and left-hand cuts may be made by reversing the hand positions.

6. Move the tool rest as necessary to maintain the recommended distance from the stock.

7. After the stock is turned to a cylindrical shape, set the outside calipers to a diameter equal to 1/8 inch greater than the desired finish size.

8. Hold the calipers in one hand and the parting tool in the other, figure 35-6.

9. Force the parting tool slowly into the wood until the calipers slip snugly over the wood. Be careful not to undercut.

10. Make cuts at several points on the spindle.

11. With the gouge, turn the stock down to the level of the parting-tool cuts.

12. Adjust the lathe for high speed according to the stock diameter.

13. Scrape or cut the cylinder to a diameter 1/16 inch over the finished size. The skew chisel may be used for this purpose.

PROCEDURE FOR SCRAPING WITH THE SKEW CHISEL

1. To scrape a cylindrical turning to finish size, lay the skew chisel flat on the tool rest. Have the cutting edge of the skew chisel parallel with the face of the stock, figure 35-7.

2. Move the edge slowly against the stock. Use the leading hand as a depth gauge. This is done by clamping the fingers tightly around the skew chisel with the edge of the hand resting against the tool rest.

Fig. 35-6 Using parting tool and calipers

Fig. 35-7 Scraping a cylindrical turning to shape

3. Move the skew chisel along the length of the stock until the desired diameter is obtained.

4. Check frequently with the calipers for the correct diameter.

PROCEDURE FOR CUTTING WITH THE SKEW CHISEL

1. Place the skew chisel on the tool rest and hold it in position, as shown in figure 35-8 or figure 35-9.

2. Adjust the skew chisel until its cutting edge is tangent to the face of the cylinder, figure 35-10. See also figure 35-8.

3. Twist the handle slightly with the right hand until the cutting edge comes in contact with the wood surface, about

Fig. 35-8 Skew chisel held between fingers for smoothing cylinders

Fig. 35-9 Taking shearing cut with skew chisel

halfway between the toe and heel of the skew.

4. Push the skew chisel forward toward the end of the stock and take a smooth, even shearing cut. After some practice, the skew may be used to cut in either direction by reversing the position of the hands.

SCRAPING METHOD FOR TURNING BEADS

1. Lay out the location of the beads on the cylinder.

2. If several beads are to be turned side by side, make a depth cut between them with the toe of the skew, figure 35-11.

3. Place the face of the skew chisel flat on the tool rest. Scrape the beads to shape with the cutting edge. Care must be taken to get a pleasing, half-round design.

CUTTING METHOD FOR TURNING BEADS

1. Make V cuts between the beads with the toe of the skew, figure 35-11.

2. Measure and mark a centerline for each bead with a sharp pencil.

3. Place the skew chisel on the tool rest with the heel of the skew lined up on the center of the bead, figure 35-12.

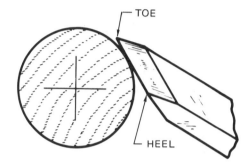

Fig. 35-10 Keeping cutting edge of skew chisel tangent to face of cylinder

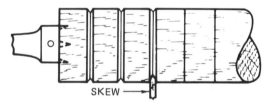

Fig. 35-11 Making V cut between beads with toe of skew chisel

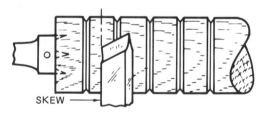

Fig. 35-12 Starting cut for bead

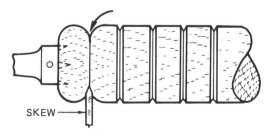

Fig. 35-13 Position of skew chisel with completing cut of bead

4. Start the cut from the centerline. As the skew moves forward, twist the handle so a rounded shape is cut to form one-half of the bead. When the cut is completed, the skew chisel should be in the position shown in figure 35-13. Depending on the bead size, it is sometimes necessary to make two or three cuts with the skew chisel.

5. Reverse the position of the hands and cut the other half of the bead. To use the skew chisel for cutting beads and other shearing cuts requires considerable skill. It is best to practice on scrap stock before making finished turnings.

SCRAPING METHOD FOR TURNING COVES

The cove is a concave cut and is opposite to the shape of a bead. If a single cove and bead of the same width are turned accurately, the bead would fit perfectly into the cove.

1. With the lathe on slow speed, lay out the width of the coves using the flat scale and a pencil.

2. Mark another line showing the center of each cove.

3. With the parting tool and calipers, make depth cuts on the centerline 1/8 inch shallower than the cove depth, figure 35-14.

4. Place the round-nose chisel flat on the tool rest. Make rounded cuts from the edges of the cove toward the centerline, figure 35-14.

5. Continue making light, scraping cuts until the exact shape is obtained.

6. Test the accuracy of the cove shape by stopping the lathe and moving the corner of a square back and forth in the cove, figure 35-15. If the edges of the square touch both edges of the cove and

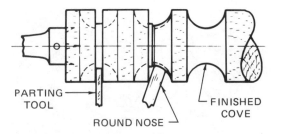

PARTING TOOL — FINISHED COVE — ROUND NOSE —

Fig. 35-14 Scraping coves to shape

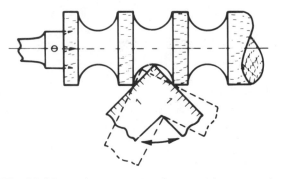

Fig. 35-15 Testing accuracy of cove with corner of square

Fig. 35-16 Starting cut for cove with gouge

the corner touches all cove surfaces as it is rotated, an accurate cove has been turned.

CUTTING METHOD FOR TURNING COVES

1. Lay out the width of the coves.

2. Select a gouge that is approximately one-half as wide as the cove.

Fig. 35-17 Position of gouge when cove cut
is completed

3. Place the gouge on edge and start the cut as shown in figure 35-16.

4. Push the gouge into the wood and turn the handle as it penetrates the wood.

5. When the cut for either half of the cove is completed, the gouge should be flat on the tool rest, concave side up, figure 35-17.

6. Make cuts from both edges of the cove until it tests true with the corner of a square, figure 35-15.

PROCEDURE FOR FACEPLATE TURNING

1. Square one face of the stock.

2. Scribe a circle on this face 3/8 inch larger than needed for the finish turning.

3. From the same center, scribe a second circle equal to the faceplate diameter.

4. Using the band saw, saw off the waste stock just outside the larger circle.

5. Place the faceplate on the smooth face of the stock. Mark around the screw holes in the faceplate with a sharp pencil.

6. Drill holes and fasten the stock to the plate with 3/4-inch No. 11 or No. 12 flathead screws. Be sure all screws are tight.

7. Remove the live center from the lathe and screw the faceplate to the headstock shaft, figure 35-18.

Fig. 35-18 Stock mounted on headstock for
faceplate turning

Fig. 35-19 Shaping lamp base on faceplate

8. Adjust the tool rest until it is 1/8 inch from the edge of the stock and slightly below center.

9. Rotate the stock by hand to see that it clears the tool rest.

10. Start the lathe at 1,000 rpm. Smooth the edge of the stock with the round-nose chisel until the desired diameter is obtained.

11. Stop the lathe and release the tool-rest tightener. Rotate it until its face is parallel with the face of the stock, figure 35-19.

12. With the round-nose chisel, smooth the face of the stock to the desired shape, figure 35-19. The next higher lathe speed may be used for this operation.

When turning bowls with thin bottoms, lids for round containers, and other pieces where both faces of the stock are shaped, it may be necessary to make a holding jig. For this method of turning, a scrap piece is fastened to the faceplate. Its face is then recessed so the stock can be inserted with a tight-press fit, figure 35-20. The stock may then be turned in the same way as other faceplate turning.

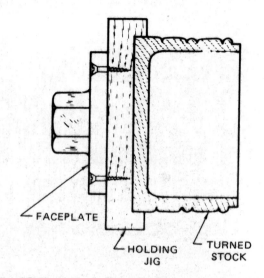

Fig. 35-20 Using holding jig for some types of face-plate turning

REVIEW QUESTIONS

A.   Multiple Choice

1. Before turning on the power, the operator should:
    a. make certain the lathe will come on at top speed.
    b. remove various items from the lathe bed.
    c. place the tool rest as far from the work as possible.
    d. rotate the lathe by hand to check setup.

2. It is necessary for:
    a. the operator to check stock occasionally to see if it has loosened between centers.
    b. the operator to revolve the work by hand to check for obstacles before starting.
    c. the stock to be cut to a circular shape where possible.
    d. all of the above.

3. The tool rest should clear the stock by:
    a. 1/32 inch.
    b. 1/16 inch.
    c. 1/8 inch.
    d. 1/4 inch.

4. When stock is held between the lathe centers, the type of turning is called:
    a. cylinder turning.
    b. faceplate turning.
    c. center turning.
    d. spindle turning.

B.   Short Answer

5. What are the two methods used to remove material from lathe stock?

6. How is the size of the wood lathe determined?

7. Name three types of turning tools and explain what each is used for.

8. When should all adjustments be made on the lathe?

unit 36
the stationary belt and disk sanders

OBJECTIVES

After completing this unit, the student will be able to:

- list five safety precautions to follow when using sanding machines.
- explain the proper sanding procedures for both the stationary belt and disk sanders.

The stationary belt and disk sanders, figures 36-1 and 36-2, are tools that may be used to smooth the ends, edges, and surfaces of stock.

The disk sander has a steel disk on which an abrasive paper is cemented. It usually has an adjustable table to support the workpiece. The sanding should be done on the part of the

Fig. 36-1 Stationary belt sander in horizontal position *(Courtesy of Rockwell International)*

233

Fig. 36-2 Stationary disk sander

disk that is moving down towards the table, figure 36-3. This keeps sawdust from being thrown into the operator's face.

The stationary belt sander has a wide abrasive belt supported on each end by flat pulleys. There is also a table that helps to support the stock while sanding. To accommodate the sanding operation, the sander may be set up in a vertical position, figure 36-4, or in a horizontal position, figure 36-1.

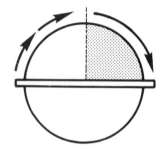

Fig. 36-3 Shaded area is the proper sanding
area on the disk sander

SAFETY PRECAUTIONS

- Use only light pressure while sanding.

- Sand only on the part of the disk sander that is rotating downward toward the table.

- Continually move the stock being sanded so the abrasive paper is not filled in any one place.

- Make adjustments only when the sander is stopped and unplugged.

- Do not sand small pieces that are difficult to hold on sanding machines.

PROCEDURE FOR USING THE DISK SANDER

1. Turn the machine on and allow it to come up to full speed.

2. Support the workpiece on the table. Slowly move the work into the sanding disk on the side where the disk is moving downward.

3. As the sanding begins, move the workpiece back and forth so you will not burn your wood or wear out or gum up the abrasive paper.

4. If possible, sand with the grain direction.

Fig. 36-4   Stationary belt sander in vertical position *(Courtesy of Rockwell International)*

PROCEDURE FOR USING THE STATIONARY BELT SANDER

1. Turn the machine on and allow it to come up to full speed.

2. Grasp the piece of stock in such a way that the fingers will not slip into the sanding belt. Slowly advance the stock until it comes in contact with the belt.

3. Move the stock from side to side to prevent burning and excessive wear on the belt.

4. Occasionally remove the stock to check progress.

5. If a large amount of material needs to be removed, it should first be cut to approximate size and then sanded. Stationary sanding machines are not meant to remove large quantities of material.

REVIEW QUESTIONS

Multiple Choice

1. Sanding should begin on a stationary sanding machine:
   a. as soon as the machine is turned on.
   b. only when the machine is warmed up.
   c. only after the sander is up to full speed.
   d. only when someone is helping.

2. While sanding on a stationary disk sander, the operator should:
   a. push hard to get done quickly.
   b. sand in the center of the disk.
   c. sand across the grain.
   d. move the piece from side to side to prevent clogging the belt.

3. On both the stationary disk and belt sanders the workpiece should be supported:
   a. by the hands.
   b. on the machine table.
   c. on another piece of wood.
   d. by one hand only.

4. Stock to be sanded on the disk sander should be placed:
   a. in the center of the disk.
   b. on either side of the disk.
   c. on the side of the disk that is rotating downward.
   d. on the side of the disk that is rotating upward.

5. Sanding machines should be used for:
   a. removing large amounts of stock.
   b. doing the final sanding just before finishing.
   c. smoothing boards to the same thickness.
   d. smoothing the ends, edges, and faces of boards after they have been cut to approximate sizes.

unit 37
the portable belt and finish sanders

OBJECTIVES

After completing this unit, the student will be able to:

- replace the belt on a belt sander and properly align the machine.
- correctly and safely use the portable belt and finish sanders.
- install abrasive paper on the finish sander.

Portable belt sanders, figure 37-1, are helpful in smoothing wood surfaces before the final hand-sanding operation. It is best, however, to remove mill marks with a hand plane or cabinet scraper before using the belt sander.

Belt sanders are available in many types and sizes. The size is indicated by the width and length of the belt. The 3-inch size with a dust collector is a good machine for most jobs.

Finish sanders, figure 37-2, are used for fine sanding where only a small amount of material needs to be removed. Most finishing sanders are designed so it is possible to use standard abrasive-paper sheets cut into one-half or one-third sheets.

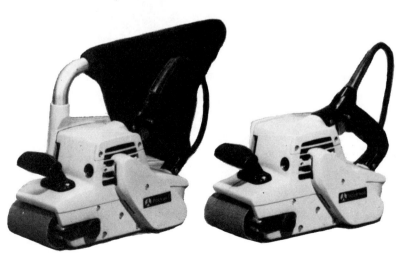

Fig. 37-1 Portable belt sanders *(Courtesy of Rockwell International)*

237

Fig. 37-2 Finish sanders *(Courtesy of Rockwell International)*

SAFETY PRECAUTIONS

- Place the power cord over your shoulder so it will not get caught in the sander.

- Properly support all work to be sanded.

- Hold the sander firmly with both hands.

INSTALLING AND ALIGNING A NEW BELT ON THE BELT SANDER

1. Lay the belt sander on its left side on the bench. Locate the tension release lever.

Move the lever so the belt may be removed, figure 37-3A.

2. Select a new belt and look on the inside to locate the arrow. Place the belt on the sander so the belt travels in the same direction as the arrow points, figure 37-3B. Release the tension lever.

3. With the sander still lying on its side, make sure the switch is off and plug the sander in. It is always best to plug in the

Fig. 37-3A Releasing tension lever on the belt

Fig. 37-3B Replacing a belt (Note direction of arrow.)

Fig. 37-4 Aligning the belt

sander when it is on its side. If the ma-machine is in this position, it will not run off the bench and be damaged.

4. Set the sander upright in its operating position and tilt it back so the belt is clear of the bench top.

5. Start the motor and adjust the belt aligning screw, located near the left-front side of the sander. Adjust the screw until the belt tracks in the center of the front pulley, figure 37-4.

PROCEDURE FOR SANDING STOCK WITH THE BELT SANDER

1. Place the stock flat on a sanding table. Fasten a thin cleat along one end of the table so the stock may rest against it.

2. Install a belt of suitable grit for the surface being sanded. A 60-grit belt is often used for the first sanding. A 100-grit belt may be used for the final machine sanding.

3. Place the power cord over the shoulder so it is out of the way while sanding.

4. Start the motor. Check to see that the belt runs true on the pulleys and adjust it if necessary.

5. Grasp the sander as shown in figure 37-5. Sand the full length of the stock. The position of the hands and the control of the sander are much the same as when using a hand plane.

6. Hold the sander level. This prevents it from making a deeper cut near the ends of the stock. It also prevents the edges of the belt from cutting grooves in the wood surface.

7. Do not apply extra pressure on the sander. This may burn out the motor. The weight of the machine is enough to get the desired results.

8. At the end of each stroke, move the sander over so that it slightly overlaps the last space sanded.

9. Continue sanding the surface until it is ready for the final hand sanding. A fine-

Fig. 37-5 Sanding the full length of stock

grade, worn sander belt is sometimes used for the final sanding.

10. When through sanding, empty the dust bag and clean the machine before storing.

INSTALLING ABRASIVE PAPER AND USING THE FINISH SANDER

1. Select the appropriate abrasive paper for the job. Generally, 100- to 120-grit paper is used for the first sanding. 180- to 240-grit paper is used for fine finish work.

2. Slip one end of the abrasive sheet under the front or rear clamping device and lock in place.

3. Fold the sheet back over the sanding pad and, while stretching it tight, clamp the abrasive sheet into the other clamp, figure 37-6. The abrasive paper must be held tight, or it will soon be ripped by the action of the sander. Retighten if necessary.

4. Place the power cord over your shoulder so it is out of the way.

5. Start the sander. Set the sander down on the work and begin moving with the

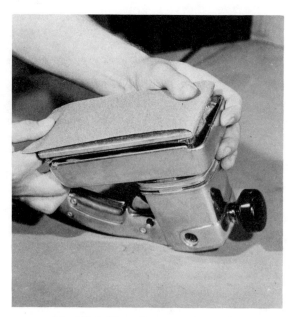

Fig. 37-6 Clamping paper to sander

grain in a back-and-forth motion in wide, overlapping arcs.

6. Do not put additional pressure on the sander beyond the weight of the sander. Excessive pressure causes the motor to overheat.

7. When sanding is complete, lift the sander off the work and shut it off.

REVIEW QUESTIONS

A. Multiple Choice

1. Before plugging in the belt sander, the operator should:
   a. check to see if the switch is off and lay the sander on its side.
   b. place the sander on the bench.
   c. turn it upside-down.
   d. hold the machine in one hand while plugging it in with the other.

2. Stock can be removed the fastest with the finish sander when:
   a. applying heavy pressure.
   b. it is operated in the left hand.
   c. allowing the sander to work under its own weight.
   d. applying very heavy pressure.

3. Before storing the belt sander:
     a. it should be turned upside-down.
     b. the belt should be removed.
     c. the alignment screw should be turned all the way in.
     d. the dust bag should be emptied and the machine cleaned.

B. Short Answer

4. Where should the power cord be located when using the portable belt and finish sanders?

5. How is the size of a belt sander indicated?

unit 38
bending wood

OBJECTIVES

After completing this unit, the student will be able to:

- list three methods of bending wood.
- explain one of the three methods of bending wood.

When constructing wood projects, it is often advantageous to bend wood to a particular shape. Some examples are skiis, seats, furniture legs, and the construction of large, curved laminated beams used to support buildings. Although wood does not bend easily, it may be bent using one of the three common methods. These methods are steaming, laminating, and kerfing, figure 38-1.

The wood to be bent should be straight grained and free of knots, checks, cross grain, or other defects. A strong form should be constructed. This allows the bent piece of wood to be held securely in place while the

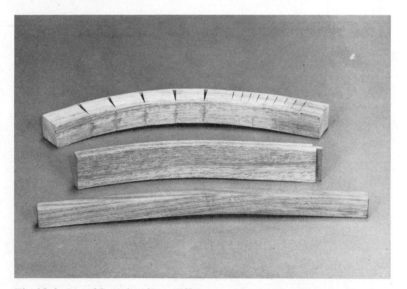

Fig 38-1 Wood bent by three different methods: steaming, laminating, and kerfing

242

piece is drying or the glue is setting. It is desirable to line this form with rubber so it applies a more even pressure to the wood.

STEAM METHOD

With this method, the wood is placed into a container where it is steamed. The steam produces heat and moisture that softens the wood fibers. This softening somewhat distorts the fibers and allows the wood to be bent around a form, figure 38-2. The wood is clamped to the form and allowed to dry. Upon drying, the wood takes the shape of the form with only slight springback. The amount of springback varies, depending on the kind of wood and the sharpness of the bend. Experience is necessary to accurately determine springback.

A large, flat-bottomed pan or cooking dish can be used to steam small pieces. It is filled with about two inches of water. A rack should be used to keep the wood above the water to prevent thoroughly soaking the wood. The container should also be fitted with a loose-fitting lid. This keeps as much of the steam in the container as possible, figure 38-3.

A better steaming device for long pieces of stock can be made by using a length of two-inch galvanized pipe fitted with a cap on

Fig. 38-2 Bending steamed wood around a form

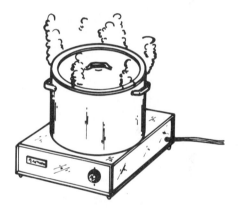

Fig. 38-3 Hot plate and large container with loose-fitting lid for steaming wood

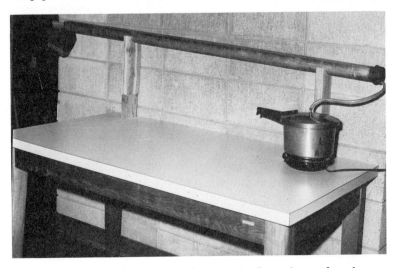

Fig. 38-4 Steaming device for steaming long pieces of stock

one end, and a connection to a hose that can be connected to a pressure cooker, figure 38-4. The upper end of the pipe should be lightly stuffed with a rag to keep as much steam in as possible. Never completely seal the pipe. This could cause a serious accident if the steam could not escape.

The best woods to select for steam bending are white oak, red oak, ash, and hickory. The time required for steaming may be estimated by allowing about one hour for each inch of thickness of the stock. For example, if the stock is 1/2 inch thick, it should be steamed for one-half hour. Steaming for a longer time does not increase the bendability of the wood. The material to be bent should be several inches longer than the required completed piece.

Do not be discouraged if some pieces break while bending. It takes considerable experience to successfully bend wood by steaming.

LAMINATING METHOD

Laminating is a layering process. Thin strips of wood bend fairly easily without steaming. If several strips are stacked on top of each other with glue between each layer, bent around a form, clamped, and allowed to dry, they will retain the shape of the form, figure 38-5. Depending on the thickness of the wood, fairly sharp curves may be made.

The laminating method is widely used in the construction industry to produce curves. Large buildings and sports arenas are often built with large, curved laminated beams. A major advantage of laminating wood is to increase its strength. The grain differences in each laminate tends to prevent splitting along any one grain line. Therefore, the strength of the laminated object is increased. In the furniture industry, laminating allows for the use of expensive veneers on the product surfaces and less expensive veneers for the interior laminations.

Fig. 38-5 Gluing laminated stock

Fig. 38-6 Kerfed stock ready for bending. (Notice the kerf does not extend completely through the stock.)

KERFING METHOD

The third method of bending wood is to cut small kerfs in the backside of the stock. These kerfs do not extend all the way through the material, figure 38-6. This allows the wood to be bent a small amount until the saw kerf comes together. If more of a bend is desired, more kerfs are cut in the back of the stock. After the desired bend is achieved, the kerfs are glued and the stock is clamped until the glue is set.

This method is fast. However, the back and edges of the bent pieces are not attractive. Veneer can be used to cover the unattractive parts. Kerfing should not be used where strength is required. It is often used to form the apron around the bottom of a table or other decorative trim that does not add strength to the furniture.

REVIEW QUESTIONS

A. Identification

1. List the three common methods of bending wood.

2. What is one of the major advantages of laminating wood?

B. Multiple Choice

3. Stock to be steam bent should be steamed for _____ hours for each inch of thickness.
    a. 1/4   c. 3/4
    b. 1/2   d. 1

4. When thin strips of wood are glued together to form thicker pieces, its strength compared to the solid piece is:
    a. weaker.   c. the same.
    b. stronger.   d. much weaker.

5. A disadvantage of cutting stock on the backside to bend it is:
    a. it takes a long time.
    b. it requires special equipment.
    c. it is weak.
    d. it has to be steamed a long time.

section 3

wood finishing

safety in the finishing area

OBJECTIVES

After completing this unit, the student will be able to:

- define flammable and inflammable and explain how spontaneous combustion can occur.
- list three pieces of specialized equipment that are needed to safely store finishes and soiled rags.
- correctly pour liquid from a gallon can.

Nearly all finishes contain materials that can catch fire. If a material is capable of catching fire, it is said to be *flammable*. However, the term *inflammable* also means the material catches fire easily. The misunderstanding of the term inflammable is the cause of many accidents. Because finishing materials are flammable, they should only be stored in a special explosion and flameproof cabinet, figure 39-1. Also, special containers should be provided for thinners and other solvents, figure 39-2.

Due to the poisonous fumes given off by most finishes, the finishing area must be well ventilated. It is also good to have a large, explosion-proof fan to use as extra ventilation. Even with an exhaust system, it is also important to wear a respirator, figure 39-3. Respirators filter out the particles of finish in the air when they are applied with a spray gun.

Fig. 39-1 Explosion and flameproof cabinet for the storage of flammable liquids

249

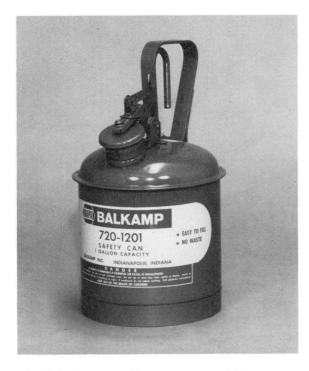

Fig. 39-2 Safety can for the storage of thinners and solvents

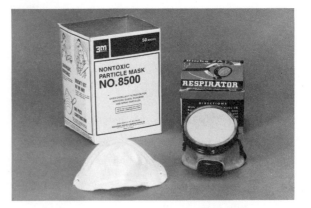

Fig. 39-3 Two types of respirators

Fig. 39-4 Metal safety container for disposing of soiled rags

Most finishing materials are not harmful to the skin, yet some newer finishes contain chemicals that irritate or burn the skin. Carefully read the container label to determine if rubber gloves are necessary.

Dispose of soiled rags, empty cans, and stirring sticks immediately after use. Rags soiled with finishing materials are particularly hazardous. If left wadded up, the oxygen in the air combines with the finish in the rag to produce heat. If the heat cannot escape, it builds up to the point where it can start the cloth on fire. This process is called *spontaneous combustion*. When through with a finishing rag, place it in a metal safety container, figure 39-4. All finishing areas should have at least one fire extinguisher. It should be easy to locate and plainly visible.

Disposing of used solvents, thinners, and other finishing liquids is a problem. Always have a special container that is plainly marked for disposal of these materials. It is not a good practice to pour thinners or finishes down the sink. They stick to the pipes and

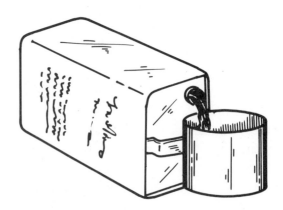

Fig. 39-5 The correct method to pour liquid from a square gallon can

eventually clog the drain. When the container is full, notify the fire department for proper disposal.

Try to keep from spilling finishing materials in the finishing area. The correct method to pour from a square gallon can is shown in figure 39-5. Keep plenty of rags or paper towels on hand to clean up spills. After cleaning up a spill, place these rags in the metal container.

REVIEW QUESTIONS

Multiple Choice

1. Which of the following terms indicates that a material ignites easily?
   a. Flammable
   b. Inflammable
   c. Nonflammable
   d. Both a and b

2. Finishing materials should be stored in:
   a. the finishing area.
   b. a flameproof cabinet.
   c. glass jars.
   d. sheet metal cabinets.

3. Dispose of rags that contain finishing materials by:
   a. placing them in a regular garbage can.
   b. waiting until there are several of them and then burn them.
   c. placing them in a special metal container used only for this purpose.
   d. putting them in the finishing cabinet.

4. Which of the following is the best way to pour liquid from a rectangular-shaped can?
   a. Rotate the pouring hole near the bottom.
   b. Turn the can upside-down and pour very fast.
   c. Turn the can upside-down and then open the lid.
   d. Turn the pouring hole so it is near the top.

5. The finishing area should be well ventilated for applying finishes. However, when spraying, added protection is provided with the use of:
   a. a respirator.
   b. a safety gun.
   c. a flameproof suit.
   d. rubber gloves.

unit 40
abrasives

OBJECTIVES

After completing this unit, the student will be able to:

- list four kinds of abrasives used on abrasive paper.
- explain the various grit sizes of abrasive paper.
- list two other abrasives used in finishing that are not coated on paper.

Abrasives are used to give a smooth finish to the raw wood surface. They are also used to smooth and polish finishing coats that have been applied to the wood surface. Some of these abrasives are coarse and cut rapidly. Others are very fine. This prevents them from leaving scratches when smoothing and polishing the final finishing coats.

ABRASIVE PAPER

The material found on the cutting side of abrasive paper is similar to sand. A close look shows that the particles are pointed rather than round like grains of sand. The term *sandpaper* does not accurately describe this material. Abrasive paper is actually crushed flint, garnet, aluminum oxide, or silicon carbide.

Abrasive Materials

Flint is a mineral that has been used extensively for abrasive paper in the past.

Flint paper can be identified by its tan color and it is the cheapest of the abrasive papers. However, it is the least durable of most other abrasives and has a comparably shorter life. *Garnet* is also a mineral with a reddish brown color. Garnet is far more durable than flint and is widely used in the woodworking trades. *Silicon carbide* is a hard abrasive that is blue-black in color. It is also used widely in the woodworking field. Aluminum oxide has a brownish grey color. This abrasive is very durable and is primarily used for machine sanding.

Crushing and Grading Abrasives

Abrasives are manufactured by first crushing the selected abrasive into fine particles. These particles are then screened into various sizes. This is done by constructing very fine screens with a different number of openings per inch. If 180-grit paper is to be made, the screen will contain 180 openings

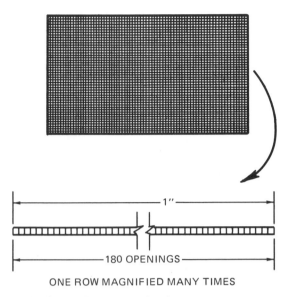

Fig. 40-1 Grading screen for 180-grit abrasive paper

Grade	Al. Oxide Sl. Carbide (Grit No.*)	Garnet (Grit No.)	Flint (Size No.)	Use
Very Fine	600 500 400 360 320 280 240 220	280 240 220	5/0 4/0	Polish, Finish
Fine	180 150 120	180 150 120	3/0 2/0 1/0	Finish Sanding
Medium	100 80 60	100 80 60	1/2 1 1 1/2	Cabinet Sanding
Coarse	50 40 36	50 40 36	2 2 1/2 3	Rough Sanding
Very Coarse	30 24 20 16 12	30 24 20		Coarse Sanding

*The grit number means that the grit can pass through a screen with the designated number of meshes to the lineal inch.

Table 40-1 Size of grits for different abrasives

per inch for each row of the screen, figure 40-1. After the abrasive has been screened, it is bonded to the paper by an electrical charge. This charge is used to force the abrasive material onto the glued paper surface.

Coated abrasives are either open coat or closed coat. *Close-coated abrasives* have all space covered with abrasive grains. *Open-coated abrasives* have some space between the abrasive grains. Close-coated abrasives cut faster, but open-coated abrasives do not plug up when smoothing finishing materials.

A sheet of abrasive paper is usually 9 by 11 inches. It is packed in sleeves of 50 or 100 sheets, or in units of 500 or 1000 sheets. They are graded in various degrees of coarseness, ranging from No. 600 grit to No. 12 grit, as indicated in table 40-1.

Abrasive papers coarser than 120 grit (medium, coarse, and very coarse) are used for smoothing wood surfaces before the final sanding with No. 120 or No. 150 grit. Garnet, aluminum oxide, and silicon carbide abrasive papers are excellent for producing smooth surfaces quickly. The coarse and medium grades are used first and the final sanding is done with the fine grade. The finer grades of abrasives, No. 600 to No. 220, are used for rubbing surfaces after the finishes have been applied. Some abrasive papers are made so they can be used dry or lubricated with water, oil, or other lubricating materials. When abrasive paper is used on a hand-rubbed finish, wet-or-dry abrasive paper should be used.

TIPS FOR USING ABRASIVE PAPER

Abrasive paper can best be used by tearing it into four equal parts. This is done by tearing it along the edge of a framing square or over a piece of wood on a bench, figure 40-2. A quarter sheet is enough for most small projects. It is best to use the abrasive over a rubbing block. When curved or irregular surfaces are sanded, the block is made to fit the surface shape.

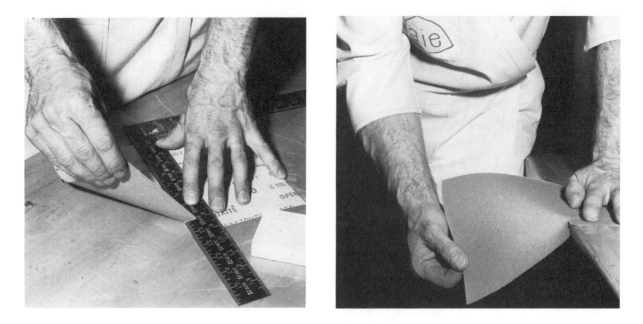

Fig. 40-2 Two methods of tearing abrasive paper

Make sure the work surface has been thoroughly planed and scraped before using abrasive paper. Before you stop sanding, make sure a smooth surface is obtained.

Sufficient sanding insures a smooth surface when finished. Be sure the abrasive paper is worn out before throwing it out.

After the final sanding, remove all dust from the surface. Give a final inspection for imperfections. If none are visible, the project is now ready for the finish to be applied.

OTHER ABRASIVES

Steel Wool

Steel wool, which is made of finely shredded steel, is used to smooth shellac and other finishes. It may leave scratches which must be smoothed with fine pumice stone or rottenstone. The coarseness or fineness of steel wool is indicated by numbers ranging from No. 0000, the finest, to No. 3, the coarsest.

Pumice Stone

Pumice stone is a powder material that is used for rubbing down finished surfaces. This

Fig. 40-3 Using pumice stone with felt pad

powder is usually mixed with water or rubbing oil to form a rubbing paste. It is white to gray in color and is available in either powder or lump form.

A felt block or felt blackboard eraser can be used for rubbing the finishing coats with pumice, figure 40-3. Keep the pumice stone and rubbing oil in separate cans. The lids should have several holes to allow the powder and rubbing oil to be sprinkled on the surface being rubbed.

Rottenstone

Rottenstone, a finely ground limestone, is used for rubbing and smoothing finished surfaces. This material is mixed with oil or water to form a paste. It is applied the same way as pumice stone. When water is used with rottenstone for rubbing a lacquered or varnished surface, it produces a high-gloss finish. If a dull surface is desired, it should be rubbed with pumice and oil.

Rubbing Compound

Special rubbing compounds for rubbing lacquer finishes are made in paste form, ready for use. Since they cut faster than rottenstone, be careful not to rub through the finish. Rubbing compound can also be used with a buffing machine.

REVIEW QUESTIONS

A. Short Answer

1. List three kinds of abrasives that are used on abrasive paper.

B. Multiple Choice

2. Which of the following grits is finer than grit number 120?
   a. 50 grit
   b. 220 grit
   c. 100 grit
   d. 00 grit

3. When tearing abrasive paper into four equal parts, the proper method to use is:
   a. to cut the paper with a pair of scissors.
   b. to place the paper over a piece of wood on a bench and tear it.
   c. to place the paper with the rough side down on the bench and tear it along the edge of a framing square.
   d. either b or c.

4. Which of the following is the finest grade of steel wool?
   a. 0000
   b. 0
   c. No. 1
   d. No. 3

5. Which of the following powdered abrasives is the finest?
   a. Steel wool
   b. Pumice
   c. Rottenstone
   d. Flint

unit 41
preparing surfaces for finishing

OBJECTIVES

After completing this unit, the student will be able to:

- point out mill marks left in the surfaces of stock that have been machined.
- list three types of crack fillers and explain how each is used.
- properly sand wood surfaces and edges for finishing.

After the project is constructed, the task of preparing it for the finishing coats and applying the finish still remains. Preparing the surface for the finish includes the removal of all machine and plane marks and defects.

The surface must be perfectly smooth and free from defects. No amount of finishing materials can produce a smooth, even finish. Finish applied over mill marks and other defects, figure 41-1, magnifies rather than hides them.

Sometimes it is impossible to scrape and sand out all defects. Nail holes, dents, checks, and pits caused by faulty grain, especially in cedar, usually cannot be removed from the surface. It is necessary to fill these defects.

REPAIRING WOOD SURFACES

If possible, the best crack filler to use is a piece of the same wood that the project is made from. Care should be taken to select a piece that matches the wood color and also

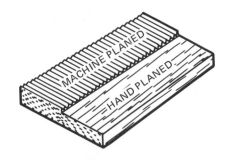

Fig. 41-1 Hand planing to remove mill marks

Fig. 41-2 Equipment for applying stick shellac

256

Fig. 41-3 Three kinds of crack fillers used for repairing wood surfaces.

the grain. Once a piece is matched, it can be carefully cut to size and glued into place.

Stick shellac is another crack filler used by finishers, figure 41-2. This material comes in a large variety of colors. It must first be heated to the semiliquid state with a hot knife before using it. Once it is forced into the

crack and allowed to cool, the surface can be sanded smooth. Make sure to select a color that will match the wood after the finish has been applied.

Plastic wood, figure 41-3, is available in several wood colors. If carefully applied, it can give very satisfactory results. Plastic wood should be forced into the crack or hole

Fig. 41-4 Raising a dent by steaming

with a putty knife or small spatula. When hard, it can be sanded smooth.

Putty stick is another material commonly used for filling nail holes and cracks in furniture, figure 41-3. These sticks are available in a large variety of shades and colors. It should be used after the finish has been applied to the project. Select the stick that best matches the finished project.

Force the putty into the opening with a small spatula or putty knife. Wipe off the excess with a cloth pad.

When filling large areas on a project to be painted, water putty is an excellent crack filler to use, figure 41-3. To prepare the putty, carefully follow the directions on the package and sand when dry.

PREPARING WOOD SURFACES
FOR FINISHING

1. Before assembling the project, remove all mill marks from the visible parts with a plane or a cabinet scraper.

2. In assembling, be sure to place waste stock under the jaws of the clamps. This prevents marring the finished surface.

3. Remove all traces of glue from around the joints because stain cannot penetrate glue.

4. If dents are found on the surface, remove them. This is done by applying a cotton pad soaked with hot water or by moistening the dent with cold water and applying a hot iron to it, figure 41-4. Make sure the iron is not so hot that it burns the wood. Repeat this operation until the defect is raised slightly above the surface next to it.

5. Remove the shallow defects by scraping lightly with a hand scraper.

6. Defects that cannot be removed, such as checks and holes, are filled with the appropriate crack filler.

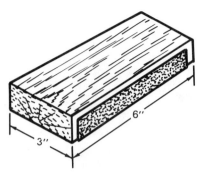

Fig. 41-5 Sandpaper block

Fig. 41-6 Sanding a flat surface

7. After the crack filler hardens, work it down until it is nearly level with the surface next to it.

8. Make a block for sanding similar to the one shown in figure 41-5. A piece of tire tube is sometimes wrapped around the abrasive-paper block. This forms an elastic base for the abrasive paper.

9. Wrap a sheet of medium-fine abrasive paper around the block. With even pressure, sand all flat surfaces with the grain, figure 41-6. Avoid a circular motion and be careful not to round the arrises.

10. Sand the edges of the stock as shown in figures 41-7 and 41-8.

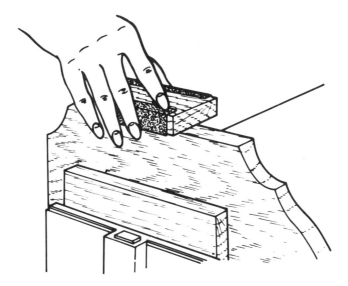

Fig. 41-7 Sanding flat edge

Fig. 41-8 Sanding rounded edge

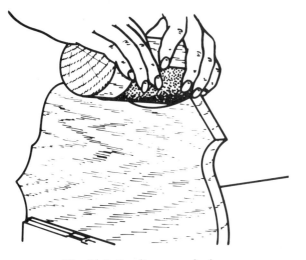

Fig. 41-9 Sanding curved edges

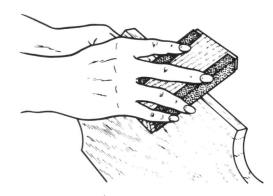

Fig. 41-10 Removing sharp arrises

11. Sand curved surfaces by fitting the abrasive paper to the surface shape. Abrasive paper is sometimes wrapped around a block shaped to fit certain curved edges, figure 41-9. When sanding curved edges, use a forward motion with the grain.

12. When thoroughly sanded, brush off the dust with a stiff brush. Inspect to make sure the surfaces are free from blemishes.

13. If water stain is used, sponge the surfaces lightly with water and allow them to dry.

14. Sand the surfaces again with a fine-grade abrasive paper. Give the arrises a light stroke or two to remove the knifelike edges, figure 41-10.

15. Remove the dust from the surfaces and give a final inspection for imperfections. If none are visible, the project is now ready for the finish to be applied.

REVIEW QUESTIONS

A. Identification

1. List four different materials that are used to fill cracks and holes in a project.

2. Which crack filler should be used when filling large areas on a project that is to be painted?

B. Multiple Choice

3. A properly applied finish:
   a. hides a poor sanding job.
   b. covers up dents and scratches in the project.
   c. magnifies the defects.
   d. covers up some of the defects.

4. Small dents may be removed from the surface by:
   a. steaming with a damp cloth and hot iron.
   b. wiping on a coat of shellac.
   c. sanding across the grain.
   d. none of the above.

5. All flat surfaces should be sanded:
   a. in a circular motion.
   b. in a straight motion with the grain.
   c. in a straight motion across the grain.
   d. with a back-and-forth motion.

unit 42
kinds and composition of wood stains

OBJECTIVES

After completing this unit, the student will be able to:

- list three common wood stains.
- properly apply all of the stains listed above.

Stains are used to bring out the grain in wood, enrich the color, and change the color of an inexpensive wood to look like a more expensive wood. For example, some furniture that is sold as walnut is red gum stained with a walnut stain.

All stains have a coloring agent and a solution of solvent to carry the stain into the wood pores. The most common stains are oil stains, water stains, and non-grain-raising stains.

OIL STAINS

Oil stains are the easiest to apply, do not raise the wood grain, and are more easily obtained in different colors. However, they do not penetrate the wood deeply. They also have a tendency to fade and do not give the clear color that some other stains do. Some shades of oil stains can be purchased ready-mixed. These are walnut, mahogany, maple, fruitwood, cherry, and shades of oak.

Pigment oil stains are made of finely ground color particles, or pigments, and mixed in a liquid such as linseed oil or mineral spirits. *Penetrating oil stains* have better penetrating qualities than pigment oil stains. They are made from dyes dissolved in materials such as turpentine and naphtha. *Wiping stains* are concentrated pigment oil stains that are used for shading purposes. The excess stain is wiped off to highlight the wood surface.

WATER STAINS

Water stains are inexpensive, are a darker, but clearer color, fade less, darken sap streaks easily, and penetrate deeply into the wood. The main disadvantage of water stain is that it raises the wood grain and, therefore, requires an extra sanding.

Water stain should be diluted with water before applying it to end grain. This prevents the end grain from becoming darker than the side grain. Water stains are applied with a rubber-set brush. They are allowed to dry without removing the extra stain.

NON-GRAIN-RAISING STAINS

Non-grain-raising stains (NGR) produce the same clear color as water stains. However, they do not raise the wood grain. They are made by dissolving colored dyes in glycol and alcohol and used primarily in industrial finishing.

Using non-grain-raising stains saves considerable time because they dry fast. When brushing these stains, use a large brush. This allows the application of the stain to the surface rapidly. NGR stains penetrate the wood very rapidly. Therefore, it is necessary to apply the stain evenly and quickly.

TIPS ON APPLYING STAINS

Stains may be purchased in a variety of colors, but it is usually necessary to change these colors slightly to fit particular needs.

Before applying stains to a project, select a piece of scrap wood similar to that used for the project. Test the stain on it. If the stain is too dark, dilute it and repeat tests until the desired color is obtained.

It is difficult to determine the results of staining until the other finishing coats have been applied. Therefore, it is advisable to apply the other finishing coats to these scrap pieces to determine the exact color.

Dry, colored powders or colors ground in oil may be used to change the color of oil stains. Colored powders may also be used to change the shades of water stain.

It is best to apply stain with a rubber-set brush, although it may be applied by spray gun. The brush should be about 2 inches wide with medium-soft bristles. Long, even brush strokes are applied the full length of the surface. The brush should be well filled with stain. A dry brush tends to leave streaks.

PROCEDURE FOR APPLYING OIL STAIN

1. Select a suitable stain.

2. Select a piece of scrap wood similar to that used for the project. Test the stain

Fig. 42-1 Applying linseed oil to end grain

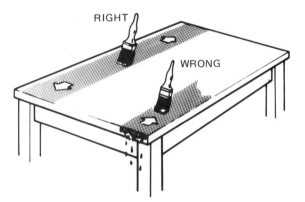
Fig. 42-2 Brushing toward arrises

Fig. 42-3 Removing surplus oil stain

on it. If the oil stain is too dark, lighten it by adding linseed oil and turpentine.

3. Apply a coat of linseed oil to the end grain of all project parts to reduce darkening, figure 42-1.

4. Apply the stain with long, even strokes from the middle of the surface toward the arrises, figure 42-2. Do not allow the stain to build up in the middle by overlapping brush strokes. Stain the top of the project first, leaving the lower and inside parts until last.

5. Leave the stain on the surface for a minute or two. Then, remove the surplus

with a dry cloth by rubbing with the grain, figure 42-3.

6. Allow the stain to dry for 6 hours.

7. Wipe the surface carefully to remove all dust particles.

8. If the wood is open-grained (woods having large, open pores such as walnut, oak, mahogany, and ash), it is now ready to be filled with paste filler. Another method is to mix the oil stain with the paste wood filler and apply it all at once.

9. If a close-grained wood (wood with small, closed pores such as boxwood, cedar, cherry, and Douglas fir) is stained, a thin coat of shellac or sealer should be applied.

PROCEDURE FOR APPLYING WATER STAIN

1. Sponge the surface lightly with water.

2. Allow 2 hours or more to dry. Sand lightly with fine-grade, worn abrasive paper.

3. Dust the surface carefully. Apply a diluted coat of stain to the sap streaks with a small, fine-bristled brush, figure 42-4.

4. After these streaks dry thoroughly, sand them again lightly.

5. Apply an even coat of stain to the entire surface. Stain the top first, leaving the lower and inside parts until last.

6. Check the edges and ends for runs and brush them out. The surplus water stain is not removed from the surface. It is allowed to dry into the surface. Therefore, make sure the stain is brushed on evenly and is free from brush marks and laps.

Fig. 42-4 Staining sap streaks

7. Allow 6 hours to dry. Then sand very lightly with fine, worn abrasive paper before applying another finish.

8. If an open-grained wood is stained, apply a coat of the proper color paste filler.

9. If the wood is close-grained, apply a coat of shellac or sealer.

PROCEDURE FOR APPLYING NON-GRAIN-RAISING STAIN

1. Select the stain nearest to the desired color. Apply it to a piece of scrap wood of the same kind as that used for the project.

2. If the stain is too dark, dilute it with denatured alcohol or a special stain thinner produced by the stain manufacturer.

3. Pour out a small amount of the stain, dilute it further, and apply it to the end grain.

4. Apply stain, mixed in Step 1, quickly and evenly to the remaining surfaces. Stain the top first, leaving the lower and inside parts until last.

5. After the stain is allowed to dry for about 1 hour, sand the surfaces lightly with a worn or very fine-grade abrasive paper.

6. Remove any dust particles from the wood pores with a stiff-bristled brush.

7. Remove any remaining dust particles with a clean *tack rag* (rag moistened

with varnish to remove dust from wood surfaces).

8. If working with an open-grained wood, the surface is now ready for the paste filler. If it is a close-grained wood, apply shellac or sealer.

Caution: Most finishes are made from flammable materials. They must be kept away from open flames. Be careful to place all oily rags in a metal container. This eliminates the danger of a fire caused by spontaneous combustion.

REVIEW QUESTIONS

A. Identification

1. List three common wood stains.

B. Multiple Choice

2. Before applying wood stain to a project, the stain should first be:
   a. diluted with oil.
   b. tested on a scrap piece of wood.
   c. applied to the underside of the project.
   d. applied only over a seal coat of shellac.

3. When staining, special treatment is required on the end grain of a project to prevent:
   a. blemishes.
   b. filling the grain.
   c. sealing the pores of the wood.
   d. darkening the grain.

4. When applying stain with a brush, drips and runs can best be avoided on the ends by:
   a. brushing from one end only.
   b. starting in the middle of the surface and brushing toward the ends.
   c. brushing the stain on all of the ends first.
   d. turning the project on its side.

5. After a stain has been applied and is dry, the next step is:
   a. to give the project a second coat of stain.
   b. to sand the surface with coarse abrasive paper.
   c. to apply the final finish coat.
   d. to sand very lightly, dust, and apply a coat of shellac or sealer.

unit 43
paints, enamels, and other opaque finishes

OBJECTIVES

After completing this unit, the student will be able to:

- list the two major ingredients of paint.
- describe what thinner should be used for oil-base and latex paints.
- properly apply paint to a project with a brush and from a spray can.

PAINTS AND ENAMELS

Paints and enamels are opaque finishes used as coatings on inexpensive woods where a solid color is desired. To produce a quality job, opaque finishes require a primer coat and at least one finish coat. The most common uses of paints are for finishing exterior and interior surfaces around the home. The two ingredients of paint, listed on the paint can, are pigment and vehicle. Also included on the paint can is the percentage of each ingredient as well as the makeup of each, table 43-1.

Pigment

The pigment is the part of the paint that gives it the color. The pigment is mixed with the vehicle to produce a certain color. Paint stores often purchase white paint and then tint or color the paint to produce the desired color.

Vehicle

The vehicle in paint allows the pigment to be evenly spread over a large surface. The

Composition by Weight	
Pigment	32.3%
Vehicle	67.7%
	100.0

Composition of Pigment	
Titanium Calcium	57.4%
Chrome Yellow	42.6%
	100.0

Composition of Vehicle	
Alkyd Varnish	44.1%
Drier	2.6%
Mineral Spirits	53.3%
	100.0

Table 43-1 Composition of paint

vehicle is made up of various oils, resins, and dryers. These aid in the paint application. If the vehicle is a varnish base, the paint is called *enamel*. Enamels produce a harder and smoother surface than other paint types. They dry rapidly and are available in high-gloss, semigloss, or flat finish. Oil-resin and latex paints use water as a vehicle. These paints are easy to apply and hold color well. They also dry quickly, making it possible to apply two or more coats a day.

THINNERS

Paints and enamels must also contain a thinner that allows for the thinning of the paint so it may be easily applied with a brush or spray equipment, table 43-2. Common thinners for enamels and oil-base paints are turpentine or mineral spirits. Turpentine is a thin, colorless, flammable liquid used to thin paints and varnishes. Mineral spirits is manufactured from petroleum. Water is the thinner used for latex and oil-emulsion paints.

COLORED LACQUERS

Lacquer can either be sprayed, brushed, or wiped on. Between each coat of lacquer, the surface should be sanded lightly or rubbed with steel wool. Lacquer produces a hard, durable surface. Colored lacquers and lacquered enamels are often used for finishing automobiles and outdoor furniture.

WATER REDUCIBLE ACRYLIC FINISHES

Water reducible acrylic finishes are a recently developed product used for the coating of woods and other materials to be finished. These finishes include spray stains, acrylic sealers, and water reducible acrylic semigloss finish for finish coating.

Water reducible finishes eliminate some of the fire hazards created by using a nitrocellulose-based lacquer. They are easier to clean than other finishes because soap and water is used. When applying water reducible finishes, carefully follow the directions on the container.

PROCEDURE FOR APPLYING PAINT AND ENAMEL WITH A BRUSH

1. To get satisfactory results when applying brush-on finishes, it is important to

Finish	Thinner
Oil stain	Naphtha, turpentine, benzol, linseed oil
Water stain	Water
Spirit stain	Denatured alcohol
Paste wood filler	Benzine, turpentine
Shellac	Denatured alcohol (190 proof)
Lacquer	Lacquer thinner
Lacquer sealer	Lacquer thinner
Varnish (oil)	Turpentine
Enamel	Turpentine
Paint (oil-base)	Linseed oil and turpentine
Paint (water-base)	Water

Table 43-2 Thinners for various finishing materials

prepare the surface to be finished as explained in Unit 40.

2. Select a place that is free of dust and has good light.

3. Cover the floor with paper that will collect paint that might drop.

4. Properly prepare the paint by stirring and mixing. Add thinner if necessary.

5. Select a good quality brush with fine bristles.

6. Dip the brush bristles into the paint one-half to one-third of their length. Remove the surplus paint with a slight tap on the bristles on the side of the can. Never drag the side of a good brush across the edge of a can. This damages the bristles.

7. Apply the paint to the surface with light, even strokes while permitting the paint to flow with as little brushing action as possible.

8. Apply the paint with the grain and then level it out across the grain with light strokes. Finish with long, even strokes with the grain.

9. Apply the paint to the lower parts first. Make sure to properly coat the hard-to-

reach places. Apply the finish to the flat surface last.

10. Allow the finish to dry following directions on the container. Apply additional coats if necessary.

PROCEDURE FOR APPLYING PAINT FROM A AEROSOL SPRAY CAN

A large variety of finishes are available in the aerosol can. Small projects and parts may be finished with aerosol cans instead of spending money for larger containers of finish. Aerosol cans also eliminate a messy cleanup. When properly used, an excellent paint job can be obtained with an aerosol can.

1. Prepare the surface to be finished.

2. Select a place that is well ventilated, free of dust, and has adequate light.

3. Place paper under the project and behind it. This avoids getting the over-spray on other items.

4. Shake the spray can vigorously for approximately two minutes.

5. Hold the nozzle of the spray can 10 inches to 12 inches from the work surface. If the can is held too far away from the surface, the spray will be too thin when it reaches the surface. This produces a spotty appearance. If the can is held too close, the paint builds up and runs result.

6. Begin moving the can and then open the valve completely by pressing it down all the way. Release the spray valve before stopping. The proper technique is to spray in a series of short bursts. Only spray while the can is moving.

7. Best results are achieved by applying several light coats rather than one or two heavy coats.

8. Hold the finger on top of the nozzle just enough to spray the paint. Do not extend the finger over the nozzle. Drops of paint will form on the nozzle and then splatter the surface.

9. After spraying the finish, turn the can upside-down and spray until the spray is clear. This cleans the nozzle so the can may be used later.

CARE OF EQUIPMENT

When cleaning equipment such a brushes, rollers, and spray guns, use the thinner recommended for each finishing material. Equipment cleaning must be done immediately after completing the job. Otherwise, the paint dries and it becomes difficult to remove.

REVIEW QUESTIONS

Multiple Choice

1. The two ingredients of paint, which are listed on the can, are:
   a. thinners and dryers.
   b. pigment and vehicle.
   c. pigment and dryers.
   d. vehicle and thinners.

2. Which of the following is used as a thinner for latex paint?
   a. Linseed oil
   b. Turpentine
   c. Mineral spirits
   d. Water

3. What is the name of the finish that uses varnish as a vehicle?
   a. Latex paint
   b. Enamel
   c. Oil-base paint
   d. Lacquer

4. Which of the following is used as a thinner for oil-base paint?
   a. Turpentine   c. Linseed oil
   b. Water   d. Alcohol

5. When applying paint from a spray can, the operator should:
   a. hold the can 10 inches to 12 inches from the surface.
   b. spray in short bursts only while the can is moving.
   c. apply several light coats rather one heavy coat.
   d. all of the above.

wood fillers

OBJECTIVES

After completing this unit, the student will be able to:
- explain the purpose of wood fillers and properly apply wood fillers.
- list the two major classifications of wood fillers.

All wood has pores which form the grain or pattern of the wood. Wood fillers are used to fill the pores of wood so there is a smooth surface before the final finish is applied. If woods with small pores (close-grained woods) such as birch, maple, gum, and pine are filled at all, a liquid filler or sealer is used. Woods having large pores that are easily visible (open-grained woods) such as oak, walnut, mahogany, and chestnut, are visible and leave the wood surface rough. These should be filled with a paste wood filler.

Paste wood filler is available in various standard wood colors or it is available in the natural color and tinted to the desired shade. When tinting wood filler, use an oil stain that has been thinned. This allows the oil stain to easily mix with the wood filler.

Before filler is applied to wood, it is thinned with naphtha, turpentine, or paint thinner to the consistency of heavy cream. At this consistency, it quickly goes through the pores of the wood. For open-grained woods make the filler thick. For close-grained woods make it thin.

Liquid filler is also used to fill and seal open-grained woods after paste wood filler has been applied. Shellac and lacquer sealer are two finishes commonly used for sealing purposes. To make a wash coat (seal) of shellac, mix equal parts of shellac and alcohol and apply it to the surface with a brush. Lacquer sealer may be thinned with lacquer thinner if necessary. Make sure to clean shellac brushes in alcohol and lacquer brushes in lacquer thinner.

When a light shade of finish is desired, it is sometimes possible to stain and fill the wood in one step. Refer to Unit 42, for a procedure for applying oil stain.

If a two-tone design is desired, the part which is to be left the natural wood color is given a coat of shellac or sealer before the paste filler is applied. This prevents the filler from coloring the wood.

PROCEDURE FOR APPLYING PASTE FILLER

1. Stir the filler thoroughly. Thin it to the consistency of thick cream.

2. Try the filler on a piece of stained, scrap stock of the same kind as that used for the project.

3. If necessary, change the color of the filler to the desired shade.

4. Using a stiff-bristled brush, clean the pores of the wood to prepare it for the filler.

5. Apply the filler by brushing it across and with the grain, figure 44-1.

    Let the filler stand until the gloss and thinner disappear. This takes about 4 minutes to 8 minutes.

6. Rub the filled surface in a circular motion with the palm of the hand. This packs the filler tightly into the pores.

7. Rub the surplus filler off with pieces of burlap or old rags, figure 44-2. Rub across the grain to prevent removing the filler from the pores.

8. When most of the excess filler has been removed, use a clean cloth to finish removing the oil and surplus filler.

9. Remove the filler from recesses and corners with a rag stretched over a soft pine stick that is sharpened to a point. For deep carvings, remove the filler with a scrubbing brush.

10. Rub the surface very lightly with the grain to remove streaks of filler that may

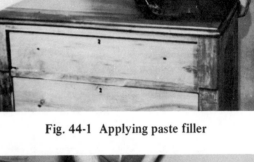

Fig. 44-1 Applying paste filler

Fig. 44-2 Removing surplus filler

have been left when the surface was rubbed across the grain.

11. Allow from 6 hours to 12 hours to dry and then rub the surface lightly with a cloth dampened with thinner (optional).

    The next step is to apply a thin coat of shellac or sealer over the filler. Lacquer, varnish, or additional coats of shellac may then be applied to the surface.

REVIEW QUESTIONS

A. Multiple Choice

1. The purpose of wood filler is to:
   a. change the color of the wood.
   b. make the wood harder so it will not scratch.
   c. fill the pores of the wood so a smooth surface can be achieved.
   d. cover up the grain pattern of the wood.

2. Wood fillers can be classified into which of the following groupings?
   a. Thin and thick fillers
   b. Liquid and paste fillers
   c. Cream and lumpy fillers
   d. Regular and special fillers

3. Paste wood filler should be wiped off the surface as soon as:
     a. the finish turns dull.   c. as soon as it is applied.
     b. after 6 to 8 hours.   d. it is not necessary to wipe it off.

4. A brush used to apply shellac should be cleaned in:
     a. turpentine.   c. lacquer thinner.
     b. paint thinner.   d. alcohol.

B. Completion

5. Paste wood filler is used on _____ (open-grained or close-grained) woods.

unit 45
shellac

OBJECTIVES

After completing this unit, the student will be able to:

- explain what a 4-pound cut of shellac is.
- list two common types of shellac and three advantages of using shellac.
- properly apply a shellac finish.

Shellac is one of the easiest finishes for the inexperienced finisher to apply. When properly thinned, it flows on easily and seldom shows streaks. Shellac dries dust free in about 30 minutes and is ready to recoat in 3 to 4 hours. A shellac finish requires several thin coats. This allows the finisher to go over the mistakes made and to smooth out blemishes caused by the preceding coats.

Shellac produces a fine finish on wood. Shellac is also used as a sealer and undercoat for other finishes such as varnish, paint, enamel, and lacquer. As an undercoat, shellac prevents some finishes from raising the wood fibers. It also prevents them from absorbing too much of the finishing coats. Few finishes have the natural adhesion quality of shellac. A finish of shellac is flexible and does not check or craze (crack in a coating) when properly applied in several thin coats. One disadvantage of shellac is that is turns cloudy if water is allowed to stand on the surface. To prevent this, liberally apply wax over the final finish.

Shellac is generally sold as 3-pound or 4-pound cut. A 4-pound cut means there are 4 pounds of powered lac, the base of shellac, dissolved in 1 gallon of denatured alcohol. For nearly all applications, shellac must be thinned to properly apply a smooth coat. Table 45-1 gives the proper thinning ratios to reduce 3-pound or 4-pound cut to thinner cuts of shellac.

Two kinds of shellac, orange and white, are available for use in wood finishing. The

If you start with:	Add this much alcohol per qt.	To make this cut of shellac
4-pound cut	1/2 pint	3-pound
4-pound cut	1 1/2 pints	2-pound
4-pound cut	4 pints	1-pound
3-pound cut	1/2 pint	2-pound
3-pound cut	3 pints	1-pound

Table 45-1 Quantities to use for thinning shellac

orange shellac is the natural color after it has been refined. This color is unsuited for finishing light-colored wood. Therefore, a bleaching process is used to make the shellac practically colorless. White shellac gives a clear, colorless finish.

Shellac has been a very popular finishing material. However, other clear synthetic finishes have replaced shellac in modern furniture manufacturing. Industry still uses shellac in the manufacture of articles such as buttons, wood cements, sealing wax, crack fillers, and for finishing leather.

PROCEDURE FOR APPLYING SHELLAC

Do not apply shellac on a surface where varnish, enamel, lacquer, or wax has been used. When applied over other finishing coats, the differences in the amount of shrinkage of these finishes cause the shellac to check and peel.

1. Make sure the stain or filler on the surface is dry. The surface must also be dust free.

2. Reduce the shellac to a 1-pound cut. At this ratio, the shellac brushes on easily and dries quickly. It also penetrates and adheres to the surface better. Thicker solutions of shellac will not dry as rapidly or be as hard.

3. Dip the brush bristles almost the full length in the shellac. Remove the excess by wiping the sides of the brush on the container.

4. Start at the top of the vertical surfaces, such as table legs, and brush downward laying the shellac on smoothly. Brush slowly so air bubbles are not made.

5. Shellac the lower parts of the project first. Leave the top until last. Shellac dries rapidly and becomes very sticky soon after application. For this reason, apply shellac quickly and evenly. Continual

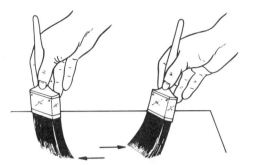

Fig. 45-1 Applying shellac

Fig. 45-2 Shellac and brush container

brushing causes shellac to pile up and turn white. Lay it on with the grain and work the entire length of the piece, figure 45-1. Avoid end laps since they show more plainly than edge laps. Avoid brushing away from the edges. This wipes the extra shellac out of the brush causing runs to form. If runs occur, wipe them out immediately with the brush.

6. Clean the brush in alcohol immediately after each use. The brush may also be suspended in a container of shellac, as shown in figure 45-2. With the tight-fitting lid, the shellac does not dry out and is ready for immediate use.

7. After the first coat has dried for 3 hours to 4 hours, sand the surface lightly with 220-grit abrasive paper. Sand with the grain using light, even strokes. Best results are obtained if an open-coated abrasive paper is used since the shellac tends to plug the abrasive paper quite rapidly. Another method is to use No. 0 or No. 00 steel wool.

8. Wipe the surface with a clean cloth.

9. Apply the second and third coats the same way as the first. If desired, slightly less alcohol may be used to mix with the shellac. This will make a thicker coat with each application.

10. When thoroughly dry, rub each coat with 220-grit abrasive paper or steel wool.

11. Rub the final coat of shellac with No. 0000 steel wool or 400 finishing paper and rubbing oil.

12. Remove all traces of rubbing compound and oil from the surface with a clean cloth dampened with benzine.

13. Inspect the surface carefully to be sure there is a smooth surface.

14. Allow 5 minutes to 10 minutes for the surface to dry. Then apply a coat of wax with No. 0000 steel wool.

15. Allow the wax to dry. Polish the surface thoroughly with a soft, clean cloth.

REVIEW QUESTIONS

Multiple Choice

1. Which of the following is not a property of a shellac finish?
   a. It provides a waterproof finish.
   b. It is very easy to apply.
   c. It has a natural adhesion quality.
   d. It does not check or craze.

2. The two types of shellac are:
   a. light and dark.
   b. white and brown.
   c. orange and white.
   d. clear and white.

3. Shellac brushes should be cleaned immediately after use in:
   a. turpentine.
   b. water.
   c. thinner.
   d. alcohol.

4. A 4-pound cut means:
   a. that the finish weighs 4 pounds.
   b. the finish will not scratch with a 4-pound weight.
   c. 4 pounds of lac is dissolved in a gallon of alcohol.
   d. 4 pounds of alcohol is mixed with 4 pounds of lac.

5. When applying shellac to a surface, how should it be applied?
   a. Quickly and evenly
   b. Very slowly
   c. Without thinning
   d. With a rag

unit 46
varnish

> **OBJECTIVES**
>
> After completing this unit, the student will be able to:
>
> - list three classifications of varnishes.
> - discuss four ways to help prevent dust particles from getting on a freshly-applied varnish surface.
> - properly apply a varnish finish.

Varnishes are a mixture of manufactured plastic resins and petroleum thinners, figure 46-1. Varnish may be applied by brush, roller, or spray gun. As the thinners evaporate, the varnish becomes a hard, durable surface with excellent wearing properties. Depending on the varnish type and manufacturer, the drying time ranges from 4 hours to 36 hours. However, most varnishes will dry dust free within one hour. Varnishes are available in glossy, semiglossy, satin, or flat mixtures.

Varnish may be classified into one of three categories, depending on the chemical composition. The categories are alkyd, phenolic, or urethane-base varnishes. The ingredients of varnish can be determined by looking at the label on the container. Generally, the alkyds are the least expensive. The urethanes are the most expensive and probably the most durable. They resist abrasion and chemicals better than the other types. Always read the

Fig. 46-1 Materials needed for applying varnish

directions and recommendations on the container carefully before selecting or applying varnish.

Many modern varnishes do not require a sealer coat to be applied to new wood before the varnish is applied. Most recommend using a thinned coat of varnish as the sealer coat.

275

The greatest difficulty in applying varnish is caused by dust. As dust settles on the finished surface, it makes small defects that remain after the varnish has dried. Follow the precautions listed below to get the best possible finish.

1. Varnish in a well-ventilated room. The temperature should be between 70 degrees and 80 degrees.

2. The finish room should be as dust free as possible. Even the slightest amount of dust will ruin a varnish finish. Place the project in the room. Leave it for at least an hour to allow for the dust to settle. When re-entering the room to apply the finish, move slowly to avoid raising dust particles.

3. Select clothing that is dust free, such as dacron and nylon.

4. Remove all dust from the project, particularly in the corners and crevices where dust can collect and be picked up by the brush.

5. Just before applying the varnish, wipe the surfaces with a tack rag.

PROCEDURE FOR APPLYING VARNISH

1. Prepare the project carefully by sanding with 240 or finer-grit abrasive paper. Watch for fingerprints or other dirt on the project. These detract from the finish.

2. If a stain or filler has been used, make sure it is dry. Move the project into the finishing area.

3. In a shallow can, figure 46-1, prepare a seal coat of varnish by mixing 1 part turpentine to 8 parts varnish. This sealer provides a better surface for the manufactured varnish to adhere to and prevents possible problems with finish coats.

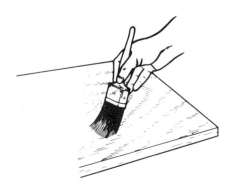

Fig. 46-2 Flowing varnish on with the grain

Fig. 46-3 Smoothing first coat
by brushing across the grain

4. Select a quality varnish brush and clean it. Make sure it is perfectly clean. This should be done even to a new brush.

5. Wipe the surface with a tack rag to remove any remaining dust.

6. Dip the brush bristles about one-third of the way into the prepared varnish and apply a full even coat to the surface, figure 46-2. Gradually raise the brush as you near the edges at the end of each stroke.

7. Work the varnish across the grain to smooth all previous brush strokes, figure 46-3.

8. Tip off the varnish using only the extreme tip of the bristles, figure 46-4. This makes the work as smooth as possible.

9. Clean the brush with turpentine. Put the remaining varnish in an appropriate container. It is not a good practice to return

any varnish back to its original container. If the varnish has dust particles, it will make the remaining varnish impure.

10. Allow the project to dry at least 24 hours or longer. Read the labels on the container carefully to determine when the varnished surface should be recoated. Some varnishes require recoating before a particular time to allow for good adhesion between coats.

11. Remove the project from the finishing area.

12. Sand the varnish coat carefully with 240-grit abrasive paper. This provides a surface for good adhesion and also levels any high spots.

13. Dust thoroughly and return the project to the finish room.

14. Pour full-strength varnish into a clean, shallow can.

15. Clean the surface with a tack rag. Apply the second coat of varnish as explained above.

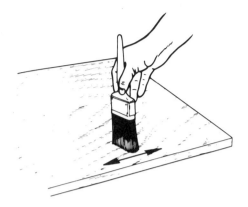

Fig. 46-4 Tip off varnish with tip of brush using light, smooth strokes with the grain.

16. After drying, the surface may be rubbed with wax or worked down with a felt pad and pumice. Mix the pumice and water to a paste consistency. Wet the surface and rub with the wood grain with the felt pad. Rub until the entire surface is dulled. Clean the surface with a clean rag. Complete the rubbing process using rottenstone and a new felt pad. Clean the surface again with a clean cloth and apply wax and polish.

REVIEW QUESTIONS

Multiple Choice

1. The manufactured varnishes now available are made from:
   a. shellac and turpentine.
   b. oil and sealers.
   c. plastic resins and petroleum thinners.
   d. pigments and vehicle.

2. Which of the following is not a category that manufactured varnishes may be classified in?
   a. Alkyd-base varnishes
   b. Oil-base varnishes
   c. Phenolic-base varnishes
   d. Urethane-base varnishes

3. When applying varnish, the greatest difficulty is caused by:
   a. dust.   c. sealing.
   b. sanding.   d. rubbing.

4. A sealer coat for a varnish finish is made by:
    a. using a white-base paint.
    b. brushing on a coat of linseed oil.
    c. mixing equal parts of shellac and varnish.
    d. thinning the varnish with turpentine.

5. If there is varnish left in the can after finishing a project, it should:
    a. be dumped back into the original container.
    b. be left to dry.
    c. be applied to the project until it is used up.
    d. be placed in the proper container for disposal.

unit 47
lacquer

OBJECTIVES

After completing this unit, the student will be able to:

- list two advantages of using lacquer for a finish.
- properly apply a lacquer finish with a spray gun.

Lacquer dries hard in 4 hours to 6 hours and produces a durable, water-resistant surface. It is available in a clear finish or several colors, figure 47-1. A special lacquer thinner is used for thinning most lacquers. It is advisable to use the same brand thinner as the lacquer used.

Do not apply lacquer directly over oil fillers, oil varnishes, and oiled surfaces. If oil unites with the lacquer, this prevents the lacquer from drying. When an oil filler is used, coat the surface with shellac or a special undercoater made for this purpose. The shellac or undercoater acts as a sealer for the stain and filler and prevents the lacquer from uniting with them.

Lacquers are available which produce a high-gloss, a medium-gloss, or a flat finish.

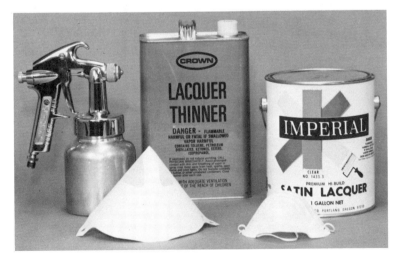

Fig. 47-1 Equipment required for spraying lacquer

279

Medium-gloss and flat-finished lacquers usually build less rapidly than high-gloss lacquers. For this reason, it is sometimes advisable to first apply a coat of the high-gloss lacquer followed by a coat of medium-gloss or flat lacquer.

If lacquer is applied smoothly, very little rubbing is required between coats. Because lacquer dries fast, dust particles do not effect the surface as much as they do on a varnish finish. Each succeeding coat dissolves and unites with the previous coat. Therefore, it is difficult to touch up surface spots, especially when applied with a brush.

The preferred method of applying lacquer is with spray equipment. With this method, an even coat is applied in a very short time.

The last coat of lacquer is rubbed smooth with a rubbing compound. Another way to do this is with either pumice stone or rottenstone and water. No. 0000 steel-wool pads loaded with paste wax may be used for rubbing the final coat. No. 500 finishing paper lubricated with water may also be used.

Aerosol Spray

Practically any finishing material can be purchased in an aerosol can. The aerosol can is held from 10 inches to 12 inches from the surface to be coated. Use a slow, sweeping motion along the full length of the surface to apply the spray. Refer to Unit 43 on Applying Paint From An Aerosol Spray Can.

Applying Heated Lacquer

To avoid thinning the lacquer and to obtain a heavy coat with one application, industrial finishers sometimes heat the lacquer before spraying it. Lacquers are highly flammable. Therefore, the heating is done by placing the open lacquer container in hot water and keeping it away from open flames.

USING A SPRAY GUN

Considerable skill is required to apply finishes properly with spray equipment. However, the spray gun has many advantages over the hand brush for applying lacquer. The finish can be applied more quickly and evenly, and the difficult parts are more easily reached.

If good results are to be obtained with the spray gun, all parts must be kept perfectly clean. It is also essential that the materials sprayed through the gun be thin and kept free from dirt specks and lumpy materials. It is a good practice to strain all material through a cloth before it is used. Special paint strainers are available for this purpose, figure 47-1.

The spray gun is generally used for applying lacquer. It may also be used for applying shellac, varnish, enamels, and paints. However, a special nozzle is necessary for handling these thicker finishes.

PROCEDURE FOR APPLYING LACQUER

Caution: Only operate the spray gun in a spray booth that has adequate ventilation. Always use a protective face mask.

1. Pour enough sealer into the spray gun cup to cover the project. Dilute the sealer one-third to one-half with lacquer thinner and stir thoroughly.

2. Fasten the cup to the spray gun and the gun to the air supply. While operating the spray gun, a constant pressure of 40 pounds to 60 pounds must be maintained.

3. Hold the trigger of the gun back. With a slow, uniform motion, apply the liquid spray to the surface in a similar manner as when using the hand brush. Spray the full length of the surface each time. Release the trigger at the end of each stroke. This prevents wasting material and applying it too heavily on the surface ends. Keep the nozzle of the gun a distance of 10 inches to 12 inches from

the surface for the full length of the stroke, figure 47-2. The operator's body must follow the movement of the gun. The body must not remain stationary.

4. Apply the finish to the lower parts of the project first. Leave the top until last.

5. Add more thinner if the liquid seems to go on dry and grainy.

6. After applying each coat of finish, remove the container from the gun. Insert the fuel pipe of the gun into a container of thinner. Press the trigger and allow enough thinner to be drawn through the gun to clean it thoroughly. After each use, take the gun apart and clean the parts with lacquer thinner.

7. Allow 2 hours for the first coat to dry.

8. Apply succeeding coats of lacquer. Additional drying time is required for each additional coat. Three coats of clear lacquer are enough to give a durable finish.

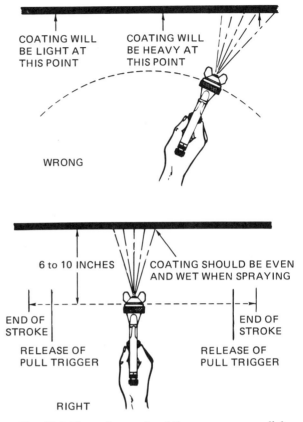

Fig. 47-2 Keep the nozzle of the spray gun parallel to the surface being sprayed. *(Courtesy of Binks Manufacturing Company)*

REVIEW QUESTIONS

Multiple Choice

1. Which of the following is not an advantage of a lacquer finish?
   a. It dries rapidly.
   b. It produces a durable finish.
   c. It is water resistant.
   d. It is easy to apply.

2. The preferred method of applying lacquer is:
   a. with a brush.   c. with a clean cloth.
   b. with a spray gun. d. with steel wool.

3. When using the spray gun, which of the following is a good practice to follow?
   a. Strain all material to be sprayed.
   b. Strain only material that has been in partially used cans.
   c. Use a pressure of 100 pounds.
   d. Use the finishes as they come from the can.

4. Which of the following precautions should be followed when using the spray gun?
   a. Only operate the gun in a spray booth with adequate ventilation.
   b. Operate the gun only with two other people.
   c. Always wear a protective face mask.
   d. Both a and c

5. When spraying with either the spray gun or the aerosol spray can, the distance between the work and the nozzle should be
   a. 2 to 4 inches.   c. 8 to 10 inches.
   b. 6 to 8 inches.   d. 10 to 12 inches.

unit 48
wipe-on finishes

OBJECTIVES

After completing this unit, the student will be able to:

- list three advantages of using wipe-on finishes.
- list the three classifications of wipe-on finishes.
- properly apply wipe-on finishes.

Finishes such as shellac, varnish, and lacquer all require considerable effort to apply them properly and in a dust-free manner. The finishing industry researched and developed new finishes that could produce quality results even when applied under dust conditions. These finishes were also developed so they could be applied easily and with as few mistakes as possible. Due to these reasons, finishing companies have products that are classified as wipe-on finishes, table 48-1.

Wipe-on finishes have the advantage over other finishes of being economical, time saving, and easily applied. This is because they are applied with a small cloth or pad which is thrown out after use.

These finishes are tough and moisture resistant. Several are resistant to heat, mild acids, and scratches. The presence of dust does not affect wipe-on finishes.

Many wipe-on finishes dry quickly, and two or three coats can be applied during a two-hour period. Other wipe-on finishes require just as much drying time as other finishing materials.

The types of finishes available are flat, semiglossy, and glossy. With so many wipe-on finishes, it is difficult to categorize them. This is because some have very deep penetration with very little body buildup, and others leave a rather thick coating on the wood surface. Wipe-on finishes are generally classified as wax-based finishes, oil finishes, and natural and synthetic resin finishes, see table 48-1.

WAX-BASED FINISH

The wax-based finish has a pleasing glow. When an eggshell gloss finish is desired, the wax-based finish is easy to apply. The wax-based finish goes well with other interior finishes and color schemes. Yet, they are not as durable as some of the varnishes and synthetic surface coatings. Therefore, carefully

Trade Name	*Classification	Producer
Beauty Lock	S	Sherman-Williams Co.
Constantine Pad-Lac	S	Alber Constantine and Sons
Constantine Penetrating Finish	S	Alber Constantine and Sons
Clear Plastic	S	Steelcote Manufacturing Co.
Deep Finish Firzite	O	U.S. Plywood Corporation
Deft	S	Deft Inc.
DuraSeal	S	International Chemical Co.
DuPont Penetrating Finish	S	E.I. DuPont DeNemours and Co.
801 Clear	S	Cook Paint and Varnish Co.
666 Perfection Oil	O	M.L. Campbell Co.
Ez-E Oil Finish	O	Golden Star Polish Manufacturing Co.
Ez-E	S	Golden Star Polish Manufacturing Co.
French Polish	S	many companies
Intex	S	American Marietta Co.
Kwik-On	S	McCluskey
Linseed Oil	O	many companies
Minwax	W	Minwax Co.
Rez	S	Monsanto Chemical Co.
Sealacell	W	General Finishes Sales and Service
Spee-D-Dry	S	Acme Quality Paints
Swedish Oil	O	R.H. Miller Co.
Tone-Lac	S	James B. Day and Co.
Wax Paste	W	many companies
Wax Stain Cabot	W	Cabot Inc.
Satinlac	S	U.S. Plywood Corp.
Watco Danish Oil	O	Watco-Dennis Corporation
Whisk-On	S	M.L. Campbell Co.
Wilco-Seal	O	Wilson-Imperial Co.
Wood-Kote	S	Spe-de-way Products Co.
Woodmate	S	James B. Day and Co.
*O = Oil Finish *S = Synthetic Finish *W = Wax-based Finish		

Table 48-1 Trade names, manufacturers, and classification of wipe-on finishes

choose the wax-based finish for the surface it is to be used on.

OIL-BASE FINISH

An oil-base finish applied to the darker woods such as mahogany, cherry, and walnut produces a very pleasing effect.

The most common oil finish is tung oil. Tung oil produces a rich color on a properly prepared wood surface.

After the tung oil is applied to the wood, it is rubbed until a dull, satin gloss appears. The degree of color depends on how much the wood absorbs the oil. Tung oil has a pleasing, darkening effect on woods such as cherry, birch, walnut, and mahogany. However, it is seldom used on light woods. For producing different colored effects, tung oil can be colored or tinted with colors in oil.

An oil-finished surface never cracks, chips, or blisters. It is particularly good for furniture which may be easily spotted or scratched. When oil finish is properly applied, the wood is resistant to water, heat, scratches, and most stains.

NATURAL AND SYNTHETIC RESIN FINISHES

There are many natural and synthetic resin finishes. In many ways these finishes are like shellac, varnish, and lacquer. The only difference is that they are applied to the wood surface with a cloth. Several natural and synthetic resin finishes can be tinted with pigment oil colors to produce various colors. Some of these finishes are deep penetrating and very little finish remains on the surface. Others build up considerable thickness. These can be rubbed to the desired sheen in the same manner as varnish and lacquer.

PROCEDURE FOR APPLYING WIPE-ON FINISHES

Since wipe-on finishes have several different properties, always follow the manufacturer's directions.

Sealacell Process

The Sealacell process consists of three finishes: Sealacell #1, Varnowax #2, Royal Finish #3, figure 48-1. These liquids are applied with small cloths that are thrown out after use.

1. Sand the surface carefully with 240-grit or finer abrasive paper.

2. Liberally apply the Sealacell #1 with a small cloth.

3. Allow 12 hours for drying. Lightly sand the surface with 360-grit paper or rub with No. 0000 steel wool.

4. Clean the surface with a clean cloth. Apply a coat of Varnowax #2 in a circular motion with a small cloth pad. Wipe off excess with the grain.

5. Allow 12 hours for the surface to dry. Again sand with 360-grit paper or No. 0000 steel wool. Wipe with a clean rag.

6. Apply the third coat, Royal Finish #3, in the same manner as the second coat.

7. Allow 12 hours for drying. Rub down with 360-grit paper or No. 0000 steel wool. If desired, apply additional coats to obtain a deeper luster. The surface

Fig. 48-1 Sealacell finish

Fig. 48-2 Watco Danish oil finish

may also be polished with a furniture polish.

Watco Danish Oil Finish

Danish oil finish penetrates the wood and combines chemically with the wood to produce a hard, durable surface, figure 48-2.

This finish is particularly recommended for walnut.

1. Sand the surface carefully with 240-grit or finer abrasive paper. Wipe clean.

2. Apply the oil liberally, flooding the surface. Continue to keep the surface wet for at least 15 minutes. This assures the proper penetration of the oil. Wipe the surface dry watching for damp spots that continue to reappear.

3. Allow the surface to dry for at least 4 hours. Sand the surface with 600-wet-or-dry abrasive paper. Use Watco oil finish as a lubricant. This sanding tends to fill the wood pores and produces a fine, satin finish. Wipe clean and dry with a soft cloth.

Deft Clear Wood Finish

Deft is an interior finish that seals and finishes the wood, figure 48-3.

1. Sand the surface with 240-grit or finer abrasive paper. Wipe clean.

2. Liberally apply Deft with a brush, roller, or with a cloth.

Fig. 48-3 Deft wipe-on finish

3. Allow the surface to dry for 2 hours. Lightly sand with 240-grit abrasive paper. Wipe clean.

4. Apply additional coats in the same manner. Generally three coats should be applied.

5. To produce a hand-rubbed effect, rub the final coat with No. 0000 steel wool and furniture polish if desired.

REVIEW QUESTIONS

A. Multiple Choice

1. Which of the following is not true of most wipe-on finishes?
   a. They are easy to apply.
   b. They must be applied in dust-free places.
   c. They may be applied with a cloth.
   d. They save considerable time.

2. The best way to find out how to apply a particular wipe-on finish is:
   a. by reading about it in a book.
   b. to have a friend tell you.
   c. by experimenting with the finish.
   d. by carefully reading the instructions on the container.

B. Short Answer

3. List the three classifications of wipe-on finishes.

section 4

careers in woodworking

unit **49**
_____

occupational
opportunities

OBJECTIVE

After completing this unit, the student will be able to:

- explain the different career opportunities that are available in the woodworking industry.

The occupations related to the various phases of woodworking are many. Only the largest classifications are discussed in this unit. A more detailed description of job opportunities is available from the *Occupational Outlook Handbook* which was prepared by the Bureau of Labor Statistics, U.S. Department of Labor.

WOOD SCIENTISTS AND TECHNOLOGISTS

Wood scientists study the biological, physical, chemical, and engineering properties of wood to define laws and principles governing its structure and behavior under different environmental conditions, figure 49-1. Wood technology deals with applying knowledge of the nature of wood to the job of developing new products and processes.

The wood scientist is normally involved in research and development projects. Commercial lumber companies and government-sponsored laboratories conduct a variety of projects, such as the architecture, nature,

and utilization of wood fiber (using optical and electron microscope techniques). A phase of research which is currently receiving

Fig. 49-1 Wood scientist testing vertical strength of wood samples

Fig 49-2   Taking inventory on logs going through a headrig

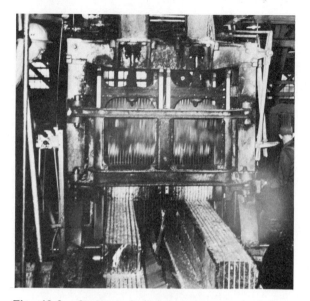

Fig. 49-3   Operator inspects gang saw turning out paneling

attention is the identification of those wood-fiber characteristics which are important in manufacturing high-quality paper and board products. By working with the forest tree breeder, the wood scientist may be able to raise future trees with the best possible types of fiber for papermaking.

While there is some overlapping with the wood scientist in types of work done, the wood technologist is usually employed in a variety of positions. These include the production and manufacturing of wood and its many products, development of new products and processes based on scientific findings, technical sales, marketing of wood products and products used by the wood manufacturing industries, and activities to upgrade the efficiency of wood-based industries.

In the manufacturing and production of wood products, the wood technologist may find employment in the primary or secondary conversion segments of the industry, figures 49-2, 49-3, and 49-4. Primary conversion consists of those firms whose principle operation is breaking down logs into lumber or veneer. Secondary conversion industries are those firms concerned with processing or remanufacturing, such as in the manufacture of decorative or structural plywood, laminated beams and arches, furniture, flooring, millwork,

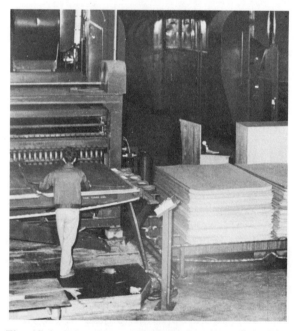

Fig. 49-4   Trimming veneer sheets to be used for plywood manufacture

flake and chipboard, hardboard and softboard, building components, and many other specialty items.

Wood technologists are required to have at minimum a college degree with a major in wood science and technology from a recognized forestry school. Fundamental high school courses should include physics,

Fig. 49-5   Workers constructing concrete forms
(Courtesy of American Plywood Association)

Fig. 49-6   Applying marine plywood to boat
framework

Fig. 49-7 Applying plywood sheathing to framework
of building

chemistry, biology, mathematics, and communication skills, as well as woodworking instruction.

BUILDING TRADES

The building trades offer opportunities in many special areas. These include concrete-form builders, rough-in carpenters, roofers, interior finishers, and interior and exterior decorators, figure 49-5.

Building interiors require the most skillful installation of panels and moldings, stairways, door and window frames, partitions and custom built-in cabinets. Many of these items are constructed in industrial plants and later installed by the general carpenter.

Carpenters represent the largest group of building trades workers, figure 49-6, employed in almost every type of construction activity. They erect the wood framework, trim, stairs, and floors in buildings, figure 49-7. The framework includes subflooring, sheathing, partitions, floor joists, studding, and rafters. The finish work, where appearance as well as structural accuracy must be considered, consists of molding, wood paneling, cabinets, window sash, door frames, doors, and hardware.

Carpenters also install heavy timbers used to build docks, railroad trestles, and similar structures. They build the forms needed to pour concrete decks, columns, piers, and retaining walls used in bridges, buildings, and other structures. They also erect scaffolding and temporary buildings at construction sites.

The ability to make working drawings and to read blueprints is essential for those in the building trades. Knowledge and use of hand and machine woodworking equipment is also a basic requirement for workers in this field. Vocational and apprenticeship training programs are normally the best way to learn a particular building trade.

PATTERNMAKERS

Wood patternmakers are highly skilled craftspersons employed in metal foundries. They build patterns used in making molds. From these molds, metal castings are formed.

The wood patternmaker selects the appropriate stock, lays out the pattern, marks the design for each section on the proper piece of wood, and saws each piece roughly to size. The rough pieces are then shaped into final form, using various woodworking machines and hand tools. Finally, the pattern segments are assembled by hand, using glue, screws, and nails. Standardized colors are used to finish the pattern.

FURNITURE INDUSTRY

Highly skilled woodworkers are employed in the manufacture of furniture used in homes, offices, schools, and many other buildings. Hand and machine carvings are used extensively in the furniture industry. Much of the work is done with precision woodworking machines. The application of stains and finishes is also an important part of furniture manufacturing.

A good introduction to the fundamentals of shaping wood with machines and a basic knowledge of furniture can be gained in a high school industrial arts course in cabinetmaking. Later, advanced training may be acquired in vocational and apprenticeship programs.

TEACHING

The teaching profession offers a rewarding career for those with skills in woodworking and a desire to work with people. Woodworking teachers may be employed in secondary schools, vocational-technical schools, two-year colleges, and special training programs for migrant workers, the aged, and the disadvantaged and handicapped. They also work in large industries as instructors of in-service training and the operation of machinery.

WOODWORKING AS A HOBBY

Woodworking is one of the most popular hobbies. This is because it offers the beginning woodworker an extremely wide range of projects that can be completed with the use of only a few tools.

In many communities, adult education classes are offered. These classes meet the demands of more ambitious woodworkers who wish to increase their knowledge and skills in the use of hand and power tools.

REVIEW QUESTIONS

Identification

1. List five different career opportunities that are available in the woodworking field and explain what each career involves.

WORKING DRAWINGS AND PICTURES

IN	MM
5	127
$5\frac{1}{4}$	133
10	254
3	76
$\frac{3}{4}$	19
$\frac{1}{2}$	13
$3\frac{1}{4}$	83
8	203
$4\frac{1}{2}$	114
$\frac{1}{4}$	6
$25\frac{1}{2}$	648

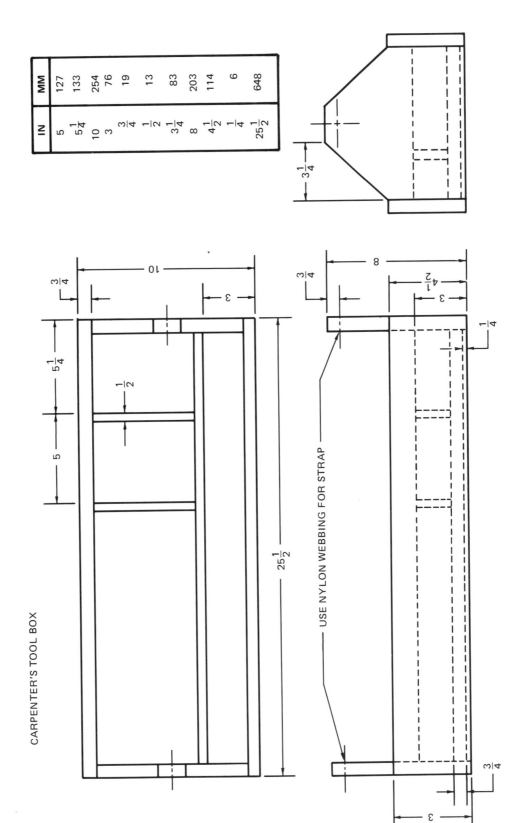

CARPENTER'S TOOL BOX

USE NYLON WEBBING FOR STRAP

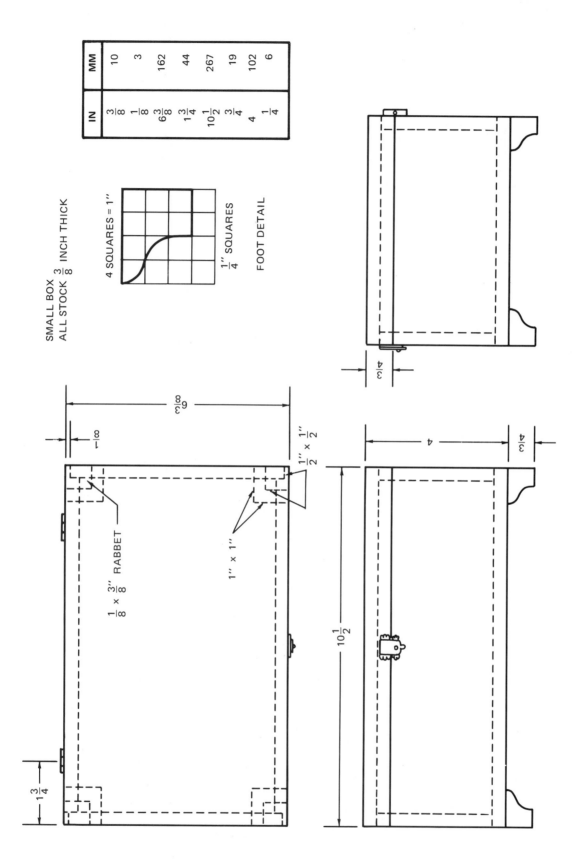

SMALL BOX
ALL STOCK $\frac{3}{8}$ INCH THICK

4 SQUARES = 1"

$\frac{1}{4}$" SQUARES

FOOT DETAIL

IN	MM
$\frac{3}{8}$	10
$\frac{1}{8}$	3
$6\frac{3}{8}$	162
$1\frac{3}{4}$	44
$10\frac{1}{2}$	267
$\frac{3}{4}$	19
4	102
$\frac{1}{4}$	6

$6\frac{3}{8}$

$\frac{1}{8}$

$\frac{1}{8} \times \frac{3}{8}$" RABBET

$1" \times 1"$

$\frac{1}{2}" \times 1\frac{1}{2}"$

$1\frac{3}{4}$

$10\frac{1}{2}$

4

$\frac{3}{4}$

$\frac{3}{4}$

TABLE TENNIS CADDY

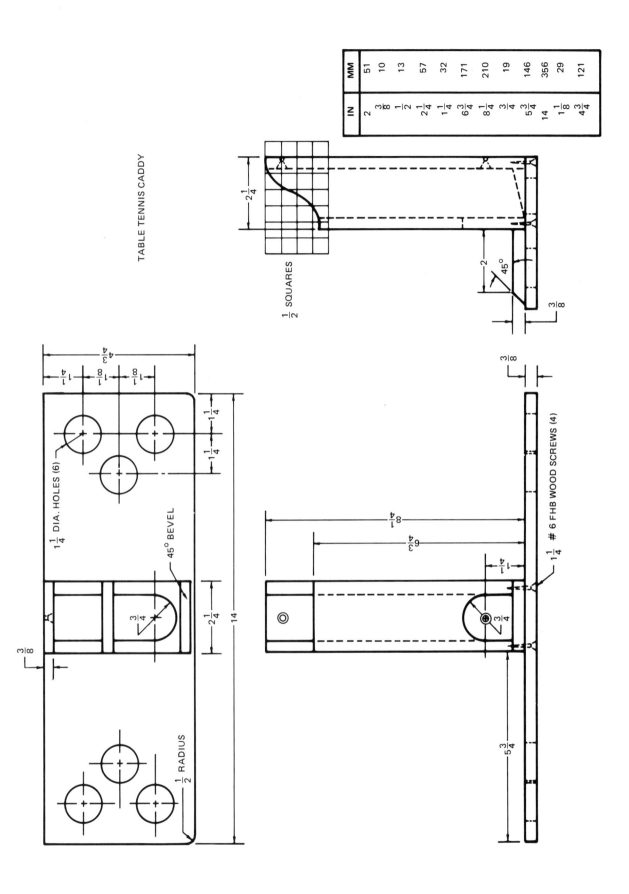

IN	MM
2	51
$\frac{3}{8}$	10
$\frac{1}{2}$	13
$2\frac{1}{4}$	57
$1\frac{1}{4}$	32
$6\frac{3}{4}$	171
$8\frac{1}{4}$	210
$\frac{3}{4}$	19
$5\frac{3}{4}$	146
14	356
$1\frac{1}{8}$	29
$4\frac{3}{4}$	121

$\frac{1}{2}$ SQUARES

1¼ DIA. HOLES (6)

45° BEVEL

½ RADIUS

6 FHB WOOD SCREWS (4)

IN	MM
10	254
5	127
$\frac{3}{8}$	10
$\frac{3}{4}$	19
$6\frac{1}{4}$	159

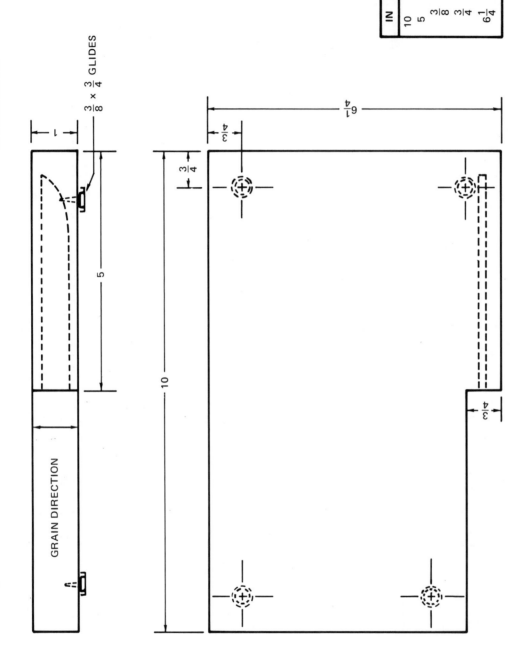

GRAIN DIRECTION

$\frac{3}{8} \times \frac{3}{4}$ GLIDES

HOT PLATE

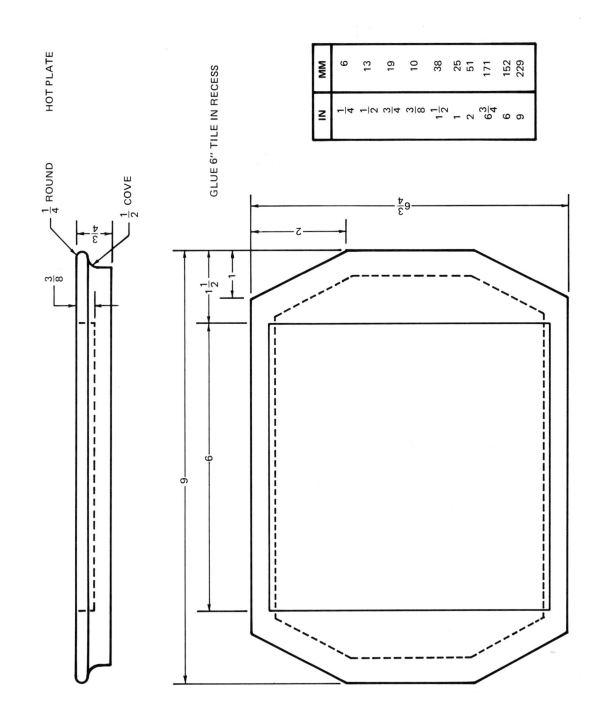

$\frac{1}{4}$ ROUND

$\frac{1}{2}$ COVE

$\frac{3}{4}$

$\frac{3}{8}$

GLUE 6" TILE IN RECESS

$6\frac{3}{4}$

2

$1\frac{1}{2}$

1

6

9

IN	MM
$\frac{1}{4}$	6
$\frac{1}{2}$	13
$\frac{3}{4}$	19
$\frac{3}{8}$	10
$1\frac{1}{2}$	38
1	25
2	51
$6\frac{3}{4}$	171
6	152
9	229

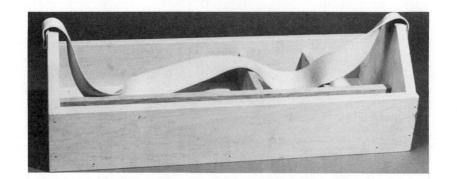

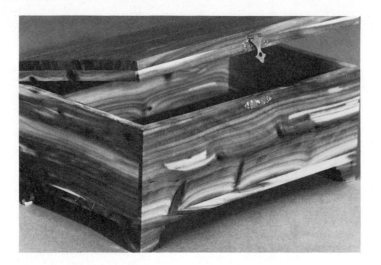

APPENDIX

BOARD MEASURE TABLE

FOR USE IN DETERMINING THE NUMBER OF BOARD FEET IN BOARDS OF KNOWN DIMENSIONS

Results given in board feet and decimal parts of a foot

(WIDTH OF BOARD)

(LENGTH OF BOARD)

Inches	1	1½	2	2½	3	3½	4	5	6	7	8	9	10	11	12	13	14	15	16	17	18	19	20	21	22	23	24
1															.08	.09	.09	.10	.11	.11	.12	.13	.13	.14	.15	.15	.16
2									.08	.09	.11	.12	.13	.15	.16	.18	.19	.20	.22	.23	.25	.26	.27	.29	.30	.31	.33
3							.08	.10	.12	.14	.16	.18	.20	.22	.25	.27	.29	.31	.33	.35	.37	.39	.41	.43	.45	.47	.50
4					.08	.09	.11	.13	.16	.19	.22	.25	.27	.30	.33	.36	.38	.41	.44	.47	.50	.52	.55	.58	.61	.63	.66
5				.08	.10	.12	.13	.17	.20	.24	.27	.31	.34	.38	.41	.45	.48	.52	.55	.59	.62	.65	.69	.72	.76	.79	.83
6			.08	.10	.12	.14	.16	.20	.25	.29	.33	.37	.41	.45	.50	.54	.58	.62	.66	.70	.75	.79	.83	.87	.91	.95	1.00
7			.09	.12	.14	.17	.19	.24	.29	.34	.38	.43	.48	.53	.58	.63	.68	.72	.77	.82	.87	.92	.97	1.02	1.06	1.11	1.16
8		.08	.11	.13	.16	.19	.22	.27	.33	.38	.44	.50	.55	.61	.66	.72	.77	.83	.88	.94	1.00	1.05	1.11	1.16	1.22	1.27	1.33
9		.09	.12	.15	.18	.21	.25	.31	.37	.43	.50	.56	.62	.68	.75	.81	.87	.93	1.00	1.06	1.12	1.18	1.25	1.31	1.37	1.43	1.50
10		.10	.13	.17	.20	.24	.27	.34	.41	.48	.55	.62	.69	.76	.83	.90	.97	1.04	1.11	1.18	1.25	1.31	1.38	1.45	1.52	1.59	1.66
11		.11	.15	.19	.22	.26	.30	.38	.45	.53	.61	.68	.76	.84	.91	.99	1.06	1.14	1.22	1.29	1.37	1.45	1.52	1.60	1.68	1.75	1.83
12	.08	.12	.16	.20	.25	.29	.33	.41	.50	.58	.66	.75	.83	.91	1.00	1.08	1.16	1.25	1.33	1.41	1.50	1.58	1.66	1.75	1.83	1.91	2.00
13	.09	.13	.18	.22	.27	.31	.36	.45	.54	.63	.72	.81	.90	.99	1.08	1.17	1.26	1.35	1.44	1.53	1.62	1.71	1.80	1.89	1.98	2.07	2.16
14	.09	.14	.19	.24	.29	.34	.38	.48	.58	.68	.77	.87	.97	1.06	1.16	1.26	1.36	1.45	1.55	1.65	1.75	1.84	1.94	2.04	2.13	2.23	2.33
15	.10	.15	.20	.26	.31	.36	.41	.52	.62	.72	.83	.93	1.04	1.14	1.25	1.35	1.45	1.56	1.66	1.77	1.87	1.97	2.08	2.18	2.29	2.39	2.50
16	.11	.16	.22	.27	.33	.38	.44	.55	.66	.77	.88	1.00	1.11	1.22	1.33	1.44	1.55	1.66	1.77	1.88	2.00	2.11	2.22	2.33	2.44	2.55	2.66
17	.11	.17	.23	.29	.35	.41	.47	.59	.70	.82	.94	1.06	1.18	1.29	1.41	1.53	1.65	1.77	1.88	2.00	2.12	2.24	2.36	2.47	2.59	2.71	2.83
18	.12	.18	.25	.31	.37	.43	.50	.62	.75	.87	1.00	1.12	1.25	1.37	1.50	1.62	1.75	1.87	2.00	2.12	2.25	2.37	2.50	2.62	2.75	2.87	3.00
19	.13	.19	.26	.32	.39	.46	.52	.65	.79	.92	1.05	1.18	1.31	1.45	1.58	1.71	1.84	1.97	2.11	2.24	2.37	2.50	2.63	2.77	2.90	3.03	3.16
20	.13	.20	.27	.34	.41	.48	.55	.69	.83	.97	1.11	1.25	1.38	1.52	1.66	1.80	1.94	2.08	2.22	2.36	2.50	2.63	2.77	2.91	3.05	3.19	3.33
21	.14	.21	.29	.36	.43	.51	.58	.72	.87	1.02	1.16	1.31	1.45	1.60	1.75	1.89	2.04	2.18	2.33	2.47	2.62	2.77	2.91	3.06	3.20	3.35	3.50
22	.15	.22	.30	.38	.45	.53	.61	.76	.91	1.06	1.22	1.37	1.52	1.68	1.83	1.98	2.13	2.29	2.44	2.59	2.75	2.90	3.05	3.20	3.36	3.51	3.66
23	.15	.23	.31	.39	.47	.55	.63	.79	.95	1.11	1.27	1.43	1.59	1.75	1.91	2.07	2.23	2.39	2.55	2.71	2.87	3.03	3.19	3.35	3.51	3.67	3.83
24	.16	.25	.33	.41	.50	.58	.66	.83	1.00	1.16	1.33	1.50	1.66	1.83	2.00	2.16	2.33	2.50	2.66	2.83	3.00	3.16	3.33	3.50	3.66	3.83	4.00
25	.17	.26	.34	.43	.52	.60	.69	.86	1.04	1.21	1.38	1.56	1.73	1.90	2.08	2.25	2.43	2.60	2.77	2.95	3.12	3.29	3.47	3.64	3.81	3.99	4.16
26	.18	.27	.36	.45	.54	.63	.72	.90	1.08	1.26	1.44	1.62	1.80	1.98	2.16	2.34	2.52	2.70	2.88	3.06	3.25	3.43	3.61	3.79	3.97	4.15	4.33
27	.18	.28	.37	.46	.56	.65	.75	.93	1.12	1.31	1.50	1.68	1.87	2.06	2.25	2.43	2.62	2.81	3.00	3.18	3.37	3.56	3.75	3.93	4.12	4.31	4.50
28	.19	.29	.38	.48	.58	.68	.77	.97	1.16	1.36	1.55	1.75	1.94	2.13	2.33	2.52	2.72	2.91	3.11	3.30	3.50	3.69	3.88	4.08	4.27	4.47	4.66
29	.20	.30	.40	.50	.60	.70	.80	1.00	1.20	1.40	1.61	1.81	2.01	2.21	2.41	2.61	2.81	3.02	3.22	3.42	3.62	3.82	4.02	4.22	4.43	4.63	4.83
30	.20	.31	.41	.52	.62	.72	.83	1.04	1.25	1.45	1.66	1.87	2.08	2.29	2.50	2.70	2.91	3.12	3.33	3.54	3.75	3.95	4.16	4.37	4.58	4.79	5.00
31	.21	.32	.43	.53	.64	.75	.86	1.07	1.29	1.50	1.72	1.93	2.15	2.36	2.58	2.79	3.01	3.22	3.44	3.65	3.87	4.09	4.30	4.52	4.73	4.95	5.16
32	.22	.33	.44	.55	.66	.77	.88	1.11	1.33	1.55	1.77	2.00	2.22	2.44	2.66	2.88	3.11	3.33	3.55	3.77	4.00	4.22	4.44	4.66	4.88	5.11	5.33
33	.22	.34	.45	.57	.68	.80	.91	1.14	1.37	1.60	1.83	2.06	2.29	2.52	2.75	2.97	3.20	3.43	3.66	3.89	4.12	4.35	4.58	4.81	5.04	5.27	5.50

Board Feet Ready-Reckoner (length in inches across rows, width in inches across columns)

Inches	1	1½	2	2½	3	3½	4	5	6	7	8	9	10	11	12	13	14	15	16	17	18	19	20	21	22	23	24	Inches
34	.23	.35	.47	.59	.70	.82	.94	1.18	1.41	1.65	1.88	2.12	2.36	2.59	2.83	3.06	3.30	3.54	3.77	4.01	4.25	4.48	4.72	4.95	5.19	5.43	5.66	34
35	.24	.36	.48	.60	.72	.85	.97	1.21	1.45	1.70	1.94	2.18	2.43	2.67	2.91	3.15	3.40	3.64	3.88	4.13	4.37	4.61	4.86	5.10	5.34	5.59	5.83	35
36	.25	.37	.50	.62	.75	.87	1.00	1.25	1.50	1.75	2.00	2.25	2.50	2.75	3.00	3.25	3.50	3.75	4.00	4.25	4.50	4.75	5.00	5.25	5.50	5.75	6.00	36
37	.25	.38	.51	.64	.77	.89	1.02	1.28	1.54	1.79	2.05	2.31	2.56	2.82	3.08	3.34	3.59	3.85	4.11	4.36	4.62	4.88	5.13	5.39	5.65	5.90	6.16	37
38	.26	.39	.52	.65	.79	.92	1.05	1.31	1.58	1.84	2.11	2.37	2.63	2.90	3.16	3.43	3.69	3.95	4.22	4.48	4.75	5.01	5.27	5.54	5.80	6.06	6.33	38
39	.27	.40	.54	.67	.81	.94	1.08	1.35	1.62	1.89	2.16	2.43	2.70	2.97	3.25	3.52	3.79	4.06	4.33	4.60	4.87	5.14	5.41	5.68	5.95	6.22	6.50	39
40	.27	.41	.55	.69	.83	.97	1.11	1.38	1.66	1.94	2.22	2.50	2.77	3.05	3.33	3.61	3.88	4.16	4.44	4.72	5.00	5.27	5.55	5.83	6.11	6.38	6.66	40
41	.28	.42	.56	.71	.85	.99	1.13	1.42	1.70	1.99	2.27	2.56	2.84	3.13	3.41	3.70	3.98	4.27	4.55	4.84	5.12	5.40	5.69	5.97	6.26	6.54	6.83	41
42	.29	.43	.58	.72	.87	1.02	1.16	1.45	1.75	2.04	2.33	2.62	2.91	3.20	3.50	3.79	4.08	4.37	4.66	4.95	5.25	5.54	5.83	6.12	6.41	6.70	7.00	42
43	.29	.44	.59	.74	.89	1.04	1.19	1.49	1.79	2.09	2.38	2.68	2.98	3.28	3.58	3.88	4.18	4.47	4.77	5.07	5.37	5.67	5.97	6.27	6.56	6.86	7.16	43
44	.30	.45	.61	.76	.91	1.06	1.22	1.52	1.83	2.13	2.44	2.75	3.05	3.36	3.66	3.97	4.27	4.58	4.88	5.19	5.50	5.80	6.11	6.41	6.72	7.02	7.33	44
45	.31	.46	.62	.78	.93	1.09	1.25	1.56	1.87	2.18	2.50	2.81	3.12	3.43	3.75	4.06	4.37	4.68	5.00	5.31	5.62	5.93	6.25	6.56	6.87	7.18	7.50	45
46	.31	.47	.63	.79	.95	1.11	1.27	1.59	1.91	2.23	2.55	2.87	3.19	3.51	3.83	4.15	4.47	4.79	5.11	5.43	5.75	6.06	6.38	6.70	7.02	7.34	7.66	46
47	.32	.48	.65	.81	.97	1.14	1.30	1.63	1.95	2.28	2.61	2.93	3.26	3.59	3.91	4.24	4.56	4.89	5.22	5.54	5.87	6.20	6.52	6.85	7.18	7.50	7.83	47
48	.33	.50	.66	.83	1.00	1.16	1.33	1.66	2.00	2.33	2.66	3.00	3.33	3.66	4.00	4.33	4.66	5.00	5.33	5.66	6.00	6.33	6.66	7.00	7.33	7.66	8.00	48
49	.34	.51	.68	.85	1.02	1.19	1.36	1.70	2.04	2.38	2.72	3.06	3.40	3.74	4.08	4.42	4.76	5.10	5.44	5.78	6.12	6.46	6.80	7.14	7.48	7.82	8.16	49
50	.34	.52	.69	.86	1.04	1.21	1.38	1.73	2.08	2.43	2.77	3.12	3.47	3.81	4.16	4.51	4.86	5.20	5.55	5.90	6.25	6.59	6.94	7.29	7.63	7.98	8.33	50
51	.35	.53	.70	.88	1.06	1.23	1.41	1.77	2.12	2.47	2.83	3.18	3.54	3.89	4.25	4.60	4.95	5.31	5.66	6.02	6.37	6.72	7.08	7.43	7.79	8.14	8.50	51
52	.36	.54	.72	.90	1.08	1.26	1.44	1.80	2.16	2.52	2.88	3.25	3.61	3.97	4.33	4.69	5.05	5.41	5.77	6.13	6.50	6.86	7.22	7.58	7.94	8.30	8.66	52
53	.36	.55	.73	.92	1.10	1.28	1.47	1.84	2.20	2.57	2.94	3.31	3.68	4.04	4.41	4.78	5.15	5.52	5.88	6.25	6.62	6.99	7.36	7.72	8.09	8.46	8.83	53
54	.37	.56	.75	.93	1.12	1.31	1.50	1.87	2.25	2.62	3.00	3.37	3.75	4.12	4.50	4.87	5.25	5.62	6.00	6.37	6.75	7.12	7.50	7.87	8.25	8.62	9.00	54
55	.38	.57	.76	.95	1.14	1.33	1.52	1.90	2.29	2.67	3.05	3.43	3.81	4.20	4.58	4.96	5.34	5.72	6.11	6.49	6.87	7.25	7.63	8.02	8.40	8.78	9.16	55
56	.38	.58	.77	.97	1.16	1.36	1.55	1.94	2.33	2.72	3.11	3.50	3.88	4.27	4.66	5.05	5.44	5.83	6.22	6.61	7.00	7.38	7.77	8.16	8.55	8.94	9.33	56
57	.39	.59	.79	.98	1.18	1.38	1.58	1.97	2.37	2.77	3.16	3.56	3.95	4.35	4.75	5.14	5.54	5.93	6.33	6.72	7.12	7.52	7.91	8.31	8.70	9.10	9.50	57
58	.40	.60	.80	1.00	1.20	1.40	1.61	2.01	2.41	2.81	3.22	3.62	4.02	4.43	4.83	5.23	5.63	6.04	6.44	6.84	7.25	7.65	8.05	8.45	8.86	9.26	9.66	58
59	.40	.61	.81	1.02	1.22	1.43	1.63	2.04	2.45	2.86	3.27	3.68	4.09	4.50	4.91	5.32	5.73	6.14	6.55	6.96	7.37	7.78	8.19	8.60	9.01	9.42	9.83	59
60	.41	.62	.83	1.04	1.25	1.45	1.66	2.08	2.50	2.91	3.33	3.75	4.16	4.58	5.00	5.41	5.83	6.25	6.66	7.08	7.50	7.91	8.33	8.75	9.16	9.58	10.00	60
61	.42	.63	.84	1.05	1.27	1.48	1.69	2.11	2.54	2.96	3.38	3.81	4.23	4.65	5.08	5.50	5.93	6.35	6.77	7.20	7.62	8.04	8.47	8.89	9.31	9.74	10.16	61
62	.43	.64	.86	1.07	1.29	1.50	1.72	2.15	2.58	3.01	3.44	3.87	4.30	4.73	5.16	5.59	6.02	6.45	6.88	7.31	7.75	8.18	8.61	9.04	9.47	9.90	10.33	62
63	.43	.65	.87	1.09	1.31	1.53	1.75	2.18	2.62	3.06	3.50	3.93	4.37	4.81	5.25	5.68	6.12	6.56	7.00	7.43	7.87	8.31	8.75	9.18	9.62	10.06	10.50	63
64	.44	.66	.88	1.11	1.33	1.55	1.77	2.22	2.66	3.11	3.55	4.00	4.44	4.88	5.33	5.77	6.22	6.66	7.11	7.55	8.00	8.44	8.88	9.33	9.77	10.22	10.66	64
65	.45	.67	.90	1.12	1.35	1.57	1.80	2.25	2.70	3.15	3.61	4.06	4.51	4.96	5.41	5.86	6.31	6.77	7.22	7.67	8.12	8.57	9.02	9.47	9.93	10.38	10.83	65
66	.45	.68	.91	1.14	1.37	1.60	1.83	2.29	2.75	3.20	3.66	4.12	4.58	5.04	5.50	5.95	6.41	6.87	7.33	7.79	8.25	8.70	9.16	9.62	10.08	10.54	11.00	66
72	.50	.75	1.00	1.25	1.50	1.75	2.00	2.50	3.00	3.50	4.00	4.50	5.00	5.50	6.00	6.50	7.00	7.50	8.00	8.50	9.00	9.50	10.00	10.50	11.00	11.50	12.00	72
Inches	1	1½	2	2½	3	3½	4	5	6	7	8	9	10	11	12	13	14	15	16	17	18	19	20	21	22	23	24	Inches

EXAMPLE: To determine the number of board feet in a board that is 9" wide and 45" long. In column 9 opposite 45 is 2.8 which is the number of board feet sought, provided the board is 1" in thickness.

If the board were more than 1" in thickness this amount, 2.8 would be multiplied by the thickness of the board in inches.

acknowledgments

Reviewer

Angelo Curci

Illustrations

The author wishes to express his appreciation to the following individuals and companies for furnishing illustrations:

American Plywood Association: Figure 49-5

Bill Ratigan: Figure 5-2

Binks Manufacturing Company: Figure 47-2

Disston, Inc.: Figures 8-2A, 8-2B, 8-4A, 8-4B, 8-10

Donald A. Pilotte: Numerous photos throughout text

Fine Hardwoods Association: Figures 3-7, 3-8

Forest Products Laboratory, United States Department of Agriculture: Unit 2

Millers Falls Company: Figure 23-9

Norton Company: Figure 35-5

Powermatic Houdaille, Inc.: Figures 23-1, 27-1, 30-1, 35-1

Rockwell International Corporation: Figures 25-5, 25-21, 27-2, 27-4, 28-1, 29-1, 35-2, 36-1, 36-4, 37-1, 37-2, title page

Southern Forest Products Association: Page viii

Stanley Tools: Figures 10-1C, 15-11, 15-12

Weyerhaeuser: Figures 1-2, 1-3, 1-4, 1-5, 1-6, 1-7, 1-8, 1-10, 3-1, 3-2, 3-3, 3-4, 3-5, 3-9

Delmar Staff

This edition of UNITS IN WOODWORKING was edited by Barbara A. Christie.

INDEX